Praise for *Little Daughter*

'Without a scrap of self-pity and with a fair dollop of humour, 28-year-old Phan describes a life mostly spent running for cover ... An extraordinary journey' *Mail on Sunday*

'Zoya is an amazing woman with a truly incredible and harrowing life all laid down clearly and movingly on the pages of this book. It's interesting, educational but enormously readable and a little piece of your heart will be left in Burma' *Jo Brand*

'Zoya's story is one of fulfilment in the teeth of terrifying odds. But the endless war grinds on' *Independent*

'Written in a very natural voice, this is an unusual story of life in Burma, a country of terrible turmoil' *Waterstone's Books Quarterly*

'A cleanly written testimony to an unending apocalypse. *Little Daughter* evokes the same despairing anger as Cambodian refugee classics such as Someth May's *Cambodian Witness*. The horrors described are all too real' *Financial Times*

'Destiny is a big, portentous, overworked word. Zoya Phan never once uses it. But for her followers, it is the only way to make sense of how she escaped persecution in the Burmese jungle and became, aged only 28, a human rights campaigner in the mould of her assassinated father, and the most powerful political activist for Burma living in Britain' *Daily Telegraph*

Little Daughter

A Memoir of Survival in Burma and the West

ZOYA PHAN

WITH DAMIEN LEWIS

POCKET
BOOKS

LONDON • SYDNEY • NEW YORK • TORONTO

First published in Great Britain by Simon & Schuster UK Ltd, 2009
This edition first published by Pocket books, 2010
An imprint of Simon & Schuster UK Ltd
A CBS COMPANY

1 3 5 7 9 10 8 6 4 2

Simon & Schuster UK Ltd
1st Floor
222 Gray's Inn Road
London WC1X 8HB

www.simonandschuster.co.uk

Simon & Schuster Australia
Sydney

Map on p. xi © Liane Payne

A CIP catalogue record for this book is available
from the British Library.

ISBN : 978-1-84739-426-2

Typeset in Palatino by M Rules

Printed in the UK by CPI Cox & Wyman, Reading, Berkshire RG1 8EX

This book is dedicated to my late mother, Nant Kyin Shwe,
and late father, Padoh Mahn Sha Lah Phan.
Z.P.

For Eva
D.L.

Zoya's father and mother, with (from left to right) Say Say, Slone, Zoya and Bwa Bwa

Contents

	Map	xi
	Acknowledgements	xiii
1	The Almost-Dying	1
2	Grandfather Bent Back	15
3	Touching the Pig	27
4	The Bamboo People	43
5	The Flower Children	55
6	River of Darkness	72
7	Victory Field	81
8	The River Spirits	88
9	The Naming	100
10	Paradise Lost	109
11	Sleeping Dog Mountain	118
12	The River of Burning Tears	129
13	Under the Big Tree	141
14	No Refuge	154
15	A Time of Darkness	163
16	The Journey Home	172

17	The New Village	181
18	The Mission Song	194
19	Running from Bullets	203
20	Refugees Again	214
21	Mae La Camp	224
22	Bangkok Daze	234
23	City Girls	243
24	Land of Evil	253
25	The Awakening	262
26	Children of Darkness	269
27	London with Bwa Bwa	277
28	In the Footsteps of My Father	288
29	In the Firing Line	301
30	The Road Home	309
31	The Final Cut	317

Statement Written by Zoya Phan and Her Sister and Brothers for Their Father's Funeral	323
Epilogue	325
About Burma	329
Burma Timeline	331
The Phan Foundation	333
Other Organizations Working for Burma	334

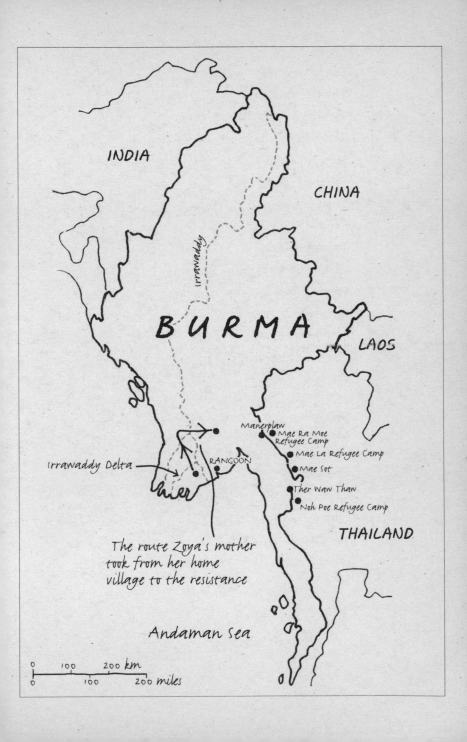

INDIA

CHINA

Irrawaddy

B U R M A

LAOS

Manerplaw
Mae Ra Moe
Refugee Camp
Mae La Refugee Camp
RANGOON
Mae Sot
Irrawaddy Delta
Ther Waw Thaw
Noh Poe Refugee Camp

THAILAND

The route Zoya's mother
took from her home
village to the resistance

Andaman Sea

0   100   200 km
0   100   200 miles

Acknowledgements

Special thanks to Mark Farmaner and Anna Roberts for helping make this book possible. Special thanks to my literary agent, Felicity Bryan, and international agents, George Lucas and Andrew Nurnberg, for their enthusiasm and belief in my story. Very special thanks to Mike Jones and Katherine Stanton at my British publisher, Simon & Schuster, Carolin Graehl at my German publisher, Droemer, and my American publisher, the Free Press, and my Canadian publisher, Penguin. Special thanks to my sister, Nant Bwa Bwa Phan, my older brother, Saw Say Say Phan, and my younger brother, Slone Phan, for their support and encouragement. Special thanks to David Lewis and Leslie Lewis for their preparation of the French retreat in which to work on the manuscript. Thanks to Christine and David Major for the Dorset writing retreat and the wonderful cooking, and to Sue Wreford for the comfort and calm of her Wynford Eagle country house in which to work.

One of the ways in which the regime ruling Burma keeps hold of power is through denying education to its own people. Without education I would not be able to do the work I do now to try to help my people. I was very lucky to be able to attend university, and for that I must thank the Open Society Institute scholarship programme, Prospect Burma, Burma Education Scholarship Trust, and other individuals including Lisa Houston, Martin Panter, Michael Woods, Paul Sztumpf and Steve Bates.

Chapter One

THE ALMOST-DYING

When I was two years old I died and came back to life again. It was my first brush with death and, sadly, there were to be many more. One morning my mother discovered me lying unconscious in our bamboo hut. I already had a high fever, and she had hoped that overnight I would have slept it off. But I was always a sickly child, and now she feared that she had lost me.

She covered me in a damp cloth, scooped me into her arms, and ran as fast as her legs would carry her to the village clinic. This was a small bamboo hut just near our house. There was one nurse running the clinic and my mother hoped and prayed that the nurse would be there, and not out treating someone.

She rushed inside in a dread of panic. Luckily, the nurse was in, but she took one look at the little unconscious bundle that was me and declared that it was hopeless.

'I'm afraid your daughter is dead,' she said. 'I'm sorry, I can't help her.'

My mother was beside herself. She refused to believe that I was gone. For years she had served as a soldier in the jungles. She was tough, and she refused to believe that I was dead.

'No way!' she cried. 'No way has my Little Daughter died, just like that. No way!'

She scooped me up again, and decided to try for the neighbouring village, to see if the nurse there might help. There was only a faint path through the jungle, but she was sure she could find her way. What made it all the more difficult was that she was already nine months pregnant with my little brother.

She left my older sister, Bwa Bwa, in the care of my big brother, Say Say, and headed out alone. It was the dry season and the Mu Yu Klo River, which ran past our village, was low, and so my mother was able to wade across. For forty minutes she fought her way through the jungle, until finally she burst into the clearing of Pwe Baw Lu village. She rushed across to the clinic, tears streaming down her face as she ran.

The nurse there was far more sympathetic. She examined me closely and declared that I was in a deep, fever-induced coma. She put me on a drip and gave me the few drugs that she had in an effort to calm the fever. Then she told my mother to be patient. I was still breathing and there was always a chance that I might come out of this alive and well.

After three days on the drip my fever started to come down. A little later on that third day I regained consciousness. My mother was sitting right beside me as I opened my eyes. She couldn't believe that I had come back to life again. None of the nurses were present, for it was Christmas Eve and they had gone to a party at the village school.

My mother gazed at me in wonder, but then she realized with a shock that my eyes weren't right. One was looking at the sky, the other down at the earth. She was convinced that I was brain-damaged. The shock sent her into labour, and the nurses had to rush back from the Christmas party to help her deliver the baby. And that's how my little brother came into the world.

My mother decided to name him Slone Phan – Shining Stone – because he brought light into the darkness of my almost-dying.

Slone and I stayed in the clinic for a few more days. My mother was with us, trying to keep us both happy. The nurses helped her, and she was so grateful for their assistance, especially the one who had saved me. But she was angry with the nurse in our village – the one who had said that I was dead. That nurse was young and inexperienced, she said, and didn't know how to do her job properly.

As children do, I recovered quickly from my almost-dying, but my eyes remained all askew. Some weeks later when my father came home he took one look at me and exclaimed, 'Oh, my Little Daughter, still so beautiful – even though you have *ta klay meh*!'

My father was only joking, but in Karen culture calling someone *ta klay meh* – 'wonky eyes' – is very rude. It is considered really ugly to have crooked eyes. From then on my sister and elder brother were always making jokes about my *ta klay meh* appearance.

My friends didn't go as far as calling me *ta klay meh*. But they would laugh at me whenever my eyes went crooked, which they did especially when they got tired. I would get very annoyed. My vision would swim, things becoming all twisted and blurred. At its worst I would be seeing a cup or a bowl of food, but my eyes would appear as if they were looking in another direction completely.

Whenever I was teased like that my mother would try to reassure me: 'Little Daughter, you're still very beautiful, despite your funny eyes.'

Over time I learned to get used to it. I learned how to bring my eyes back to normal by looking down at the ground, and then slowly bringing them up again. Luckily, the older I got the less wonky they became, and by the time I was in my teens they were almost back to normal.

In the culture of my people, the Karen, families don't usually have surnames. Children have only the one name that they were given by their parents, and there is no name passed down through the generations. A person's name can be made up of more than one Karen word, and it almost always means something. For example, one of my best friends at school was called Tee Ser Paw – 'sweet water flower' in our Karen language.

But when my father left his home village and came to join the Karen resistance, he broke away from that tradition. He abandoned the one name that his parents had given him, and chose a resistance name instead. Resistance fighters did this largely to protect their families back home from reprisals by the Burmese military regime.

My father chose the name Mahn Sha Lah Phan – Mr Star Moon Bright. He chose 'star' and 'moon' because he believed the heavens were the light of the future; and 'Phan' because he believed that future would be a bright one – for the Karen, and for all the people of Burma.

When my father was young there was a Karen leader called Mahn Phan Shaung – Mr Bright Unity. He was a great military commander and resistance fighter, and he was my father's role model. He believed in freedom for the Karen people and human rights and democracy for all. My father chose to take 'Phan' as his own 'surname' – to keep this man's spirit alive. When we were born he passed that name on to us, to sustain his memory through future generations.

I called my father 'Pah' – which is 'Daddy' in our language. My mother was 'Moe' – 'Mummy'. My older brother was called Say Say, which means 'silver silver'. But I called him 'Joh Joh', Karen for 'older brother'. My older sister was called Bwa Bwa – 'white white' in Karen. My parents called her this because she was snowy white when born. But I always called her 'Nor', which means 'older sister'. And of course Bwa Bwa would call me 'Day Mu', which means 'younger sister'.

When my little brother, Slone Phan, came along, I called him 'Day Kwa', which means 'younger brother'. Whenever Slone called out 'Nor! Nor!' – older sister, older sister – both Bwa Bwa and I would come running, as we wouldn't know which of us he was after.

My father was a loving, gentle man and I was very close to him. Out of all my siblings, mine was the only birth at which he was present. He managed to stay with the family for six months when I was born, and I think that in part explains the special bond between us.

He was of average height, slim but strong. He had brown eyes framed by laughter lines and black hair. He would be clean-shaven whenever possible, and he'd use a cut-throat razor to shave. He always seemed to be dressed the same: a checked shirt, rolled up at the sleeves, with a Karen longyi – a *Hteh Ku* – wrapped around his waist.

The longyi is a length of Karen material worn about the waist like a kilt. It is a multipurpose piece of clothing. In the rainy season it could be hitched up to form a pair of 'shorts' for wading through the floods, and it doubled as a towel and even a makeshift blanket.

Like most people in the resistance my parents had precious little money. So my father wore plastic flip-flops, the unofficial footwear of the Karen resistance. For ages one of his flip-flops was broken at the toe; he repaired it by fashioning a thong out of bamboo rope.

One day when I was little my father tried to teach me to swim in the mighty Thu Mweh Klo River. Few Karen can swim, and it's not something that comes naturally to us. My older brother and sister were screaming and laughing with joy, but I was crying because of my fear of the water.

My father tried to soothe me: 'Little Daughter, don't worry, you are with me right here in my arms. Don't worry, Little Daughter, you're safe.'

Still I screamed, but after a while I did let go of my fear and stopped clinging to him so tightly. I allowed my father to pull me along, with my legs kicking through the clear, fast-flowing water. I soon forgot my worries.

Once I had learned to swim properly I used to love playing in the river and resting on the riverside beach. Say Say would climb on top of one of the giant water buffaloes, which wallowed in the shallows, and start dancing on their horns. These huge, placid creatures are used by the Karen to pull carts, or to plough their fields.

At dusk Say Say would grab some nets and take me on a fishing trip. He'd cast them into the river and leave them out overnight. Very early in the morning he'd wake me and we'd go to see if we'd caught anything. Usually, the nets would be full of little tilapia fish and we'd carry them home to show my father. My mother would curry the fish, or mix them with water spinach to make a delicious stew.

But these happy times with my father were few and far between. Mostly, he was away on his resistance work. He was absent for ten months of the year or more. I didn't have the time to play with him or to get to know him properly, and sometimes it felt as if he was a stranger. When he returned, Say Say, Bwa Bwa and I would have all but forgotten him. But I'd always be the first to go to him, and soon I'd be following him around everywhere.

When it came time for my father to go away again my mother would have to trick us into letting him leave. She would take us to play with the animals under the house, so he could sneak away without us knowing. Without a goodbye he would just be gone. If she hadn't done that we would never have let him leave.

'Don't go!' we'd have cried. 'Don't go, Daddy! Please don't go!'

At times I wondered why my father was absent so much. I resented it, and I used to ask myself – *why*? Why was he so rarely with us? Why?

My little brother, Slone Phan, didn't take very kindly to my father's absence. One day when Slone was around three years old, my father returned from a long period away. But Slone didn't know who this strange man was. He started to beat my father with a bamboo rope, to make him leave the house.

My mother tried to stop him. 'That's your father! Your father! Stop it! Stop it!'

Eventually, she had to take the rope away. It was the only way to make Slone stop. My father laughed and laughed, but inside I think he felt very sad. It must have been so hurtful realizing that his children didn't know him, or recognize him, or feel he was their father even.

In spite of his absence, my father tried to show his care for us in many ways. Whenever he came home he would bring us something that he'd crafted with his own hands: a woven bamboo hat; spoons, forks and bowls made out of wood; maybe even a carved toy. These we would cherish as our most precious possessions.

Every day that he was home my father would show his love for us by grabbing us and kissing us on the cheek. He might reach out and catch us for a hug and a kiss at any time, sometimes five times a day. I used to complain about his stubbly face, but in reality I adored his kisses.

My father wasn't particularly handsome, but he was very intelligent, and he had a great sense of humour. He'd gone to university in Burma's capital city, Rangoon, and graduated in history. We had few university graduates in the Karen resistance, and in my mother's eyes this made him extra-special.

My mother was tall for a Karen woman, almost as tall as my father. She'd wear a red Karen longyi – and red must have been her favourite colour, for she wore it every day. She had straight jet-black hair, which she kept clipped up on her head in a bun. She would only let it down when she washed it, when she'd leave it free to dry.

I used to marvel at her hair. When she let it down it fell in a glistening, glossy waterfall right to the small of her back.

My mother's complexion was a little darker than my father's; I had inherited his lighter colouring. Every day she would wear Tha Na Kah – a traditional Karen face cream – on her cheeks. She used to make the Tha Na Kah from the bark of the Tha Maw Glay – the tamarind tree.

She would take a smooth-worn stone and roll a length of bark backwards and forwards on it, adding a little water as she did so.

Gradually, the bark would dissolve into a light yellow paste – the Tha Na Kah cream. She would rub it on to her cheeks using a circular motion, until it left a little yellow sun on each one.

We Karen believe that Tha Na Kah makes a woman look beautiful, and it also protects our skin from the sun. My mother would rub Tha Na Kah on to my cheeks, arms and legs, to keep me cool in the hot season. And when she grew old and less capable, we children would do the same for her.

My mother was considered to be a real beauty. She was also unusual, in that she was so much more than 'just' a housewife. In the past she had been a renowned resistance fighter, commanding a company of women soldiers, and after that she had continued working for the struggle.

From my earliest memories my mother worked in the information department of the Karen resistance. She had to use an old manual typewriter as there were no computers. With my father away so much, she had no one to help look after the children. I'd go with my brothers and sister to her bamboo-walled office, and we'd play quietly whilst she banged away on that ancient typewriter.

My eldest brother, Say Say, was adopted. He had a pointed face, whereas my mother and father had rounded features, more like my own. He came to our family when he was about ten, and I was just four months old. He was considered one of the most kind and helpful people in our village. If anyone asked Say Say, he would be sure to assist them.

Whilst my father was a serious man, he was also quick to see the funny side of things. Whenever we were unhappy he would tell us funny stories, in an attempt to cheer us up. But for difficult matters he would be serious, and iron-willed in his intentions. Say Say followed the more earnest side of my father, and he was conscientious and hard-working.

With my father away so much, Say Say helped my mother with the chores. And when both my parents were away on their resistance work, Say Say took over. He would wash, cook and clean for the three of us, as if he was our mother and our father. And he would carry me everywhere he went strapped in a longyi on his back.

One day when I was little my father told me the story of how Say Say had come to be with us. My father was talking to my mother about his work in the Kler Lwee Htu district, from where he had just returned. It was far distant from us, and much closer to the front line where the Burmese military were attacking our villages. I knew this was the area that Say Say had come from, so I pricked up my ears.

The Burmese regime had a notorious policy called the 'Four Cuts', which was designed to crush the Karen. The Four Cuts policy was brutally simple: it would cut off all supplies, information, recruits and food to the Karen resistance.

The policy was beginning to bite deep. Whole villages in the Kler Lwee Htu district were on the brink of famine. Burmese troops had destroyed their crops, and burned their food stores down. Starving families were reduced to eating the flesh of banana trees.

When my father had returned home this time I'd noticed that he looked exhausted and drawn. I'd watched as he devoured the leftovers from the previous meal. My mother had told him that she was making a fresh curry for him, but my father had insisted on eating every last scrap of the leftovers. There was no food where he had just come from, he said, and people there were being forced to eat putrid, rotten rice.

The Four Cuts policy was hurting people terribly, he explained. I tried hard to listen, but as a small child I couldn't understand everything he told us. I knew my people were starving to death; I also knew there was an enemy doing this to us, and that they were human, just like us. But I was scared and I didn't want to think about it.

In an effort to reassure myself I'd whisper: 'Well, we've got food, and it's a long way away . . .'

I could see that my father was suffering, but I tried to close my mind to that. We were all closer to our mother at this time, for the simple reason that she was around. I'd grow close to my father when he was with us, but hurt, and distant, when he left.

The Four Cuts policy had driven families to ever more desperate measures. One day a man who worked for the resistance had approached my father. Over their time spent working together they had grown to like and respect each other. He told my father that he had seven children, and that he wanted one at least to get a proper education. But the Four Cuts policy had destroyed all the schools in the area.

He asked my father to take one of his older sons, Say Say, and give him an education in our home village. My mother and father only had one child at this time – my older sister, Bwa Bwa – and my father felt a deep sympathy for his friend. He agreed to take Say Say as one of his own children, and so Say Say became my parents' adopted son.

Once a year Say Say's parents would try to visit, if they could afford the time to make the long journey. Whenever they did they were so happy and proud to see how well their son was doing in his studies at school.

When Say Say came to live with us he started attending the village junior school. He was a 10-year-old boy in Year One, and most of the other children were half his age. But Say Say didn't mind. He was happy just to get an education, and he studied hard and tried to make up for lost time.

When I was four years old Say Say started taking me to school with him, so I could be looked after. The schoolroom was little more than a bamboo-walled hut with open windows, and rows of rough wooden desks. There were no childcare facilities in the village, so whilst Say Say studied hard I would play quietly at his feet. By now Say Say was in his fourth year, and people used to joke that I was barely four years old, but already in Year Four!

My favourite game was making mud pies on the classroom's earthen floor. I'd start with a mound of earth, prod a hole in the middle and spit into it – and that was my cooking pot. I'd stir the contents around, imagining that I had my favourite food – pork curry – bubbling away in there. When it came time to go home I'd be covered in mud, but I didn't mind. I loved playing mud pies in Say Say's class.

Say Say came from an isolated jungle village, and he understood the nature of the forest – its moods, its promise and its dangers. Whenever my siblings and I went to the jungle without Say Say, invariably we'd get lost. We'd leave from one side of the village and return from another, never knowing where we'd been. But Say Say had a sixth sense – he always knew the way home.

My sister, Bwa Bwa, took after my mother in looks, being taller than me. But emotionally, she was like my father. She cared about everyone, was touched by their suffering, and felt their pain in her own heart. People said that I was my father's favourite, but Bwa Bwa was his firstborn child. He was away on the front line when she was born, yet his love for her bloomed in his heart. Even before he had set eyes on Bwa Bwa he used to smile at the very thought of her existence.

Bwa Bwa's hair was jet-black and die-straight, like mine, but my father used to like us to cut it in a bob. Bwa Bwa was fine with that, but not me. Her lips were thinner than mine, and her face rounder, but people used to say that Bwa Bwa and I were equally pretty. She was very clever, and was always at the top of her class. I looked up to my sister, and it was her example that I wanted to equal at school.

My sister had been born the wrong way round, feet-first. It was a difficult birth for my mother, and her next child miscarried. For the first six months of her pregnancy with me I barely moved, and my mother feared that she would miscarry again, or that I would be stillborn. As it was, I was a very frail baby – as exemplified by my almost-dying. I would faint easily and my heart was weak. Sometimes, my mother would beat Bwa Bwa if she was naughty, but never me. She was too fearful of causing me a heart attack.

My little brother, Slone Phan, followed me in frailty. He was the spitting image of my father in looks, but he was such a small child. Compared to his friends, he was tiny. Most Karen have a sharp, teasing sense of humour, and we nicknamed him 'Maung Bala' – 'Muscle Man'. It's a nickname that has stuck; even today, people still call him Muscle Man.

Slone Phan was thin and small, but he was totally fearless. He seemed to compensate for his size with his temper. He was always angry. At times he would lie down and bash his forehead on the ground repeatedly. If he couldn't get my mother's attention he'd keep smashing away, making a loud slamming noise. We'd get so worried.

His friends soon learned to respect his temper, and mostly they followed his lead. He was the boss of his gang because of his bravery. If they were to climb a tree, Slone would dictate which one they climbed. He'd be first up, directing the others to various branches, and ordering them which fruit to pick.

I was Slone Phan's big sister, and I loved having a little brother. The day he was born, as told to me by my mother, was unforgettable. He came out of my mother's womb complete with a strange kind of skullcap. The whole of the top of his head was covered in a 'hat' of white, hairless skin. Everyone in the village came to gaze at baby Slone, as no one had seen such a thing before.

Gently, my mother peeled away the skin cap, revealing a head of soft, fluffy, jet-black hair. My mother carefully folded up that skin cap, and kept it safe. In our animist belief system someone born with such a distinctive feature is blessed – it signifies that they have a special future ahead of them.

My mother and father were born animists. This is a traditional belief system that assigns things in nature – trees, rivers, mountains, the sky and stars – souls and a consciousness. My parents came from a village that was mixed animist, Buddhist and Christian. It was typical for Karen people of differing religions to live happily side by side.

My parents rarely explained to us the nature of animist beliefs: instead, they preferred to show by example. There were no set scriptures or prayers, and no holy book: it was all about an individual's personal relationship with the spirits of the universe. Karen animists believe that everything on earth – a tree, a plant, a river, a mountain – has a spirit. If a boy drowns in the river, we believe that the river spirit must be angry. You have to make an offering to the river spirit, and ask for forgiveness.

My father marked the day of my birth with a traditional animist ceremony. The name of our village, Per He Lu, means 'Mountain of Teak'. Above it rears a dark hill cloaked in teak trees. My father took my umbilical cord and proceeded to climb, and when he reached the very top he searched for the biggest tree. Karen animists believe the bigger the tree the more powerful the spirit that resides there.

He buried my umbilical cord under an ancient giant of a tree, and then he prayed for his Little Daughter. He prayed to the tree spirit on the mountaintop, because it is high and has vision and can see into the future. He prayed that when I grew up I would be strong, and that I would help my country and my people. My father was only able to do this for me, as he was absent for Bwa Bwa and Slone's births.

Whenever we had visitors he used to tell this story. 'And with my Little Daughter, when she was born I took her umbilical cord and climbed Teak Mountain—'

I'm sure my brothers and sister must have got sick and tired of hearing about it all the time!

I knew I was special to my father in another way, too. My name, 'Zoya', is not a Karen name. People were always asking how I had come by such an unusual name. My father would explain that the original Zoya was a Russian partisan who had fought against the Nazis in the Second World War, and been captured and executed. And she was the Zoya that he had named me after.

But none of this meant much to me when I was little. I wasn't really interested in that Zoya: I was interested in me. And I had no idea where Russia was, who the Nazis were, and what the war had been about. It was only years later that I would understand just how prophetic it was for my father to have named me 'Zoya'. For he had named me after who and what I was to become.

Chapter Two

———————

GRANDFATHER BENT BACK

Our legends tell that in ancient times Pu Tau Meh Pa, the first leader of the Karen, led his people south from Mongolia searching for a new homeland. On the way the Karen divided into two. One group, known as the 'mother side', or Pwo Karen, travelled through central Burma and settled in what is now the Irrawaddy Delta.

The 'father side', the Sgaw Karen, followed the Salween River and settled in an area of mountainous jungle in what is now the border region of Burma and Thailand. Many centuries later the British officially created that border and split our tribe in two. We called our new home Kaw Lah – Green Land.

A Karen elder led us to the area of present-day Rangoon. His name was Pu Ta Ku – Grandfather Bent Back. There, we saw a beautiful, lush plain. He made a makeshift flag, by hoisting a fishing rod with a traditional Karen tunic on it, and that was how Rangoon was founded. Back then the settlement was called Way Ta Ku – Bent Back City – after Grandfather Pu Ta Ku.

Centuries later the British came along and renamed it Rangoon.

Our own name for ourselves is Pwa K'Nyaw – and it means, quite simply, 'the people'. When the Burmans – now the predominant ethnic group in Burma – arrived, they gave us the name 'Kayin'. 'Karen' is most likely a name that the British adapted from Kayin.

Over the centuries the different ethnic groups in Burma expanded, and more people settled in the country. As they did they came into conflict with each other. The Karen people were subjugated and persecuted by the ethnic Burman and Mon groups. When the British colonized Burma the Karen were treated more equally, and many Karen considered that life was better under British rule.

Many Karen were converted to Christianity, and the British exploited ethnic and religious differences in Burma in their effective divide and rule strategy. The perceived closeness of the Karen to the colonizing British exacerbated the existing prejudice that many Burmans had against the Karen.

These differences became more extreme when the Karen sided with the British in fighting the invading Japanese during the Second World War. Aung San, leader of Burma's independence movement, had joined forces with the Japanese to drive the British out of the country. He later switched sides and fought against the Japanese, but some Burmese considered the Karen to have collaborated with their oppressor.

During the Second World War the British promised the Karen they would be given an independent country once Burma gained independence, and so would be free from oppression. But the British broke their promise, and left the Karen in Burma when the country gained independence in 1948. So began decades of oppression and discrimination against the Karen people.

Many people talk about the problems in Burma as starting in 1962 when the first dictator came to power, or in 1988 when students protesting in Rangoon were massacred on the streets and an even more brutal dictatorship took over. But for the Karen persecution has been going on for centuries, and escalated from the moment Burma gained independence.

Karen people were not given equal rights in 1948, and the government incited communal clashes, accusing the Karen of being lackeys of British colonialism. Peaceful protests were ignored, with the Burmese Prime Minister, U Nu, even telling Karen leaders the only way they would win the rights and independence they called for was if they fought for it. Attacks escalated, with Karen villages being burned, villagers shot and women raped. Karen organizations were outlawed and Karen leaders arrested. In January 1949 Karen leaders called on their people to take up arms to defend themselves.

Freedom's struggle was led by the Karen resistance movement, the Karen National Union (KNU). The Karen resistance gave their traditional lands the name of Kaw Thoo Lei – Land of No Evil. It was to this Land of No Evil, and the wider resistance struggle, that so many were drawn – my parents among them. I was born in Manerplaw, the headquarters of the resistance – and in our language Manerplaw means 'Victory Field'.

My parents loved telling us stories of their differing journeys to join the resistance. There was a wild romance about my parents' journeys to Kaw Thoo Lei and their finding love there.

My parents came from the same village, one situated deep inside Burma on the Irrawaddy Delta. When my father was a young boy the Burmese Army attacked, and he and his family fled into the forest where they hid for many days. There he lost his younger sister to dysentery and, soon after, his mother succumbed to smallpox – a dreaded, and highly contagious, disease. It made her skin fall off in great lumps, and because of this she was unable to hug her children goodbye when she sickened and died. My father never forgot the pain and trauma of losing his mother in that way.

After their deaths, my father was brought up by his father. He owned a plantation of betel nut palms on the outskirts of the village. The Burmese Army had burned down the village, but the plantation had survived. All across Burma people chew the nut of the betel palm, mixed with lime leaves and betel pepper, as a mild stimulant a little like coffee. My father's father used the money he earned from selling betel to give my father a proper education.

After high school my father went to university in Rangoon. He was nineteen years old, and studying hard for his history degree, when in 1962 Army General Ne Win seized control of the country. All student unions were banned, as were trade unions, and my father led angry students demonstrating on the streets. The military cracked down hard, and there were hundreds of arrests.

Luckily, my father escaped the soldiers, and he went on to join the KNU. Of course, that organization – like all resistance movements – was banned, and so it had to operate in secret. As soon as my father graduated he decided to go and join the resistance proper, in Manerplaw, and it was there that he rediscovered his childhood affection for my mother.

As a child my mother was so poor that she only ever owned two dresses. She was the eldest daughter of impoverished parents with seven children. She was twenty years old by the time she finished Year Seven of her studies. Her parents didn't have the money to keep her at school, and so she decided to do something to help her family.

Although the Burmese government did not provide training, she had heard that the KNU ran courses training young women to be nurses. They lasted for two years and they were free. My mother planned to return to her village after the training, to work as a nurse, and to earn money to help put her siblings through school.

With her parents' support she went away to start training as a nurse. As a trainee nurse my mother was drawn into the struggle, helping those who had been injured in attacks by the Burmese Army as well as injured soldiers or people who were sick. The more she saw at first hand of the suffering of her people, the more committed she became. Although she had planned to return to her village after the course, because she was in the KNU – even as a nurse – it was not safe for her to return. She was only in her early twenties, and was never to see her home village again.

Instead, my mother joined the KNU, and was a member of a company operating in the south-west Delta region. Her talent and commitment were appreciated by her commanders, and she was promoted to command a company of female soldiers. As the Burmese Army sent more soldiers into the region, it became more and more difficult for them to operate, and the order came from KNU headquarters that they should join the main Karen Army in the east of the country to avoid them all being killed.

My mother was heartbroken to be leaving the Delta, for she feared she would never see her mother or father again. In Karen culture parents depend on their children when they are old and infirm, and she felt terribly guilty. But equally, she had a responsibility to the struggle and the soldiers in her charge.

There was no direct route by which my mother's unit, Delta Battalion, could join the main Karen Army in the east, and so they embarked upon a perilous journey into lands most had never seen before. My mother never for one moment imagined that the journey ahead would take five years, and be one of the most challenging undertakings of her entire life.

Several hundred fighters travelled north into the rugged Arakan Mountains. Some months into the journey they met a Karen fisherman and his son. The commander in charge of Delta Battalion asked the fisherman if he knew the way ahead. Father and son said they did, and they led the Karen soldiers along hidden paths and secret valleys towards the far side of the Arakan Mountains.

During that journey the fisherman and his son decided to join the Karen resistance, and travel with them all the way to Manerplaw. But as they left Karen lands far behind them the soldiers started to run short of food. They came to a place where there were herds of wild elephants. Elephants have a special place in Karen culture, and no one would ever normally think of killing and eating one. But the soldiers were desperate. It was either that, or starve to death.

Two of them were shot and killed. Whenever she told me this part of the story, my mother used to stress how odd the elephant meat tasted. It smelled pungent and musty, like the jungle, and was tough as old leather. The trunk was the oddest thing to eat, for it was all cartilage and bony bits. There were around 200 soldiers in Delta Battalion, and the two elephants were barely enough to keep them going.

It was at around this time that the Burmese Army discovered their whereabouts and set about wiping them out. My mother had some thirty female soldiers under her command. She was determined that not one of them would die of starvation, or get killed by the enemy. One morning she went out from the camp searching for vegetables and fruit. All of a sudden she spotted something in the undergrowth – an enormous python. It was asleep, and it hadn't seen her.

As quickly as she could she returned to the camp and explained to her soldiers what she had in mind. Four of them would go and kill the snake; any more and they might wake it. She would creep up and jump on the beast's neck, in an effort to hold it down and keep it from swallowing anyone. The others would rush in and beat it with bamboo sticks. By the time my mother was back at the python's nest, she had realized what a truly scary prospect it was. She didn't fancy wrestling with such a beast.

She steeled herself and on the count of three she jumped. As soon as she landed on its thick and powerful neck the python awoke. It was surprised and angry, and it thrashed about trying to get its jaws around my mother, but she held on with all her strength. Whilst my mother tried to strangle the python, the others beat it with bamboo sticks. On and on the battle went, the python thrashing and the women screaming and beating it, until eventually they overcame the giant snake.

The story of her battle with the python was one of my mother's favourites. She used to tell it to us of an evening when my father was away, and Say Say, Bwa Bwa, Slone and I were sitting with her near the cooking fire. She used to act out the battle, with the python thrashing and thrashing and squirming beneath her. We children would be listening in rapt attention, marvelling at how she could ever have been so brave. She was such a soft and loving mother, and I used to wonder how she could have been so fierce.

Often, my mother would end up laughing so much over the fight with the giant python that she couldn't continue the story! After they had killed it, the four of them rested to recover their strength. It had been an exhausting battle. Then they hoisted that heavy python on to their shoulders and carried it back to camp. When they got there the other soldiers eyed the python hungrily. The Burmese Army was closing in on all sides, and they were trapped in the jungle with the pangs of starvation gnawing al their stomachs.

My mother made a fire and hung the python over it to smoke. Then she cut it into lengths and placed the python meat in pots of boiling water. They had no spices or anything to flavour it, so they ate the boiled flesh just as it was. But that python meat didn't last for ever. A day or two later my mother went out on another food-gathering expedition with some of her fellow soldiers.

By this time Delta Battalion's commander had fallen sick. He remained in the camp, along with the main body of soldiers. It was now that the Burmese Army chose to attack, and the camp was quickly overrun. When my mother and her soldiers returned from their food-gathering expedition, they found the commander dead. He had been killed with a knife thrust to the stomach.

My mother and her troops knew there was nothing to stay for and that they had to try to make their escape. They set off into the jungle, with the aim of scaling a high peak that lay to the north of their position. Many exhausting days later they discovered a beautiful cave, which seemed totally deserted. There was no sign that any humans – the enemy included – had ever been there. They decided to rest up in that cave and try to recover their strength. They made a fire at the entrance, and as darkness descended they told each other what had happened to them when the Burmese Army had attacked.

All of a sudden there was a deafening roar, and a huge tiger came bounding out of the darkness. Before anyone could react, it snapped its jaws shut around the head of one of the soldiers sitting by the fire. As it tried to drag him away the man thrashed and fought through the flames, and the fire flared up fiercely. The tiger kept shaking the man's body, making the flames grow higher and higher. The cave was filled with smoke and sparks, the tiger's roaring and the man's screaming echoing horribly all around. Eventually, the tiger succeeded in dragging his victim away. My mother and the rest of the Karen soldiers knew then why the Burmese Army had never used that cave as somewhere to camp.

Once more they set off into the forest, and finally they came out of the Arakan and Pegu Mountains into the central plains of Burma. All they had to do was cross the Sit Taung River, and they would be into the eastern highlands, which were controlled by the Karen forces.

It was the rainy season and the Sit Taung River was high and strong. It was impossible to wade across, and the soldiers set about building rafts to ford the river. My mother ordered her troops to work quickly, as she feared the Burmese Army were still on their tail. The forests of Burma are full of bamboo, and in the intense, steamy heat each can grow to the thickness of a man's thigh. For its weight bamboo is incredibly strong, and the Karen are renowned for building just about anything with it – including rafts.

It started raining hard, a torrential downpour drumming on the leaves. The harder it rained the more difficult it became to cut the bamboo and lash together the rafts. They had to weave rope from bamboo fibres and craft paddles from split bamboo stems. My mother sent the first raft into the strong current, soldiers climbing aboard and striking out for the far side. But just as it neared the centre of the river, shots rang out from the jungle behind. The Burmese soldiers had found them.

My mother asked for volunteers, and soldiers stepped forward to face the enemy. They headed off to set up a defensive cordon, and buy those escaping some time. My mother mustered her remaining troops for the crossing. At her side was her close friend, a male soldier who had led the way in cutting the giant bamboo. There was not enough space for all on the rafts, and so he volunteered to swim across.

On his back he strapped his weapon and a rucksack full of ammunition, and in one hand he carried a sack of rice, some of the little food they had with them. My mother watched as he headed down to the water's edge and hooked his arms around a long length of bamboo, to provide flotation. As he went to launch himself into the current my mother asked if he would be okay. He turned back to her and smiled confidently.

'Yes, I'll be fine,' he answered.

He turned away from her again and kicked out into the water. Almost immediately he was caught by the river's mighty flow, and within seconds he was swept downstream. A moment later he was tugged into the angry depths, the weight of his backpack pulling him under fast. My mother searched and searched with her eyes for an arm or a head to reappear above the swirling waves, but there was no sign of him. Her brave companion was gone.

My mother boarded a raft that was crammed with people. As they pulled away from the riverbank she shouted orders that the volunteers holding off the enemy should try to swim for it. Most had never seen a river as wide or as powerful as this. They thought they would be able to make it, but many did not. When my mother reached the safety of the far side she counted how many she had lost. Fifteen had drowned in the river, many of whom were from her own troop.

My mother had vowed not to lose a single one. She was heart-broken, for she felt like she had failed them. There was a mother and daughter team in her troop, and she discovered to her horror that they had both drowned. My mother would often tell me how she would never forget that loss, no matter how long she lived. That, and seeing her friend swept away to his drowning.

But those who had died hadn't given their lives for nothing, my mother explained to us. A few months after that fateful river cross-ing she and her soldiers reached the safety of Karen territory – the heartland of the resistance. At last they had made it. My mother loved telling us these stories. This had been a time of real adven-ture, and she wanted us to know all about it. As for me, I had never met anyone who was as brave as her before.

But I did use to wonder why she hadn't just shot that python and killed it. Surely, it would have been far easier – and safer – than beating it to death? One day I asked her as much. It was then that she explained to me how ammunition was in such short supply. Karen soldiers had been rationed to a few bullets each. They were only ever allowed to use a bullet in an effort to kill the enemy. Shooting the python would have been seen as a dereliction of duty.

My mother was thirty-two years old when my father and she met again, in Manerplaw. They had known each other as child-hood playmates, back in the home village. My father started to court her, and he was romantic in a way that no Karen man would normally be. He would pick fresh flowers and deliver bunches to her door, which was unheard of in Karen society.

Normally, a man would write a letter to the woman he liked. It would be worded very simply: 'I feel love for you; d'you feel the same for me?' The man would get a go-between to deliver the note, and the courtship would be pursued through the exchange of such letters. Eventually, if they really liked each other, they might meet.

But my father did things very differently. He gave her flowers, wrote romantic poetry, and offered her a pillowcase with a message of love embroidered on it. It is a Karen tradition to give pillowcases between lovers – for the pillow is the place where they might both eventually lay their heads. But the woman is supposed to give it to the man, not vice versa! My father was a true romantic, and over time he won my mother's heart.

It was 1976 when my mother and father were married. My father was proud of the way he had won my mother's love. He often told me the story of how he had done so, and all throughout their married life he never stopped bringing her fragrant bunches of flowers.

By the time my mother and father had re-met and fallen in love, she had given up her life as a soldier and started working as an information officer for the Karen National Union. In spite of those tough years fighting in the jungle, my mother was a soft and gentle person. And my father was open-minded and educated. Together, they tried to teach me to be good and to stand up for what I believed was right.

My mother had never forgotten the tricks she learned as a resistance fighter. It wasn't that unusual to find snake curry on the menu at home, although it was never giant python! Most of the snakes we ate were about the length of a man's arm, and they were captured in the bush that surrounded the village. My mother would smoke the snake meat over the cooking fire, before frying it in oil, with onions, garlic, salt and chilli. The curried flesh tasted like fish crossed with chicken, and was quite delicious.

One night a snake came to our house to steal some eggs. The house was built of bamboo, with a raised bamboo floor supported on stilts. Beneath this our chickens and ducks would roost for the night. At that time Pu Baru – Grandfather Baru – was staying with us. He was an old man, but his hearing was still sharp, and he detected that snake slithering into the chicken house. He headed out into the darkness and beat it with a stick.

We called that snake Ghu Hsaw Di – the egg snake. As it was an egg-eater it wasn't poisonous, and we knew it was good to eat.

But we avoided eating venomous snakes – and there were lots of those where we lived – for we feared they might poison us.

But in reality it wasn't the venomous snakes we had to fear. It was the gathering darkness of the war.

Chapter Three

TOUCHING THE PIG

Despite what was happening in the rest of Burma, our village, Per He Lu, was a tranquil paradise. It nestled right on the banks of the Mu Yu Klo, a tributary of the mighty Moei River. The Moei was fringed with towering mountains, and it was deep, with dark emerald-green waters. Our area was not so mountainous, and the Mu Yu Klo was shallower, with a lighter, jade-green hue.

Manerplaw was just an hour's walk away from our village, on the far side of Teak Mountain. On one side our village was fringed by the river waters, and on the other it was penned in by the steep, jungle-clad hillside. The village consisted of bamboo huts strung out along the riverbank, each set on stilts some six feet above the ground, with a bamboo ladder leading into it. The space underneath was both a wood store and a place for animals.

No one had locks on their doors. What would have been the point? We had a culture of honesty, and no one would have dreamed of stealing. Even if we went away for days on end we wouldn't bother locking anything. The only reason we had latches on the doors was to prevent the chickens from going into the house when everyone was out and pooing everywhere, or eating leftover food.

We didn't have any clocks in the village, either. The cockerel was everyone's timekeeper. He would crow at specific times of the day. The first crow was around two o'clock in the morning, and we called it *hsaw oh oh ter tablaw* – 'the first crowing of the cock'. That was the signal for the farmers to get up and start pounding their rice for breakfast.

At three o'clock he would crow again: *hsaw oh oh kee blaw tablaw* – the second crowing of the cock. This was the time to start cooking breakfast. On the third crow, at four o'clock – *hsaw oh oh ther blaw tablaw* – people would eat and go to their farms. The cockerel was known to us as 'the Karen clock'.

Most years during the rainy season the Mu Yu Klo would flood its banks, thick brown water gurgling into the village. But we would sleep safe and sound above the flood, in our bamboo house on stilts.

My mother would travel to Manerplaw in the week, for her work, leaving us in the village. If it was the wet season, she could get there easily by 'long-tail' boat. These are like enlarged canoes, with a car or truck engine mounted on the back, and a long shaft with a propeller on the end dipping into the water. Traditionally, the Karen would travel on foot, or by paddling dugout canoes. But in recent years long-tail boats had become a common means of transport, both for villagers and the resistance fighters.

During the wet season, the river journey to Manerplaw would take thirty minutes or so, as the waters were deep and easily navigable. In the dry season it would take longer, as the boatman would have to find a way through. Sometimes, the rivers would be impassable by long-tail boat, and my mother would have to take the path that led over Teak Mountain. There were wild elephants living in that forest and they could be dangerous.

My father and mother had built our house all by themselves. In fact, my father was a great craftsman, and he'd make tables, chairs and beds for friends and neighbours. He'd make huge hats woven out of young, supple bamboo and interwoven with leaves. They were meant to cover the whole of the body when worn, so as to keep off the sun in the hot season and provide shelter during the rains.

One day my father took me into the forest to show me how to cut bamboo. This was an important lesson, for bamboo is central to the lives of the Karen. We use it to make the floor, walls and roof of our houses. We use it to construct bridges over rivers. We use it as fuel for cooking, to construct water pipes and water-carriers, and to make furniture. We use bamboo staves as weapons, and bamboo leaves are the favourite food of the elephant.

Bamboo is the heart of the Karen people, and we have many names to describe the types of bamboo found in the forest. There is Wa Glu, quite simply the most giant bamboo you could ever find; Wa Blaw, a type that has a long separation between each of the internal walls; and Wa Klay, which is in between the two of them.

We even have a traditional dance called Ta Si Kli – 'the bamboo dance'. Two lengths of bamboo are laid on the ground, parallel to each other, with a man at either end. The men lift the bamboo poles in unison and bash them together, making a hollow clashing sound. The dancers have to jump in between the bamboo to that rhythm, whilst avoiding getting their ankles crushed.

But bamboo is only ever useful to those who know how to use it. It grew in huge groves many feet high in the forests that surrounded our village. My father showed me how to use a *gheh* – a machete – to clear the small branches and shoots away, so as to get at the choicest stands of bamboo. Often, the person cutting it would have to shin up the chosen bamboo stem, and cut it halfway. Otherwise, if it was cut at the base it might fall and injure or kill them.

During the dry season I would help my parents collect firewood in the forest and store it under the house. Once we had filled up the space under the ground floor, my father would build an outer 'wall' of firewood around each side of the house. This was to keep the rain out, and the wood inside dry.

The walls of our house were made of flattened lengths of bamboo. You had to work out the length you wanted the wall to be, and the number of bamboo flats you would need. After cutting the bamboo you had to lay it on the ground, and score marks along its length with a machete. You split it open and removed the pith. Then you got a boulder and rolled it along the length of bamboo, flattening it as you went.

We called the bamboo planks that resulted *pu dah*. In order to make them more durable we would stack several together, and place them in the river, with stones on top to stop them floating away. We would leave them there for a week or so, during which time the water would wash away the sap. This made the bamboo less attractive to *ta ghah* – 'the destroyer of things' – or termites, as they're called in English. Termites love bamboo, and a bad termite attack would leave nothing but crumbly powder.

The frame of our house – on to which the bamboo floor and walls were attached – was made from solid wood. This was mostly offcuts from a nearby sawmill. We called these offcuts *thay bah kay* – 'the leftover wood'. My father used to take me collecting offcuts, but he'd warn me to be careful, for it could be dangerous.

The sawmill stood on the banks of a river. The building was made of a wooden frame, with a roof thatched with leaves. Logs would be floated downstream, and pulled into shore at the sawmill. There, domesticated elephants would drag the logs up the riverbank, so they could be sawn into planking. To one side was a huge pile of *thay bah kay* – the offcuts. The sawmill workers were forever throwing out more to join that heap of discarded wood.

The biggest danger when collecting *thay bah kay* was that

someone might not see you in among the high mountain of wood. They'd throw a discarded plank out and you'd have to dodge it, so as not to get hit. The other 'danger' was that I used to love watching the elephants at work. I'd stand there daydreaming, and fail to collect any of the *thay bah kay* that we'd come for!

Elephants have a very special place in Karen culture. In fact, just as the British might once have been characterized by roast beef, Yorkshire pudding and cricket, the Karen are known for elephants and bamboo. Just about everything we needed we could make using bamboo, and for all our transport needs there was the elephant.

In Karen culture, a man who owned an elephant was called *theh hti* – 'a rich man'. Elephants can live a very long time, longer than humans, in fact. Usually a *theh hti* would have inherited his elephant from his father. Occasionally, young elephants would be captured in the forest. Obviously, it is far from easy to capture an elephant. In order to do so a hole would be dug in the ground and covered in branches. Wild elephants would be driven in that direction and one might end up trapped, which was the start of the domestication process.

Our village had its very own elephant. She was called Mo Ghay Bay – 'the elephant with the beautiful skin'. Mo Ghay Bay's main task was to pull heavy wood out of the jungle, so it could be cut into firewood. Mo Ghay Bay lived in an elephant house made of bamboo and thatched with leaves, on the outskirts of the village. She could stay in her house and keep dry, or wander out to forage for young bamboo leaves, her favourite food.

Mo Ghay Bay had a keeper, whom everyone called Ka Hsaw Kwah – 'the elephant man'. It was Ka Hsaw Kwah who had named her 'the elephant with the beautiful skin'. It was his job to look after Mo Ghay Bay, keeping her scrubbed, healthy and well fed. He would ride on her neck, and on her back was a wooden cradle for carrying heavy loads. He had a metal hook, and he used this to steer her by tapping her on the side of her head.

Growing up with an elephant in the village was completely normal for us. As children we didn't even call her 'the elephant' – everyone called her Mo Ghay Bay. If we saw her lumbering towards us, we'd cry out: 'Look! Look! Here comes Mo Ghay Bay!' We'd run and chase around her feet, and she'd be very gentle. She never harmed us, not even when we got in her way. It never once struck me that Mo Ghay Bay was an odd name for an elephant: the idea that an elephant could be beautiful just seemed right, somehow.

Mo Ghay Bay was older than most of the people in Per He Lu, so she was like a wise grandmother to the village. There were no vehicles and no roads, and so everything had to be transported by elephant or on the river. Sometimes, elephants would come from neighbouring villages to help Mo Ghay Bay with her work. It was nice to see her having some elephant company.

One day a male elephant came to help Mo Ghay Bay with her work in the village. Like all male elephants, he had big, curved tusks of milky-white ivory. When he caught sight of Mo Ghay Bay – the elephant with the beautiful skin – he started to get all excited. Mo Ghay Bay didn't pay much attention though.

Our house was right in the centre of Per He Lu, next to the village square. The bamboo steps led up into a living room to the left, and to the right was a bedroom. We used to sleep on rush matting laid out on the bamboo floor. If my father was home he would sleep on one end of the row, next to the door, to stop the monsters getting in. I always wanted to sleep with him. I'd happily let my brother and sister sleep next to my mother, if I could have my father all to myself.

As a tiny infant, my favourite position was lying on his chest, with my head on top of his. We didn't have anything like nappies, so if I peed in the night it would go all over him. In the morning he'd wake up, and he'd have to wash his clothes and the blanket. But my father was never angry with me. When I was a little older he would wake me in the middle of the night and take me out for a pee.

To the right of our bedroom was a spare room, with a couple of bamboo-framed beds in it, for guests. At the back of the house was the kitchen. It had an earthen floor for a hearth, and three stones arranged in a triangle. Firewood would be pushed into the space between the stones, and a cooking pot balanced on top.

Above the hearth was a shelf for drying foods – chilli, vegetables, meat and mushrooms. This was a way to preserve things when you didn't have a fridge or a freezer. My father also put his bamboo hats up there to cure. My mother did most of the cooking, but my father was always interfering.

My mother might be cooking a chicken curry – frying the meat with onions, garlic, turmeric, oil, chilli, sweet basil leaves and lemon grass. But when her back was turned my father would taste it, and add in some extra ingredients – salt and lemon perhaps. If my mother caught him she would scold him, but it was only ever in jest. In fact, I think he used to interfere like that deliberately to tease her!

'You! Always interfering!' my mother would say. 'Are you trying to teach me how to cook!'

My father would burst out laughing. 'No, no, no – it's the other way around. I'm not your master – you're mine!'

One time my father added some salt to my mother's soup, from a bottle beside the cooking fire. She returned to the pot to find it frothing over with bubbles. She couldn't understand what had happened, until she checked the contents of the 'salt' bottle. It actually contained the dregs of some washing powder. She had no choice but to throw it all away.

'I can't believe it,' she exclaimed. 'Washing powder in the soup! Whoever mistakes washing powder for salt!'

We were sitting there hungry, and now the food was ruined. But it was so funny that my mother couldn't help laughing. She had a laugh like me: it sounded like the sharp cry of a bird. In spite of our hunger we started laughing along with her. You had to see the funny side of it, after all.

We would eat seated on the bamboo floor at a round wooden table. We were free to sit anywhere we liked, and mealtimes were very informal. In Karen culture mealtimes generally pass with little or no conversation. In fact, it's considered rude to talk in the middle of a good meal – the time for conversation comes after. Normally we'd have a vegetable soup, followed by a salad of water spinach, cucumber and tomatoes, with the main dish being a chicken or pork curry. Or we might have a fish curry, if my brother Say Say had been fishing.

Most importantly, every meal had to include chilli powder and fish paste. Breakfast, lunch or dinner, those two things had to be present. We grew our own chilli, and pounded it with a pestle and mortar. As for fish paste, it is one of my favourite foods. The fish is fermented and pungent and mushy, and most Westerners dislike it. But it's a very popular Karen dish.

We'd each eat from our own wooden bowl. On special occasions we might use those made by my father, but we worried we might damage them, and they were precious to us. We'd each take some rice, some curry and chilli and mix it together with our hands, and then place the wad of food into our mouths.

If my parents weren't at home, we'd have to wait until Say Say came back from school to eat. He was the only one old enough to deal with the cooking fire, and big enough to prepare the food. But first we'd have to help Say Say feed the chickens and ducks, and make food for the pigs – usually banana shoots pounded into a mash. Say Say didn't mind doing the cooking, and he tried to look after us well. That was one of the reasons my parents loved him so much.

Most evenings all Say Say would manage to prepare was rice, fish paste and a water-spinach salad – but it was good enough for us. On the rare occasions when he had time, Say Say would cook his speciality – a rich chicken curry. But for that he'd need meat, and meat was a special treat. The staple food for breakfast, lunch and dinner was rice and fish paste. We looked forward to mother coming home at the weekend, for she'd try to cook us something special. But even when she did, we'd only get to eat meat once or twice a month.

On a weekday, Say Say would get up very early in the morning – at the third crow of the cockerel – and start his first chore of the day, pounding the rice. Beneath the house was an ancient-looking rice pounder, which my father had crafted out of wood. It consisted of a wooden bucket, into which the rice was poured, and a long wooden beam with a pivot at the far end. Say Say would have to stand on the end of the beam, using his weight to lift it and then letting it drop into the bucket. A lump of hard wood set at right angles to the beam would smash down on the rice, so breaking the husks away from the grains.

The pounder would make a slow, rhythmical thump-thump-thump. The noise would echo around the sleeping village, the thumps muffled by the trees and the mist rolling in from the Mu Yu Klo River. The only problem Say Say had was that he wasn't heavy enough to operate the pounder properly. My little brother, Slone, was too small to add enough weight, and my sister was too big, but I just happened to be the perfect size.

Early in the morning he'd wake me up, strap me on to his back, and start the rice pounding. As he worked, Say Say would sing me back to sleep:

> Sleep, sleep my Little Sister . . .
> Sleep, sleep my Little Sister . . .
> Sleep, sleep my Little Sister . . .
> Sleep.

By the time he had pounded enough rice for the day, I would be sound asleep. Say Say would winnow the rice, to separate the grains from the husks. He'd hold a wide, shallow basket above his head and tip out the contents. As the rice fell, the lighter husks would blow clear, the heavier grains collecting in a basket below. Next, he would blow on the embers in the hearth, spark up a cooking fire, and boil rice for the day.

By seven o'clock Say Say would have left for school. Bwa Bwa, Slone and I would wake around then, and eat the breakfast that he'd left us. We used to tease Say Say about how he was too thin to pound the rice. But when Bwa Bwa, Slone and I grew up we were teased in turn, as none of us found it any easier.

My parents could not go back to their home village because, as members of the resistance, it would have been too dangerous. We had few possessions and little wealth. We planted our own rice paddy and vegetable gardens, and reared chickens, pigs and ducks. I loved the chickens, especially when they hatched out their chicks. I'd go into the chicken house with some leftover rice. I'd sit on the straw and hold out my hand, making little clucking noises, and waiting for them to peck the rice right from the palm of my hand.

But my mother's ducks and chickens seemed to like nothing more than to scratch around in my father's beloved flowerbeds. He had planted small flower gardens around the house, and these were his pride and joy. He'd also dug a small fishpond, which was lined with flat pebbles taken from the riverbed. The pond was purely for ornamental purposes, and the fish he put in it weren't for eating. My father was more the romantic and intellectual, whilst my mother was the practical, pragmatic side of the partnership.

Of course, my mother's ducks made it their mission to try to catch my father's fish. And when he went away on work the fishpond became neglected. The water wasn't replaced often enough, and the ducks colonized the pond and began to use it as their toilet. One morning Bwa Bwa and I discovered that the water had turned sickly green, and the fish were dead. My mother was away in Manerplaw and so we pulled out the dead fish ourselves. It seemed such a waste to throw them away, and Say Say cooked them for dinner.

As it wasn't a fishpond any more, Bwa Bwa and I decided to make it our swimming pool. The water was sun-warmed, and it seemed like a good idea to us. We swam in it every day, and in our mind's eye it *was* our swimming pool. Finally the water became so dirty and smelly that we had to stop. Several months later my father came home, but all he found was a dry, fishless dustbowl. No one owned up to eating the fish. In a way we were very naughty children, and my father was quite upset.

No one in our village was wealthy, and we did our best to ease each other's hardship. One of the big events of the year was the roof-building time, called *dut htaw hee koh* – 'the time of covering the house with leaves'. It took place before the start of the rainy season, and it demonstrated how much easier our lives were when everyone pulled together. Word would go around the village that it was so-and-so's time to do their *dut htaw hee koh*. No one would pledge to come – it was all very informal – but on the allotted day there was always enough help.

The roof needed replacing every year, and the aim was to get the whole job completed in one day. Very early in the morning we would head off into the forest to collect the leaves of the Tur Lah – the 'tree of leaves'. It is similar in size to a teak tree, and it has similarly large leaves. The leaves would be piled into woven bamboo baskets, each with a strap attached. With the strap pulled taut around the forehead, my mother and father would each carry home a basket of leaves balanced on their back.

Upon arrival, the basket would be emptied out and the leaves laid flat on the ground. Each was about the size of a small dinner plate. We'd fetch bowls of water and weight the leaves down with a rock to soak. This would make them last longer as a roofing material, but it would quickly spoil their beauty.

My father and Say Say would be first up on the rafters, whilst we prepared the leaves down below. One by one the able-bodied boys and men of the village would come to join them. Each leaf would be passed up and its leaf-stem hooked over a bamboo roof spar. The stems were lashed to the spar with bamboo rope, for extra strength. Row upon row of leaves were added to the roof, each overlapping the other.

My mother would prepare a special meal, *lu kay tha dot hsaw nyah* – 'pumpkin and chicken curry'. In Karen tradition this is the dish you feed to those who help with the roofing. She kept everyone well fed as they worked. The more people came to help the quicker the roof would go up – but the more pumpkin and chicken curry was required!

People would be talking, cracking jokes and laughing, and sometimes those above would be working at different speeds from those below, and the roof would start to go all wonky. Some would have to stop and help others catch up. By nightfall, the roofing would be done.

Such communal activities were the social glue that held the village together. Each year in August, the whole village would come together for the most important event in the Karen calendar, Lah Ku Gee Su – 'the month of wrist tying'. The wrist-tying ceremony takes place alongside Pwaw Htawt Ker Pa – 'the ceremony of touching the pig'.

This was a bittersweet time for our family. On the one hand, we enjoyed the way in which these ceremonies reaffirmed our Karen culture and identity. But on the other, they reminded my parents of how totally cut off we were from their home village and their extended family.

Both ceremonies are animist in origin, and have been adopted as symbols of Karen identity. For the wrist-tying ceremony, the whole village would gather in the local monastery. The elders would sit in a row at the front, with the youngsters of the village facing them. In between would be baskets crammed full of mouth-watering food: coconut, sweet sticky rice and delicious 'bamboo-cooked' rice. We Karen even have a special way of roasting rice inside a length of bamboo.

The elders would remain seated where they were, and the young would come across to stand before them. The elders would proceed to tie a white cord around the youngsters' wrists, one woven together in the traditional Karen way. After that they would offer a blessing, invoking the spirit of the young boy or girl to ensure they had good fortune in the year ahead.

'Spirit, come back, come back to the body,' the elder would say. 'Spirit, come back to this boy, in peace and in hope, to give the body long life, health and happiness. Don't stay under the bamboo or the tree, but come back to the body.'

All the while the elder would be stroking the rope along the young person's wrist. Once the elder had completed the blessing, the youngster would do the same for them. Once everyone had been tied and blessed in this way, we would eat the feast, and the adults would drink rice whisky and rice wine. Rice whisky is fermented from boiled rice, and rice wine from sticky rice. The eating and drinking would last long into the night.

After the village ceremony there would be a private family gathering called Aw Gheh. This was the time of real poignancy for so many families. It was vital that all living family members returned to the family home for Aw Gheh. If there were family members who were absent, then the spirits could never be properly accommodated. This was a very bad thing in animist culture; little was worse than the family being disunited at the time of Aw Gheh.

But, of course, it was impossible for my mother and father to return to their family home. On becoming resistance fighters, they had been forced to sever all family ties. Any contact at all could be fatal as the Burmese regime had spies everywhere. No mercy would be shown to a family that was found to have links with the resistance.

My mother and father had been absent from their families for years now, and for all that time their families had been unable to hold a proper Aw Gheh ceremony. The only way round this impasse was to hold a ceremony to expel the missing family member, and then Aw Gheh could be held without them. But parents were obviously reluctant to do this to their children.

One day a cousin of my mother came to visit. It had taken her months to find us, for all she had been able to do was go from village to village, asking after my mother's whereabouts. Whilst her family knew she had joined the resistance, they had no idea where she was living, or even if she was still alive. That cousin had come to ask if my mother was willing to come home, so that a proper Aw Gheh ceremony could be held.

I was very young at the time, but I still remember how miserable my mother was. She was inconsolable. At first she had been so happy to see her cousin, for it was the first family contact she'd had in many years. She wanted to see her parents and her siblings so very much, but she was torn.

'What will happen if I do try to go home?' she said. 'I might never see my children again.'

We were so upset at the thought of losing her, and we didn't want her to go.

'Don't go, Mummy,' I told her. 'Don't go. Don't leave us.'

I told my mother about a dream that I'd had. Maybe it was a premonition of the future, for I dreamed that my mother had disappeared. My father was away on work, and she had left the four of us – Say Say, Bwa Bwa, Slone and me – all alone. It was evening and we were hungry and lonely, yet still our mother didn't come. I was so sad and worried, because I was used to being with her.

The four of us sat by the door waiting as the evening sky grew dark and night arrived with all its loneliness and fears. We were wondering whether we should go to bed and see if she came home the following day, but I knew I wouldn't be able to sleep. I felt abandoned.

All of a sudden my mother appeared out of the gloom. She was carrying a bundle of the long grass that we use as an alternative kind of roof thatch. I ran up and hugged her and told her how sad we were that she had left us. I was crying and crying.

'Pomu Sit – Little Daughter – I didn't leave you,' my mother replied. 'I had things to do for the house: see, I came back with some new thatch.'

My mother lit the fire and started to cook some rice. And it was then that I had woken up from my dream. I looked wildly around for her, wondering if my dream had been real somehow. But all along she had been sleeping beside me, and she had woken with my cries. She gazed at me in sleepy concern.

'What's wrong?' she asked. 'Pomu Sit, have you had a bad dream?'

I thought to myself that if my mother ever left me, or died, I would go mad with the grief, or die myself. But I didn't tell my mother this. I just kept crying and crying, and eventually I cried myself to sleep.

My mother had reassured me that she would never, ever leave us. And now, even though she faced being 'expelled' by her family, the same was true – she could never leave. She realized that she couldn't go back to her village; it was too much of a risk. She had no choice but to agree to be 'expelled' from her family. Of course, it was in name only: if ever she had gone back they would have welcomed her in. But still she was extremely sad for a very long time afterwards.

As we were separated from our extended family my father decided that we should have an Aw Gheh ceremony at home. Traditionally, a fat pig would be killed and roasted on a spit over a fire. Each family member would touch the roasting pig, starting with the eldest and finishing with the youngest. We couldn't afford a pig, so we performed our Aw Gheh ceremony with a turkey, instead.

As he was the elder of the family, my father led the ceremony. He tied the traditional white cord around my wrist and started to pray.

'Spirit, come back to my Little Daughter; come back and make her healthy, make her happy, and make the year before her a good one . . . Spirit, do not live under the tree; spirit, don't stay under the bamboo grove; spirit, don't hide on top of the mountain. Spirit, come back instead to my Little Daughter . . . Come back, come back to my Little Daughter . . .'

After the tying and blessing, we ate roast turkey with sticky rice, and we drank the cool, sweet milk of coconuts with the tops lopped off. We couldn't 'touch' the turkey though, because that part of the ceremony *had* to be done with a pig.

My father was adamant about it: it had to be 'touching the pig'. Anything else just wasn't good enough.

Chapter Four

THE BAMBOO PEOPLE

One day when I was around three years old, we headed into the forest to clear a field to plant rice. Bwa Bwa, Slone and I were too young for this kind of work, so we were left at the bottom of the hill to play. We decided to make some toy guns from banana shoots. We had no real toys as such, but banana shoots were soft enough to carve, yet tough enough to last a good while. We had a packed lunch, and I took out the knife to shape the trigger and the barrel of my gun.

Even at this age I'd see Karen soldiers passing through our village with their weapons slung over their shoulders, so I knew what guns looked like. But as I went about shaping the end of my toy gun, the knife slipped. All of a sudden blood was spurting out of my finger and I was screaming. Bwa Bwa took one look and set off at a run to fetch help.

'Come quick! Come quick!' she cried, as soon as she saw my mother. 'Little Sister has cut her finger!'

My mother rushed down the hill, and discovered that I had all but sliced off the end of my index finger. It was hanging by just a flap of skin. She was horrified, especially as it was she who had put the knife in with our lunch.

'Oh, my Little Daughter, I'm so sorry,' she cried. 'It's my fault! I shouldn't have left those knives with you.'

She grabbed a handful of leaves from the Sit Poe Kwee, a wild bush. She rolled them into a compress, and bound it tightly around my finger with a length of cotton torn from her longyi, to stop the bleeding. Two weeks later she unbound it, and my injured finger had knitted back together again almost as if it had never been cut. Like most Karen, my parents knew what in the forest could be used to cure illnesses and heal wounds.

But the person in our family with the greatest knowledge of forest law was Say Say. When he first started taking me on expeditions into the jungle I was barely a toddler, and he would carry me strapped on his back. He knew all the free foods one could find there. We'd climb the hill above the village in search of mushrooms. The best time to find them was at the end of the rainy season, when the forest was hot, musty and damp – perfect mushroom-growing conditions.

There were many that were poisonous. Say Say would show us which were good to eat and which were not. One of the commonest edible ones was called Gur Wa Koh – 'the bamboo mushroom'. It grew in clumps on the shadowy roots of the bamboo, a flash of white umbrellas with water splashes of grey. The biggest was the size of a child's hand, the smallest the size of a thumb. Say Say would show us how to turn over the bamboo mushroom, to check if it had its distinctive fan of grey gills. If it did, we knew it was good for the pot.

But the real prize was the Gur Toh Pwi – 'the bird mushroom'. It grew in the wet, shady places on the forest floor, and it looked like the outstretched wings of a bird. There was no mistaking a clump of bird mushrooms; it was like a flock of white doves taking to the air. The flesh was soft and tasty, and it was my favourite. My least favourite was Gur Thay Pu – 'the wooden mushroom' – which grew on rotten tree stumps. You had to cook it for a long time. It was tough and chewy, but tasty and good for soups.

When my little brother Slone Phan was old enough, the four of us would go mushroom-hunting together. We'd also be on the lookout for edible leaves and vegetables. At the start of the rainy season we'd go hunting for bamboo shoots. We'd find them spearing forth from the soil all around the bamboo groves. The biggest that were edible were around a foot high; any larger, and they were too tough. We'd dig a little way down before cutting, as the most delicious part was under the ground.

We might eat them right away, boiled and smeared in cooking oil. Or my mother might fry them with onions and garlic and a little spice. Alternatively, you could dry them on the rack over the cooking fire, or pickle them in salt water. Say Say knew where to find the tastiest mushrooms, the crispest bamboo shoots, the juiciest fruit and the most beautiful wild flowers. The forest was like a second home for Say Say, and he taught us all that he knew.

At dusk he would take us locust-hunting. We'd pop the insects into a bag and take them home with us. In the morning we'd eat them as a deep-fried snack – crunchy and sweet and bursting with fat.

At night in the midst of the rainy season we'd go looking for frogs. We'd creep around in the darkened bush, listening to the deep croaks reverberating through the leaves. Say Say would point a torch in the direction of the noise, and two pinpricks of light would jump out of the darkness – the frog's eyes!

The frog would be mesmerized by the light. As Say Say held the torch steady I would creep up and grab it. They were dark green in colour, slippery to the touch, and some were as large as an adult's fist. We'd put them into a pot, cover it with a lid, and place a heavy stone on top to stop them escaping. In the morning we'd throw in boiling water, which quickly killed the frogs.

The best way to cook frog was to curry it. We'd fry garlic and sliced onion with turmeric and salt, until the onions were golden brown. Then we'd add the frog, frying it until the spices and salt had been absorbed into the meat. We'd add water, check the taste, and then boil it for fifteen minutes or so. At the last minute we'd add some lemon grass or sweet basil leaves. This helped to kill the smell of the frog, which was pungent and fishy.

In the dry season when there were no frogs, we'd go hunting for water snails. They could be found grazing on algae on the smooth stones of the riverbed. The biggest were the size of a fat wine cork. When we had collected enough, we'd cut the top off each of the conical shells. We did this for two reasons: one, because it contains the snail's faeces; and two, because it enables you to suck the flesh of the snail out of the shell. We'd prepare them in the traditional Karen way, making Ta Ka Paut – 'water snail porridge'. Water snail tastes like squid, and the Karen are famous across Burma for eating Ta Ka Paut.

Near our house a clear stream came tinkling off the mountain, and there we would hunt for freshwater prawns and crabs. The biggest prawns were about the size of your finger, and far too fast to catch by hand. We'd drive them into a small net or a piece of cloth. If we caught enough, my mother could make prawn curry. The crabs were bigger, about the size of a child's hand. It was great fun hunting for them under the rocks. They made a lovely crab soup, or you could peel off the hard bits and pound them with chilli, to make spicy crab paste.

Sometimes, Say Say went hunting alone for food in the forest. One day he came home proudly bearing a whole ants' nest. He explained that these were Tur See – 'the sour ant'. Each was about half an inch long and fire red. The nest itself was woven together with leaves, and it was bulging with ant eggs. Say Say gave it to my mother and she boiled it up to make soup. You could see the ant eggs swimming about in the liquid, like grains of rice. It tasted sour, and I couldn't understand what Say Say was so excited about. But he and my mother really loved that ants' nest soup.

If my father was home, Say Say would go hunting in the forest for tree orchids. The orchids grow in the forest canopy, and sometimes they would be forty or fifty feet above the forest floor, but that never stopped Say Say. He was incredibly agile and sure-footed, and I never once saw him slip or fall as he gathered up whole orchid plants in his arms.

When Say Say gave the orchids to my father he would break into a wide smile like sunshine. He would sit on the steps of the house and admire the orchids, pointing out the various parts of the plants and explaining what each was for. Say Say, the orchid hunter, would be beaming from ear to ear.

My father would weave hangers for the orchids out of coconut husk, and we had scores of them swinging from the rafters. But my mother would pretty much ignore them, as she wasn't so into flowers. She was more concerned with growing things that we could eat.

Each morning my parents would be awake by five o'clock at the latest. My mother would head for her vegetable garden and to feed the animals, whilst my father went to tend to his flowers. First light was his happiest time in the garden. Often, he'd bring my mother a beautiful bunch of cut blooms. She would act all embarrassed, but secretly she was very happy. My father's romantic gestures helped keep their love fresh and alive. We nicknamed my father Paw Ka Sar – 'the flower man'.

When my parents had first moved into the village they had nowhere to stay, and so they had lodged with the family of Ter Pay Pay, a Karen man in his thirties. Ter Pay Pay lived with his parents, who were getting on in years. Over time he became a close friend of ours, and his parents became our honorary grandparents. Of course they weren't related to us, but we loved them as if they were family, and they were the nearest we ever had to a real grandpa and grandma.

Their house was on the opposite side of the school from us, so just a short walk away. In Karen culture, adults are usually nicknamed after their oldest child. My father would be called Bwa Bwa Pah – 'father of Bwa Bwa' – and my mother would be Bwa Bwa Moh – 'mother of Bwa Bwa'. Everyone called grandpa and grandma Ter Pay Pay Pah and Ter Pay Pay Moh, after their son, Ter Pay Pay. We never knew their real names.

Grandpa was a quiet man, but grandma was the opposite. She seemed never to stop talking, and was always telling us stories about her youth. She and grandpa were in their eighties, and they had lived through the British colonial times. When she was in her twenties, grandma had worked as a teacher at a school founded by the British, called Per Ku School.

Generally, the Karen and the British colonizers had got along well. The British did their best to respect Karen culture, and the Karen reacted well to that. For the first time in the modern history of Burma, the Karen were granted the right to have Karen New Year recognized across the whole of the country. Under the British, it was declared a nationwide holiday. It had been a long, long fight to reach this point, and it meant a lot to the Karen people.

The Karen calendar is different from the Gregorian calendar used by most of the world. It is a lunar one, each month lasting one cycle of the moon. There are twelve months each of thirty days, making a 360-day year, so each year entails a five-day slippage. Each month has an evocative name; for example, month three is Thway Kaw, 'the month when cicadas sing'; ominously, the twelfth month is Lah Plu, 'the month when the spirits of the dead walk the earth'.

Karen New Year happens on the first day of The Lay, the first month in the year. It was this day that the British had formally recognized and declared a public holiday.

One of grandma's favourite stories was about when the Japanese came to attack, during the Second World War. One day aircraft appeared overhead and bombed the school, and everyone had to flee. The Japanese soldiers came next, with the Burma Independence Army (BIA) – the Burmese forces that had made common cause with the Japanese – in support.

The BIA had joined forces with the Japanese to drive the British colonizers out of Burma. What they had failed to realize was that in doing so, they would replace one colonizer with another.

The Japanese and BIA forces visited horrific cruelties on the Karen villages. Grandma told us how they would snatch Karen babies, throw them into the air, and impale them on their bayonets. Or they would get a pregnant Karen woman, force her to lie on her side, and pound her stomach with a rice pounder. It was so horrible. It seemed impossible that people could be so merciless.

The attacking forces hated the Karen, because they knew we were sheltering their enemies – the British and Allied soldiers. More than anything, the Japanese were trying to force the Karen to give up the leader of the British troops, Major Hugh Seagrim. Major Seagrim was leading a joint force of British and Karen soldiers, who were fighting a guerrilla war from the jungles. They would launch surprise attacks then melt back into the hills.

The Karen steadfastly refused to betray Major Seagrim, but when he realized that the Japanese were taking revenge on innocent Karen villagers he gave himself up. He did so knowing that the Japanese would execute him for leading such a spirited resistance. We Karen had an affectionate name for Major Seagrim. He was so tall compared to most Karen that we called him 'Grandfather Longlegs'. We didn't agree with Grandfather Longlegs giving himself up, but he was a brave and principled man. He wouldn't stand by and see innocents suffer.

The Japanese executed Major Seagrim and several of his Karen brothers-in-arms. Even then, the Japanese and BIA continued to oppress the Karen people, burning villages and crops and shooting people on sight. Yet still the armed resistance grew. The British airdropped weapons and soldiers into the Karen jungles. The parachutes fell most thickly around Thaw Thi Ko Mountain, the centre of the resistance movement at that time. This was the area where grandma was born, and where she had fled to during the fighting.

One night under a silver moon grandma saw many things fall from the sky: it was an airdrop of men and crates of weapons and ammunition. Karen soldiers who had been training and fighting alongside the British in India had returned to free their homeland.

Under the leadership of a handful of British officers, they came to rouse the Karen resistance and lead them in battle.

The Japanese knew that a force had fallen from the sky, and they massed to attack. But the mountain was very high, and only the locals knew the way to climb it. They were helping the British and Karen force build underground shelters and trenches. The Japanese advanced, but they had underestimated the mountain and the severe weather. As they climbed conditions steadily worsened.

Several thousand Japanese troops launched the attack, but they were much weakened by the cold. The battle raged for days as people fought and died on the mountain. Finally the fighting came to an end when the Americans dropped the atom bomb on Hiroshima, and the Japanese troops were ordered to abandon the offensive and return to their barracks.

The Japanese commander decided the quickest route to do so would be to follow the Salween River south to Moulmein, the capital of Mon state and their headquarters. The Japanese went about commandeering boats from the Karen villagers. There were strong, river-worthy craft that the villagers used to navigate the mighty waters of the Salween, but the Japanese commander decided that these weren't good enough. He wanted craft with proper roofs to provide shade to his soldiers on the long journey ahead. The Karen villagers were ordered to build new ones, and quickly, even though they warned the Japanese that they wouldn't be river-worthy.

When the flotilla was ready, the Japanese force set off along the Salween. Everything was fine until they reached the notorious rapids at Papun. Here the boats started to rock wildly, and one after the other they were torn apart. Of all the Japanese soldiers only one survived; he was thrown clear and on to the bank of the river. Villagers found him, and sent him on to the Japanese headquarters, on foot. That lone survivor had been struck dumb by his terrible experiences.

Grandma told us lots of tales like this. She did so because she never wanted it to be forgotten how the Karen had fought and suffered. I liked listening to these stories; somehow, I felt it was important to hear such things. The British had promised the Karen some degree of autonomy in a post-war Burma, as they had done with other ethnic groups who fought on their side. This would be their reward for helping to drive the Japanese out of the country.

But by the time the war was over those promises seemed to have been forgotten. In 1947, shortly after the Second World War, the Karen National Union had been founded, and this went on to become the heart of the resistance movement. After centuries of oppression as part of Burma, the KNU wanted an independent state for its people. They saw this as the only way to guarantee their rights and preserve their culture.

KNU leaders travelled to London to ask the British Prime Minister to keep his promise that the Karen would have their own state. But when Burma gained independence, in 1948, no such guarantee was given. And so had begun decades of conflict and hardship for the Karen people.

Whenever I walked to grandma's house I had to pass through the turkey field. Normally, I'd be with my elder sister or brother, but one day I set out alone. I reached the turkey field, and all of a sudden I was a little girl surrounded by these giant birds. Sensing my fear and uncertainty, the turkeys fluffed out their feathers and started to hiss at me. As I shrunk back they advanced and started to peck. I screamed as loudly as I could, and grandpa came running. He scooped me up in his arms and carried me off to safety. I felt so loved and cared for. 'Wow, Little Granddaughter!' grandpa exclaimed, once he'd heard what had happened. 'You are so brave – this little, and still you come to visit us all alone!'

Grandpa smoked a wooden pipe, and he was always asking me to go and fetch his lighter from the bedroom. Grandma also smoked, and her lighter and his would be lying side by side near the bed. I knew which was which, and I would always return with the right one. Grandpa would put me on his lap and light up, the tobacco smoke hanging blue and fragrant in the air. As he puffed away I would drop off to sleep in his arms. Often, Say Say would have to carry me home fast asleep.

When I was nearing my fourth birthday grandpa died quite suddenly. He was the first person that I had ever known to die. My mother explained to me that grandpa was dead, and that once he was buried I would never see him again. I was very sad. I loved grandpa even more than grandma. She was forever chatting away, but it was with grandpa that I got the best snoozes and cuddles.

I had spent much time playing at grandpa's feet when he was alive, and I wanted to touch them one last time. I went to their house, and found grandpa laid out in the living room, his body surrounded by candles. He was covered in a white cloth, with just his face showing. He looked so peaceful, and if I hadn't known better I would have thought him fast asleep. I went and tweaked the cloth, so it revealed just his toes. I played with each in turn, until I was sure they were all there.

After he was buried I asked my mother where grandpa had gone. She didn't give me any easy answers – like he was in heaven and we'd meet him again. Karen animists believe that once the body has died the spirit remains on earth, so in that sense grandpa was still with us. This is what my mother explained to me, and somehow I liked the idea that grandpa was here, watching over me.

Grandpa died at the approach of the rainy season. June to September was the time of the heaviest rains, and during those months it rained day and night, seemingly without end. Just prior to the start of the rains was the time for clearing and planting rice fields. November to December was the driest part of the year, and the harvest time. The rice planting and the rice harvest were the two big milestones of the Karen year, and each stage of the rice-farming process was marked with a ceremony.

We farmed by cutting a patch of forest, burning it, and planting in the ash-rich soil. Our rice was a rain-fed crop, and it was often grown on steep hillsides. Prior to cutting the first tree, my father would perform an animist ceremony called Pet Ku – 'the tree cutting'. He would take some food and pray over this, before offering it to the forest. My father would ask the tree spirits to forgive him for cutting them, and explain that he needed to grow food for his family.

After the forest had been cut and burned, my father would hold a second ceremony, Thu Bu – 'the rice planting'. Again, he would offer food, whilst asking the spirit of the farm to look after the rice. This was to ensure a rich and bountiful harvest. When I was little I used to try to help Say Say with the rice planting, but instead of dropping four or five seeds into each hole I'd throw in a whole handful. Say Say had to follow after me taking the extra seeds out as we couldn't afford to waste any!

The third ritual, Kut Bu – 'the rice harvest' – worked in a similar way to the roofing ceremony. We would announce that we intended to harvest our rice fields in so many days' time. On the allotted day the neighbours would gather and we'd head off to the fields. My mother would cook chicken and pumpkin curry, but this time she would do so in a temporary shelter adjacent to the rice fields.

Prior to starting the harvest, most animist Karen would give thanks to the spirits. We would offer little dishes of food, as a token of appreciation. My father and Say Say would organize the work force, and a row of bodies would bend with their *htat gheh* – the rice-cutting knife – and begin. Each person would take a handful of bright green stems, slice at just above ground level, tie the cut bundle with a rice stem, and place it to one side.

When you had enough cut bundles, you'd lay them out on a woven mat beside the hut. After three days drying in the sun, you had to walk backwards and forwards on the bundles, until all the rice had fallen off the stalks. You'd remove the rice stalks and take them to feed your animals, or put them on the vegetable garden as fertilizer.

The harvested rice would be separated into parts: the largest, for the family to eat; another, as seed for planting the following year; a third, to say thank you to those who helped with the harvest. The family's rice would be placed inside a giant rice store, a *bu paw*. This was the size of a small car, and it was made from woven bamboo rope covered in a cow-dung-and-mud plaster. The plaster would dry hard as rock, and it provided a tough, waterproof exterior. A ladder led up the outside to a cover, which gave access to the interior.

My father and Say Say had made our *bu paw*. They'd plastered the outside with their bare hands, and their handprints could be seen in the hard covering.

There was a popular joke that we used to tell about the dung plaster. This is how it went: one day a Karen scientist and a Karen philosopher were inspecting a rice store. The scientist said: 'I'm confused -- how did the cow get up so high to defecate on the side of the rice store?' 'It's easy,' the philosopher replied. 'Just give me your hands and I'll show you how it's done!'

Normally, the *bu paw* would sit beside or under the house. But since the Burmese Army had launched its Four Cuts policy, people were increasingly building their rice stores in hidden places. Of course, in our village there was no danger of Burmese soldiers burning our rice stores down. At least, not yet there wasn't.

In my childish mind the war was all a long way away, and we lived in a beautiful, peaceful place. It was inconceivable to me that it would ever change. I had seen grandpa die, but he was an old man – and I knew that all people had to die in the end. There was nothing dark or horrific about his death.

And in any case, grandpa's spirit was still with us.

Chapter Five

THE FLOWER CHILDREN

When I was five years old I started primary school. The school building was very basic – a large bamboo-framed hut, with open sides and rows of sawn log benches facing the single blackboard. Still, it was all we knew and from the very first I loved it. Whilst my mother was more the warrior, my father was the thinker of our family, and I took after him.

In Year One we had Karen language lessons, basic English and handwriting. There was a set school uniform – a blue skirt and white blouse – but a number of families were so poor that they couldn't afford it. Their children were allowed to come to class in whatever clothes they had. I felt sorry for them in their make-do half-uniforms. Luckily, I had my sister's hand-me-downs.

During that first year the teacher asked us what we wanted to be when we grew up. I said 'a teacher', because that was about the most important profession that I could think of. Of course, my teacher was very pleased. In those first few months I learned to write my name, 'Zoya', in Karen. But I often got it wrong, and spelled it 'Zo-gah' instead. I kept getting the Karen 'y' letter upside down, which turns it into 'g'. Zo-gah means 'broken', and my friends would laugh and tease me mercilessly. I was already unhappy, because my name wasn't a traditional Karen one. This just made it worse.

The school doubled as the village church and the village hall. Boys and girls had to sit in separate rows. We were told that the atmosphere was not to be one of competition between pupils, and we should be pleased when others did well.

There was a school bell made of a triangular iron rod. Each morning the headmaster would bash a metal pole backwards and forwards inside it. The harsh ringing would echo across the village, and that was the signal for morning assembly. It was also rung at the end of the school day, and for Sunday school.

Our village was mixed Christian, animist and Buddhist. No one ever tried to convert anyone directly, but Sunday school was an overtly Christian affair. We were taught that if you weren't a Christian then you would go to hell. When the teacher told me this I feared it might be true, and that was scary.

My parents were very relaxed about religion. Whenever they were asked their religion, they would say that they were Pwa Aw Gheh – 'the people who believe in the spirit'. That is how Karen people describe their animism. But my parents never preached to us. They always said that I was free to choose my own faith. So I listened carefully to what the Sunday school teacher told us, and tried to make up my own mind.

Mostly, the different religions in our village coexisted without tension or conflict. A good example of this was people's attitude to my almost-dying. I first heard about my almost-dying when I was five years old. We had visitors, and my mother decided to tell them the story. As I listened I realized that she believed it was truly a miracle that I had lived. It was as if I had been given the gift of life.

As for the visitors, they were amazed to meet someone who had been unconscious for three days and survived. We had no proper medical facilities in our area, and in their minds I should have died. Each person would view the story from the perspective of their faith – Christian, animist or Buddhist – interpreting the miracle of my survival from within their own belief system.

The lack of proper medical care in our village was so acute that people turned to alternative cures. My mother was a healer of sorts, and the method she used was acupuncture. She called it Ter Ru Tat – 'the Chinese needles'. She had been taught basic Ter Ru Tat during her nursing training. People would come to our house from far and wide, complaining of back pain or joint aches. Most were poor villagers or farmers, and she never turned anyone away.

She would get the patient to sit on a rug on the bamboo floor. Then she opened a little wooden box and removed her needles. She'd sterilize each in a cup of boiling water. As she did so, she'd ask the patient to tell her exactly what was wrong. I remember one man who had terrible back pain. He was a farmer, and he explained that he had been suffering for so long. There was no clinic in his area, but he had heard about my mother, and so he had come.

My mother asked him if he was sure he wanted her to proceed. He told her he did. She searched for the right spot and inserted the needles in his back. Every now and then she tweaked them, to make them sensitive again. He lay there for an hour or so like that, and then she told him that his pain would be healed. He got up from the floor and smiled. He seemed to be moving much more easily. A few days later he came back with a gift of a chicken. His back was better and he could work again.

Sometimes injured Karen resistance fighters would come for treatment. I'd ask my mother how the needles worked. Normally, a needle was used for an injection, and you could see the medicine going in. She told me that her needles already had medicine in them. But you had to concentrate and be steady with your hand, or the needles wouldn't hit the right spot. It looked very scary to me when I saw someone stuck full of needles, like a pincushion.

But it must have worked, for my mother was famous for using her 'Chinese needles'.

Because our school was a village one, most of my classmates were also my neighbours and my playmates. My closest friends were Day Nyah Paw – Lily Flower; Tee Ser Paw – Sweet Water Flower; and Nightingale. Nightingale was called Nightingale in English, and she didn't have a Karen name. It wasn't that unusual for Karen children to be given English names, especially among the families of the resistance.

Nightingale lived next door, and she was the same age as me. Her house was between the river and ours. Her mother was a housewife and her father worked in the resistance. We were very close, and we'd always be playing at each other's house.

I would call out from mine: 'Nightingale, are you there?'

If she was in she'd hear me, and her voice would come floating back: 'Yes! Yes! Are you coming over to play?'

Nightingale's hair was cut very short. Like me she was curious, and always up for an adventure. One time she and I sneaked into the neighbour's garden and stole some mangos from her tree. We returned to Nightingale's house and headed for the toilet. It wasn't the nicest place for a mango feast: it was a simple hole dug in the ground with a bamboo wall around it, and it smelled horrid. But we couldn't think of anywhere else to eat them without getting caught.

We devoured the fruit and threw the stones down into the dark, smelly pit. Unfortunately we'd been found out already. Nightingale's older sister had seen us sneaking into the loo. She caught us as we were coming out, our hands all sticky with mango.

'You naughty girls!' she scolded. 'You stole mangos from the neighbour's garden! I saw you! Don't you know she can work magic, and now you've eaten them you'll have horrible pains in your tummy?'

I was so scared that I wanted to vomit up all of the mango, but of course I couldn't. We didn't even try to deny it. We were both too worried, and in any case we knew it was wrong to lie.

'Don't you know that lady counts her mangos every day?' Nightingale's sister went on. 'She'll know how many she's lost, and then she'll work her spells on the thief.'

We were even more afraid now. We vowed that we wouldn't ever steal mangos again.

I was the leader of my girl friends, and most likely the mango-stealing mission had been my idea. The mangos were very tempting. The problem with the plan was the toilet; it wasn't a very nice place to eat a mango, and it was far too public to do so in secret.

On the other side of my house from Nightingale lived Tee Ser Paw – Sweet Water Flower. Although she was thin and dainty-looking, she could be loud and competitive. But Sweet Water Flower was still part of our 'gang'. Her aunt was both the school maths teacher and our Sunday school teacher, and I'd often go to their house for lunch.

Sweet Water Flower had a beautiful voice, and in church she would invariably sing the solo. She and I were in the Sunday school choir, along with many of the other students, and I did enjoy singing the songs we learned.

Jesus loves me yes I know,
For the Bible tells me so,
He came to free me from sin,
And now I am his child again.

The third friend in our gang was Day Nyah Paw – Lily Flower. Her house was a little separated from the three of us, and further towards Teak Mountain. She was the opposite in appearance to Sweet Water Flower, as she was a big, strong-looking girl. Others used to say she was bossy, but she wasn't ever like that with me. She was the biggest girl in our class, and she used to order Nightingale and Sweet Water Flower around. But she could also be kind and generous, too.

My fourth girl friend was Naw Paw – Miss Flower. Her father

was a political prisoner so the family were very poor. But the problem for her was that she lived down the far end of the village. The village was squeezed between the river and the mountain, strung out in a long line along the riverbank. From one end of the village to the other was a real trek. All of us liked Naw Paw, but she just didn't live close enough to be with us all the time.

I was the gang leader most of the time. In part this was because I was always thinking up new games to play. But I also had an advantage in that the floor of our house was unusually high, leaving plenty of room beneath it for us to play. Often, our gang would go climbing the guava trees. Bwa Bwa might be with us, and Slone might come with Nightingale's brother, his best friend. If Miss Flower was there then we would be eight – all of us swinging in the branches, grabbing the fruit, and playing.

On a steep slope beneath some trees we made a mudslide. Nightingale and I would go careering down the muddy shoot on our backsides, laughing fit to burst. We knew it was naughty, because we'd get covered in mud from head to toe. But there was no way we could be good: playing on the mudslide was just too much fun.

I was good friends with the leader of the boys' gang, Lah Ka Paw – Moonlight. Moonlight was a bit of an angry child, like my little brother, Slone. He channelled that anger into being in firm control of his friends. If Moonlight made a decision, the others had to follow. Like my brother, Slone, he wasn't a particularly big child. But he was very smart, and that's how he kept control of his gang.

Moonlight lived next door to Sweet Water Flower, so he was my next-door neighbour but one. One sunny day we broke lessons for lunch. On the way home Moonlight and I started playing in the sun, wheeling around with our arms outstretched as if we were birds. I soon forgot completely about lunch. Once afternoon school was over, Moonlight and I finished off our flying game. By the time I got home my mother was worried sick. She'd even sent Say Say to search for me.

'Little Daughter – where have you been?' she exclaimed. 'You didn't come for lunch, and you're home so late.'

'I wasn't anywhere, Moe,' I said. 'I was just playing with Moonlight in the sunshine.'

After that everyone was convinced that Moonlight and I had a little romance going, and that we were destined to become sweethearts. His family and my family teased Moonlight and me remorselessly. My sister was the ringleader, amply assisted by Say Say and Slone. I was shy, and I didn't like being teased like this. As for Moonlight, when his brothers and sisters teased him that I was his girlfriend he used to get so annoyed.

One of the members of Moonlight's gang was called Winston Churchill. None of us had ever heard of the famous British prime minister of the same name, so to us his was just another English name. Winston Churchill's father was called Saw Htoo – Mr Gold. He had seven children. First was a boy called Eh Kaw Htoo – Love Country Gold. Next were four girls named Keh Blu Htoo – Helpful Gold; Ba Blu Htoo – Useful Gold; Ghay Nay Htoo – Better than Gold; and Mu Yu Htoo – River of Gold.

By then the parents must have run out of names relating to gold, for they named their next-born Winston Churchill. The final child was a girl, and she also had an English name – Running Shell. Winston Churchill's parents had given her that name because the Karen people were always running from shells, bullets and bombs. But I never heard an explanation as to why Winston Churchill was named thus!

One day Nightingale and I went on our craziest-ever adventure. Because my sister was older I used to follow her lead most of the time. Bwa Bwa announced that she was going to collect mangos, and I said that Nightingale and I were going, too. Bwa Bwa argued that it was a long, long way and we were too young. But we refused to be left behind. When Bwa Bwa and her friends set off we followed. Soon we were deep in the forest. The path petered out, and no one was sure in which direction the mango trees lay.

We'd been walking for hours when we reached a small rice farm. One of my sister's friends said she thought the mango trees were just downhill from there. My sister tried to send us back, but I kept insisting that we were fine. We went down the steep hill, clinging to bushes and branches as we descended a slippery slope. All we had with us was a basket and a knife for cutting the mangos. We had no water, and we were so thirsty.

We paused whilst my sister cut into the side of a banana tree. We cupped our hands and drank the banana water as it came pouring out. It tasted like diluted, ripe banana, and was wonderfully cool and refreshing. We pushed on and eventually we reached the mango trees. Fruit was lying everywhere. These were a small variety of mango, about the size of a plum, and they were delicious. We collected up the mangos and ate our fill. By the time we were done there weren't enough left to fill the basket.

Someone suggested that we should whistle up the wind, so that it would blow down more of the ripe fruit. Many Karen believe that by making a whistling noise like the wind in the trees, you can cause the wind to blow. We all tried to whistle, but no matter how hard I tried I couldn't manage it.

'It's probably because your lips are too big,' Bwa Bwa announced. 'Look at the size of them! No wonder you can't whistle.'

The others followed Bwa Bwa's lead and started to tease me about my lips.

'They may be big, but they're beautiful,' I retorted. 'In fact, they're the perfect size for calling up the wind!'

Just then and as if by magic the wind started to blow. It blew and blew and down fell the mangos. We collected up as many as we could, and then we turned for home. We tried to retrace the route we had taken on the way out. But we'd lost track of the time, and dusk settles quickly in the forest. At night the forest is a completely different beast from the day, and we didn't want to be out in the dark. We hurried ahead, fearful of losing our way. It was a huge relief when we reached the village in the gathering darkness.

We had left in the morning and spent the whole day mango-hunting. In a sense it was a crazy thing to have done, but we were only thinking of the mangos! There were so many dangers in the forest: snakes, scorpions, poisonous spiders, tigers and wild elephants. All we'd been wearing was T-shirts, cotton shorts and flip-flops. My parents had warned us about going into the forest without Say Say. We decided it was best to keep that mango-hunting expedition very quiet.

At school I quickly mastered my English ABCs and moved on to learning basic sentences. The teacher would write the words 'this is' on the blackboard and hold up an item – for example, a piece of chalk or an apple. We had to fill in the missing words. But poor Nightingale found it so hard to master 'this is'. She had a lisp, due to a gap between her two front teeth, and she pronounced it 'thi i'. It was so funny, and we teased her when she got it wrong.

We didn't appreciate it at the time, but we were so lucky to be learning Karen. In areas controlled by the Burmese regime – which is dominated by the Burman ethnic group – no one was allowed to study Karen or any other ethnic language.

In Burma there are eight main ethnic groups: the Shan, Arakan, Mon, Kachin, Chin, Karen, Karenni and Burman. Then there are dozens of smaller ethnic groups, and each has its own language. But the only language other than English taught in schools controlled by the regime was Burmese. Rather than celebrating the nation's cultural riches, the regime tried to crush its diversity.

Each week on a Friday we would have a lesson called Citizenship Education. In it we were taught to respect older people, to respect our parents and to help people who might be in need of assistance. If we were walking on a path and we saw an old woman carrying firewood, we were taught to go and offer help. It was common sense really, and a reminder to us about how we should behave towards others.

I came top of my class in the Year One exams. There was a big prize-giving ceremony on the school playing field. My mother was there, as were most of the other parents. When I was called to the front to receive my prize I was thrilled. Of course, I was wearing one of my sister's hand-me-down skirts and it was far too big for me. I went running up to the stage, all the while holding up my skirt with my hands. But when I went to reach for the prize I let go in my excitement, and down my skirt fell.

Everyone burst out laughing. It was so funny that the teachers laughed, the parents laughed, the pupils laughed, and my brothers and sister laughed. Even my mother couldn't help laughing. I was shocked and confused, and I didn't know what to do. Should I first take my prize, or pull up my skirt? Finally, it was the teacher who reached down and did it for me. She told me to grip my skirt with one hand and take my prize with the other. I did just that, and turned around and went back to join my mother. She was glowing with a mixture of pride . . . and embarrassment.

It was more than worth all the humiliation when I examined my prize – it was six exercise books and three pens. We had little or no money to buy such things, so these were precious to me. The funniest thing was that the following year I did a repeat performance. I came top of the class in Year Two, and sure enough the same thing happened – down my skirt fell! By Year Three it had become something of a prize-giving tradition: Zoya would come top of the class, and her skirt would fall down. Each year people were just waiting for it to happen.

In the village I soon became known as 'the-girl-whose-skirt-fell-down'. We Karen have a wicked sense of humour, and we are always laughing at each other's misfortune – as long as it isn't serious. Even when I got a lot older people remembered my falling skirts, and still they teased me about it.

Ever since I can remember I was very independent, and when I won the school prize I kept my winnings to myself. I used to store my things in a rucksack that I kept by my bed, and I didn't like other people touching it. In that bag were my few clothes, a wooden bowl my father had made me, a handful of precious photos that had been taken at village weddings, and my school prize materials. And those were all my worldly possessions.

At school we studied the Karen flag and learned its meaning. It is made up of three stripes of red, white and blue, with a rising sun with nine rays set over a Karen drum in one corner. During colonial times the Karen had to fight to get their flag recognized by the British, just as they had done with the Karen New Year.

We learned that the red stood for the courage of the Karen people. The white signified purity of purpose and honesty. And blue in our culture means loyalty. The rising sun signified that the Karen were a new nation, and its nine rays stood for the nine regions inhabited by the Karen people – Irrawaddy, Mirawaddy, Tennasarim and so on.

As for the Karen drum, that is used for the Done Dance – a traditional Karen procession and an archetypal symbol of our people. In the early morning before the sun rises, drummers would begin their beating to signify it was time to start the rice harvest. They would beat the drum to call people to the fields. Whenever a person heard the drum beat it signified the strength of the Karen spirit.

Some of our teachers were nice, but one or two were very strict and scary. If any of us pronounced a word wrongly, or made a spelling mistake, we might get a bamboo stick pushed into our tummy button, twisted around and pulled sharply out again. This was the worst form of punishment as it was so painful.

When Slone Phan started school *theramu* – teacher – Lah Say Wah tried the tummy button punishment on him. But Slone was having none of it. Instead, this 4-year-old boy turned the tables by grabbing the bamboo stick and hitting *her*, to the great amusement of the class. *Theramu* Lah Say Wah told my mother that her young son was uncontrollable and that she couldn't handle him any more. My mother couldn't help laughing when she heard what Slone had done.

But the worst was Thera C Win, known simply as 'Teacher C'. We used to play a game called *ta htaw ler* – 'the stone game'. You had to throw a piece of gravel into the air, pick up another piece and catch the falling stone, all with the one hand. Once you'd managed it with one stone, you'd throw two into the air, then three and four and so on. The stone game was addictive and I loved it.

One morning during assembly Winston Churchill's sister Keh Blu Htoo – Helpful Gold – and I were playing the stone game. The school assembly hall had a wooden floor, upon which the stones made a hollow crack. Everyone was quiet, listening to Teacher C speaking from the stage. All of a sudden Teacher C went quiet. He'd caught the noise of our stones clacking on to the floor. He bounded down the room and was standing over us.

We stared up at him, guiltily. There was no time for explanations. He just grabbed us each by the hair and banged our heads together. The sound of our heads colliding was far noisier than the falling stones! It was so painful. I felt as if my head were about to explode. Teacher C demanded to know if we'd learned our lesson. Indeed we had: no more playing the stone game in school assembly!

Not long after this someone broke wind during morning assembly. It smelled horrible, and the nasty aroma quickly filled the room. Teacher C became red-faced with anger, and he demanded to know who had broken wind. We were all so scared, and we knew that whoever had done it would be punished severely. A deathly silence filled the room, but no one would own up to it.

'We know someone has done this!' Teacher C thundered. 'Now own up! If you don't own up, I will punish everyone, because you have lied to me.'

Teacher C made us stand on the wooden benches for the whole morning. No one was allowed to leave, not even to use the loo. Students who needed to pee either ended up wetting themselves, or peed into a plastic bag. I knew that none of the pupils my age could have made such a horrid smell, one that filled the whole assembly hall. That made the punishment even less fair. The person who had made that bad smell never did own up, so we never knew who the culprit was.

In our culture breaking wind is considered the height of bad manners, although most Karen will admit a loud one can be very funny. But burping is seen to be more a sign of enjoying one's food. Feet are considered to be a potential source of offence, because they are the 'lowest' part of the body. If you stick your feet out before you, or into someone's face, it is a particularly rude thing to do. By contrast hair is considered the 'highest' part of the body, and it is almost sacred. That's why Karen women rarely if ever cut their hair.

As children we never had enough money to buy school supplies, and so we had little for the luxuries of day-to-day living. I had no toothbrush or toothpaste. Instead, Say Say taught me how to use wood ash from the cooking fire to clean my teeth. A finger of ash rubbed vigorously around my mouth tasted horrid, but once it was rinsed away it left my teeth shining.

As for washing, we used Sat Pya Tha – 'the soap fruit'. Soap fruit is the size and shape of a chicken's egg. It comes from a tree in the forest, and Say Say was an expert at finding it. You'd take the pulp of the fruit and rub it over your skin, producing a thin lather. As for shampoo, we'd use turmeric root, mixed with Thay Blo Blay, the 'slippery plant', plus the seed of the Poe See – 'the sour fruit tree'. We'd boil it up and leave it overnight, and by morning the water would be thick and slimy. We'd wash our hair in the liquid, and rinse it with clean water.

We believed that this shampoo would take away your sadness. There was a special ceremony we had for doing so. Once a year my mother would make sure she washed our hair with this special shampoo, and we in turn would wash our mother's and father's hair with it. Following that we'd give them a bath, using water perfumed with flower oil. In this way we showed our love, care and respect for them, and our parents gave us their blessing in turn.

Our bathroom was open-sided, with a bucket on a bench and a leaf roof overhead. A number of bamboo poles split in half lengthways formed a series of interconnecting pipes that siphoned water from the stream above downhill to our bathroom. When I was little I wasn't too concerned about staying clean, so I would copy Slone. Slone just whizzed a few dishes of water over his head, and declared himself done.

Our primary school teachers taught us the legends of the Karen people. One of the most important was a poem that narrated the story of the earliest times of our tribe. It tells that in the beginning there was an animist god, called Ywa. Ywa was neither man nor woman, and was not in a human form. Ywa was the creator of the world and a force for good. To balance Ywa there was also a force for evil, called Mu Kaw Lee.

Ywa created three sons in human form. The eldest was a Karen, the second a Burman, and the youngest was a white man. To the Karen son Ywa gave a golden book, to the Burman a silver book, and to the white man Ywa gave a book bound in normal paper.

When the rains began and the Karen son went to plant his rice field, he placed the golden book nearby, on a tree stump. But his youngest brother, the white man, had grown jealous and coveted his beautiful golden book. When the Karen man wasn't looking the white man came along and took it, replacing it with his own. Then the white man built a boat and escaped to a far-off country. He carried his prize with him – the golden book that contained the teachings Ywa had given to his eldest son.

After a long day working under the heavy rain, the Karen man went to fetch his golden book. The book that the white man had left in its place had fallen apart in the rain, and there was nothing left. A chicken had been scratching around the stump searching for food, and all the Karen man found was chicken scratch marks. He concluded that the golden book had been replaced by the scratch marks, and that those must embody the message that Ywa had left him.

And so the Karen man taught himself to read and write in chicken scratch. Over time, he learned the truth about the golden book being stolen, but by then it was too late – chicken scratch had become the official language of the Karen. The Karen man wrote down the story of how the golden book was stolen, and the word

of Ywa lost, in a new book. He called this book Li Hsaw Weh –
'the book of chicken scratch teachings'.

Centuries later the first white missionaries came to Burma.
Many Karen believed that this was the younger brother returning,
bringing the golden book in the form of the Bible, and so they welcomed them. Many Karen believe this story absolutely, and that
one day the younger brother – a white man – will come again to
help save our people.

The traditional 'chicken scratch' writing of the Karen has all but
died out. With no recognized written language the missionaries
found it hard to convert people to Christianity, especially as they
couldn't read the Bible. So the missionaries invented a written
language for the Karen, based upon the Burmese alphabet. That
is what we use today.

Many of the Karen are Buddhist, and it is the predominant religion in Burma. Once a year my parents would take me to the
Water Festival, which happens every April. We'd take a long-tail
boat to Ka Paw Lu – Spider Hill Village – on the bank of the Moei
River. It was called Spider Hill Village because the villagers found
many huge spiders when they cleared the bush to build the first
houses. The Water Festival was held in the Buddhist monastery
that overlooks the village.

The Water Festival is like a captivating carnival. It takes place
at the hottest time of year, and people are supposed to pour water
over each other to cool down. But, invariably, it turns into a big
water fight! The monks would dress in their saffron robes, and
ring their little hand bells, as they started chanting, chanting,
chanting. There were trays piled high with delicious food – rice,
curry, biscuits and traditional snacks. And the smoke of burning
incense with its spicy scent would hang heavy in the air.

But best were the hot air balloons, each as big as an elephant.
The monks made them out of brightly coloured paper, with a
small wood fire at the neck of the balloon. Hanging down was a
long rope strung with gifts – children's clothes, soap and sweets.
The monks would release a balloon and it would soar skywards,

everyone watching to see its direction of flight. As the fire died down, so the balloon started to descend. People tried to guess where it was going to land and set off at a run, balloon-chasing. The first to find it could take their pick of the presents.

Of course, we loved it. It was a wonderful adventure for us, but my parents went to show their respect for Buddhism. Throughout our childhood my parents would take us to hear the chanting of the Buddhist monks and the preaching of the Christian pastors, whilst at home they would follow their animist traditions. In this way they exposed us to the main faiths in Burma, leaving us free to choose our own.

The highlight of the Christian year was Christmas, and our village made it a very big deal. As with the Water Festival, it was a magical time of year. With the help of Mo Ghay Bay, we'd drag a big tree out of the forest. Mo Ghay Bay was so strong she could pick up a tree using only her trunk. With her help we'd erect the tree in the school playground, and decorate it with balloons and presents. The presents would be wrapped in old exercise book paper, for that was all we had, and tied up with string.

On Christmas Eve we had a nativity play, with one student acting as Joseph and one as Mary, and a model stable with a baby in a cradle. Others acted as the Three Wise Men, following the star to the stable, and as angels, shepherds and sheep. For some reason I always wanted to be a sheep, covered in a white cloth and crawling on all fours. But eventually I got bored with that, and then I wanted to be an angel, singing with an angelic voice in the choir.

Christmas morning was for present opening. Parents didn't generally give their children many presents, as no one could afford them. Instead, our parents would buy us gifts of biscuits, sweets or soap, which we were supposed to give to our friends. The teachers would write the names of all the children on scraps of paper and put them into a hat. Each of us had to pick a name, and that was the child to whom you gave your present.

By lunchtime the entire village would have congregated at the school. Each family would have brought their own Christmas lunch – usually bamboo-cooked rice, sticky rice and chicken. Bamboo-cooked rice was my favourite food at Christmas. To make it one had to cut a bamboo the width of a man's arm and about three or four feet long. The inside would be packed half full of rice and topped up with water.

Then you'd lay the bamboo in the glowing embers, so that 75 per cent of it was in the fire and you could keep turning the free end. As the bamboo blackened in the fire, the rice inside would get cooked. Finally, you'd remove it and split it open. The rice would come out in a pillar contained in the inner membrane of the bamboo. It would be steaming hot and delicately flavoured.

Another of my favourite foods on Christmas Day was a dish made with sticky rice. The sticky rice had to be mixed with sesame seeds and pounded in a pestle and mortar, until it became like a sticky, hard mash. Once it was ready you'd cut it into slices and eat it like savoury cake.

But the best thing about Christmas was Santa Claus. Santa would be dressed in a red suit made of light cotton, and wearing a pointed hat with a white ball on the end. As he ho!-ho!-ho!-ed he'd throw handfuls of sweets and biscuits. We'd go mad fighting to get them, running and falling and laughing fit to burst.

Sometimes Santa would start doing a silly dance, which would make us laugh all the more. He wore an enormous white beard, and at first I believed absolutely that he was for real. In my mind he was a kindly human from a far distant land who came to make Karen children happy on Christmas Day.

In my village it seemed to me we lived in a kind of paradise. But, sadly, not even paradise lasts for ever.

Chapter Six

RIVER OF DARKNESS

When we weren't at school we had to invent our own entertainment, as there were no televisions, computers or cinemas in our village. One of our best games was called *moh geh tha* – 'the seed game'. The seed we used was hard and woody, with a smooth, tough exterior. It was about the size of a domino, with a flat, streamlined shape.

We'd start by placing a line of seeds in the earth, balanced on their ends. You'd move back to the start and shoot a seed at the line, flicking it off your palm in a spinning trajectory, a bit like a tiny flying saucer. If you hit the line of seeds just right they would all go tumbling down, like a line of dominoes. Both boys and girls played, and however many you knocked over would be your score.

I had a classmate called Saw Htoo Say – Mr Gold Silver – who was the champion of the seed game. Saw Htoo Say's father was the keeper of Mo Ghay Bay, the village elephant. But in Year Two at school Saw Htoo Say suddenly became very sick. He'd broken out in what we called 'the boil sickness', with painful pustules all over his body. Poor Saw Htoo Say died in complete agony. All he would have needed to cure him was antibiotics and antiseptic dressings, but in the village clinic we had only a few very simple medicines.

People died in our area because we lacked even the most basic medical supplies. To us this seemed normal, for it was all we had ever known. Death was no stranger; it was a companion that we lived with daily. But it was still very sad when someone as young as Saw Htoo Say died. He was a lovely, kindly boy and very gifted at school. After his death the whole village – teachers, family, children and the elderly – went into a kind of collective mourning.

I remember very clearly the first 'proper' clinic that was ever held in our area. I was around five or six years old when two French nurses, a man and a woman, came to our village. They were running a mobile backpack clinic: all the medicines they had with them had to be carried on their backs through the jungle. But to us it was just as if a real hospital had come to town, so impressive were their medical supplies.

It was also the first time that I'd seen white people. I was told they were 'French', but that meant nothing to me. All I knew was that they were Gaw La Wah – 'white people'. Their hair was whiter than elephant ivory, and their eyes were bluer than the sky. As I gazed at them with their pale faces and long noses, I couldn't believe how scary they looked.

They sat on pillows provided by the villagers, and spread out their medical supplies. I had no idea why they were sitting on the pillows like that. In Karen culture a pillow is the highly respected place where you lay your head to rest. That's why we gave them as presents to lovers. No Karen person would ever place their bottom on one!

The French nurses called together the adults and announced that they'd come to vaccinate the children. We sat on the ground and waited, nervously, as the village nurse called us one by one. Eventually it was my turn. I went and sat on my teacher's lap, and waited to see what would happen. A lot of the children before me had cried. The French lady turned to me and gave me an injection in the arm. It didn't really hurt, and I thought to myself 'If that's it, it's not so bad.'

I gazed up at her as she dabbed at my arm with a piece of cotton wool. It was her nose that I just couldn't get over. It was long and white and pointed, and burned red on top from exposure to the sun. I realized then that the other children hadn't been crying because of the pain of the injections; they'd been crying because of their fear of the nurse! I found her scary, too, but I didn't cry. I just wished my mother had been there to hold me.

When we weren't playing our seed game, we might be playing 'the marble game'. Of course, we didn't have proper glass marbles, so we had to make our own. On the outskirts of the village was a pit where you could find sticky reddish clay. We would search for the right kind of clay. If it contained small stones or sand it wouldn't work, as the marbles would fall apart in no time. We'd hoof out the pure clay with a digging stick and mix it with water. Then we'd take bite-sized lumps, roll them into individual 'marbles', and leave them to bake in the sun.

Once they were as hard as rock we'd build marble pyramids, with a base of three and one on top. Then we'd take up our positions and throw one marble after another to knock them down. Whichever pyramid you destroyed you won – those were your marbles to keep. The competition to bash down the pyramids was fierce, and the tension of the marble game could make it quite exhausting!

Whenever we tired of the marble game, my sister might lead us in our own imitation of the Karen Done Dance. Bwa Bwa would start by striking a lump of wood with a stick to beat out a slow rhythm. One of her friends would join in, bashing an empty tin can to quicken the beat. We'd form up in line, and then my sister would count 'One, two, three!' On the count of three each of us would take a step forward, bow and start to dance and sing. We thought we were doing the real Done Dance, but ours was only a silly made-up children's version.

Those of us who were truly adventurous would play in the forest and rivers that surrounded the village. There was one area where the trees were draped in vines of all shapes and sizes, and it was like a natural playground. There were thin ones and ones as thick as your wrist, and smooth ones and knobbly ones, and even vines that were covered in spines. The latter were best avoided, for our favourite game was to climb a tree and go whooshing down one of the vines.

If we were feeling really brave we could jump on a vine and swing out over the river, hanging on for dear life as the water flashed past below. Of course, this game was very dangerous as the vine could break and we'd end up in the middle of the river. But we didn't consider such things as children. We had little sense of fear.

My father, however, was quite aware of how dangerous it could be, and so he built us a wonderful tree house in the garden. He constructed it in the heart of a beautiful, spreading tamarind tree, using offcuts from the sawmill, plus bamboo. I think he figured if we fell out of his tree house at least we'd end up on the ground, and not be swept down the river.

The tamarind is an evergreen that bears yellow flowers streaked with red and has an edible seed pulp. We loved that tree house so much. Slone and I spent hours playing in it, and Bwa Bwa, too. We pretended it was our home. We allocated some of the branches as bedrooms, and others as the kitchen or living room. We'd climb out to collect the tamarind fruit and bring it back to the house. Then we'd dip it in salt and chilli and have a tamarind feast. We'd eat and dip, and eat and dip, until we couldn't eat any more.

Beneath the floor of our house my father built us another plaything, a kind of giant wooden cradle. It was suspended from the rafters above with bamboo rope, and it was big enough for five or six of us to cram into. With one person allocated to push, we'd swing backwards and forwards, backwards and forwards, laughing as we did so. Eventually we'd always swing too high, or lark about too much, and someone would go tumbling out.

One time I fell and ended up under the cradle as it came swinging down again. It crushed my left arm, and I suffered for months in real pain. I couldn't lift my arm above shoulder level, or move it backwards or forwards very much. But I didn't want my parents to know, for then they might ban me from playing with my friends. So I did everything I could to disguise the fact of the injury.

We used to eat with our right hand, and take spoonfuls of curry or other food with the left. As I couldn't use my left arm very much, I had to use my right for both. But in our culture that's very rude, because your right hand is invariably covered in food from where you've been eating. When my mother noticed me doing this she asked me where all my manners had gone. Eventually, my arm seemed to repair itself of its own accord.

We had other favourite games, too. There was a giant flying beetle – the Kywee – that infested rotten bamboo. It was a glossy greeny-black in colour and about the size of a slice of apple. Whilst the male had two horns on its head, the female was hornless. Slone was an expert at climbing the bamboo and catching them. He'd give me one and share the others out with our friends, and then we'd make the males fight each other. Whoever's beetle ran away would be declared the loser.

The game wasn't without its risks. Usually, the person who lost the game had to drink a glass of water. If you lost ten times in a row you'd have to drink ten glasses of water. Much more risky was if the beetle managed to catch a finger with its pincers. Then it would close them tight and pierce the skin. It was agony. You had to hold the beetle at the back, and try to avoid that happening. We used to tie a piece of thread around the base of the beetle's horns, so it couldn't escape. Then you could let it fly about like a tiny helicopter on the end of a string.

When we tired of playing with the beetles it was time to eat them. We'd put them in the embers of the fire and watch as they crackled and sizzled. When the shell was burned, we'd take them out and let them cool a little. Then you could peel away the hard bits, including the head and legs, and eat the body. It tasted like the locusts we ate, only not quite so delicious.

Both the male and the female beetle could be used for either a game or a snack! There was a similar-looking beetle that lived in cow dung. I could never bring myself to eat that one, although lots of people did.

And then there were the games we would play all together as a village. I've no idea how it came to be so, but one of the most popular for the Karen is volleyball. Every village would have a team, and competition between villages was fierce. My mother was in the Per He Lu Village Volleyball Team. At the Karen New Year there would be a volleyball tournament, which was great fun.

But the sport that is unique to the Karen is our martial art – Ta Ker Met Su, 'hitting your opponent with fists and feet'.

Ta Ker Met Su is only for the men, and the tournament is the biggest event of the New Year. Young men fight wearing only lengths of cloth wrapped around their fists and a pair of shorts or a tucked-up longyi. Usually, we'd build a stage for our Ta Ker Met Su tournament, but elsewhere the fighting would take place on a bare earth enclosure with a rope around it. The entire community would come out to watch, with people cheering for their relatives, friends or neighbours.

Ta Ker Met Su has rules – no biting, no holding, no gouging out eyes – and both hands and legs can be used. Every bout goes a number of rounds. But at any time one or other fighter can declare that he is giving up, at which stage the judge declares the winner. But in reality that rarely if ever happened. More often than not both would end up with faces cut and covered in blood, and one might even be knocked unconscious.

Ta Ker Met Su marked our biggest yearly celebration, and it was a chance for the young men to prove they were men. The winner would get a small prize – a little money, and maybe some soap and shampoo. But it was really the honour they were after winning. It was a chance for men who weren't married to show off to the women who would be watching.

But when I was about six years old our happy games suddenly turned very dark. I was playing with my brother and sister down by the river. It was the hot season, and we were splashing about in the cool shallows. The roots of a big tree formed an underwater loop, and you had to dive down, swim through the loop and up again. It was a tight squeeze, even for someone as small as me, and you had to wiggle a lot. Neither of our parents knew we were playing this game, or I don't think they'd have been very happy.

It was nearing evening and the sun was dipping down below the mountains. As we played in the darkening water, we suddenly caught a whiff of something very bad. None of us had ever smelled anything like it before. Instinctively I was scared, but at the same time I was curious, and I wanted to know what it was.

I let my big sister and brother go first as we edged our way forwards, closer to the furthest tree roots. All of a sudden we were screaming in horror. In front of us was a man face down in the river, his body all swollen and bloated. He was lodged under a tree root, which was what was stopping him from floating away downstream. The smell was totally sickening, and we turned as one and fled back to the house.

When we reached the house we grabbed our father.

'Daddy! Daddy! Come! Come!'

'There's a dead person in the river!'

'It smells so horrible—'

He led us back towards the river. I didn't go too close this time, as I was scared. But Slone and Bwa Bwa were braver and they went close enough to show my father exactly where the body was. My father told us all to keep back, as he went to deal with it. I watched in horrified fascination as he grabbed a stick and leaned out and pushed the body until it went under. A moment later it bobbed up again, a little further out, and slowly it was dragged into the current.

As it floated away I could see that the man's back was torn to shreds and crisscrossed with angry red slash marks. It was so horrible I had to look away. What on earth had happened to him?

I wondered. Had he been attacked by a wild animal? Even though I had turned away and hidden my eyes, the horrible image stayed in my mind. I knew for sure then that I was going to have nightmares.

My father told us it was time to come in now and he led us back to the house.

'How did that man fall in the river and die?' I asked him, quietly.

My father glanced at me. I could tell that he was trying to decide what answer to give me. Finally, he must have decided to tell me the truth.

'Far away up river there are other Karen villages,' he explained. 'Sometimes, the Burmese Army go into those villages and kidnap people. They use them as forced labour – as porters to carry their heavy loads. Those poor people get no proper food to eat nor any rest. When they are exhausted and cannot continue carrying the loads of weapons or food, the Burmese soldiers throw them in the river. That's how that man ended up here.'

'But why was his back so horribly hurt?' I asked. 'How did that happen?'

'The Burmese soldiers beat the porters, to make them keep going,' my father replied. 'When they cannot go on any more, sometimes they do very bad things to them. They do it to show the other porters what will happen to them if they stop carrying their loads. Once they're done, they throw them into the river to die.'

It was so horrible. And somehow, even as a child, I was so upset with the soldiers who had done this. This was my most direct experience of the war to date, and it was so up close and personal. We had found that dead body, and we'd found it in one of our sunniest, favoured play spots. And I had seen the bloody, scabbed scars on the man's back from the beatings he had suffered. My father knew that the dead man had to be a Karen, as the villages upstream were all populated by our people.

It was not something that a child should see, and for many

weeks it cast a dark shadow over us. One night I overheard my mother and father talking about it in hushed tones. They sounded worried, and this in turn worried me. They were discussing the fighting, and how it was coming closer than ever to our own lands.

My mother seemed to be the most disturbed; whenever the war lurched a little nearer she felt its threat and its darkness imping-ing upon our happy lives. Perhaps this was because she had been a soldier herself, and she knew from bitter experience the trauma of war. She herself had fought against the Burmese Army soldiers who were doing such things, and I used to think that she was so very brave.

I used to think that I could never be a warrior like her, a true Karen hero. Seeing that dead body in the river had made me even more fearful. The image of it stayed in my head for a long time. It haunted my dreams.

After that we stopped playing in the river for a long, long time.

Chapter Seven

VICTORY FIELD

With my mother working so much in Manerplaw, my father decided that we needed a house there. So we built a bamboo one, similar to the one in the village. Next to it was a small rice paddy, which my father converted into a flower garden. He did so for two reasons. The first was because he loved flowers. He loved their beauty and their spirit, and he loved them because the very sight of them and their scent made people happy.

The second reason he planted the flower garden was because we didn't need to grow so much rice any more. In the past, Karen resistance workers had been given food rations by the KNU instead of wages. But it was always rough, unhusked rice, so my mother and father had to grow extra food. But in recent years things had improved: now the KNU ration included proper husked rice, salt, tea and fish paste.

Whilst my father nurtured his flower garden, my mother used the land around the house to grow vegetables. She planted coriander, water spinach, onions, garlic and green beans. She teased my father that when it came to mealtimes he could eat his flowers. So he planted pineapple, mango, lemon, plum and banana trees, so he had an excuse that he was really making an orchard. But his real passion remained his flowers. He would exchange seeds with his friends, and was forever cultivating new varieties.

My favourite food as a child was fruit. Slone and I would climb into my father's mango trees and stay up there for ages feasting on the fruit. We used to pretend we were animals in a tree. When my father found us he would scold us. He was worried that we'd fall out and hurt ourselves, so we used to do this mostly when he was away. Often, my little brother would throw the mango stones at me. He knew my father wasn't around to catch him. I didn't like it, but I couldn't help loving my naughty little brother.

My sister and I spent hours in my father's flower garden catching butterflies. We'd pop the prettiest ones into a clear plastic bag, until we had a rainbow of fluttering colours in there. Once we had enough we'd set up a 'market stall' selling butterflies and using sweet wrappers as money. The yellow one was 'the golden butterfly', and so it was the most expensive. Blue was the 'sky butterfly', and less expensive. Green was the 'leaf butterfly', and so the least costly of all.

My friends would come and try to barter flower petals for our butterflies. For some reason purple flowers were worth the most, followed by red and then yellow. From the flowers we bartered for our butterflies we'd make a petal-and-lily-leaf salad and pretend to eat it. The butterfly and flower market was one of the best games of all.

My father's flower garden ran right down to the banks of the Moei River. People travelling on the busy river used to comment on how lovely it looked, and wonder who might live there. One dry season my father built a bamboo summerhouse in the midst of the garden, with a view of the river. When it was hot we'd go there to read, and it was somewhere to take visitors. This was my father's idea of how to make people feel truly welcome.

VICTORY FIELD

For my father, no flower garden was complete without its ornamental pond. Undeterred by the fate of his first fishpond, my
father built one at our Manerplaw home, and filled it with pretty
grey and silver fish. But when my parents were at work there was
no one to protect it. The ducks got very excited, went into the
pond and quacked with delight as they caught and ate all the fish.
When my father came back from work all he saw was the ducks
waggling their backsides contentedly, and an empty pond.

He turned on my mother in exasperation. 'Look! Look what
your ducks have done! I gave up all that time to dig that pond and
put those fish in there, and—'

'Why didn't you put a fence around it?' my mother countered.
'Anyway, you're happy to eat duck whenever I cook it, aren't
you?'

'Well, don't you like sitting around the pond and watching the
fish? How're we going to do that now?'

My mother snorted. 'As if I ever get the time! I'm always working in the garden, growing the vegetables to cook with the duck
curry!'

It was a rare occasion when my parents argued like this, and
when they did we just kept quiet. The arguments never became
that heated, and the most that would happen was that one of
them would storm out. After the ducks ate all his fish my father's
ornamental pond became a duckpond, and the water got very
dirty – so it suffered a similar fate to the one back in the village!

The Karen soldiers used to dock their long-tail boats in the
lagoon below our house. It was like a little harbour, and often they
would pause for a rest in my father's flower garden, before continuing up the hill to their base. Since my mother had been a
soldier, and often told me her soldier's stories, I knew what they
were fighting for. They were the army of the people, and they
were very brave.

There was always a lull in the fighting during the rainy season,
as the jungle would become impassable. Then, there would be
military training on the sandy beach below our house. One soldier

would swim across the river and tie a rope around a tree on the far side. It would be hoisted out of the water and tied to a tree so it was stretched taut. One by one the soldiers had to link their arms and feet around the rope and climb across. Once they'd done so, they had to swim back again. From our garden we had a ringside seat, and we'd watch in fascination, hoping that no one would fall.

There was no primary school in Manerplaw, so Per He Lu remained the centre of our lives. If it was approaching exam times my mother would remain in the village, tending the animals, cooking meals and watching out for us. My father used to tell me that if I got the first prize in the exams, then I'd get a special treat. This made me try even harder as I wanted to please my father and see what he might give me.

In my third year at primary school I was top of the class again, and my father gave me a wonderful pink dress. It was in the style of a Western party dress, and I had never seen anything so pretty or so exotic. Normally, I only ever got my sister Bwa Bwa's hand-me-downs. I'd never owned a new item of clothing in my life, and I'd certainly never had a dress to wear.

All I ever used to wear at home were cotton shorts and a T-shirt, and these would be my sister's cast-offs. I didn't really mind. Everyone in the village wore the same kind of thing, so I wasn't the odd one out or anything. I knew why we never had new clothes; my parents couldn't afford to buy them. Those who joined the Karen resistance were volunteers, and as such they earned no wages. All they got was the food ration and some domestic items.

The only way to earn any money was to have a little business on the side. My mother ran a small shop in Manerplaw. It was a little stall under the house, which she opened in the evening and at weekends. She sold fruit, home-made snacks of rice flour and raw, juicy sugar cane, and chunks of crunchy brown sugar, called *ghan da gah*. And she stocked *tha blu yah* – betel nut mixed with lime paste and a red spicy powder, the mild stimulant that people chewed. Doing so produced mouthfuls of saliva and stained the teeth a dark red.

With what little money she earned my mother would buy some cut-price Moh Htoo – Burmese cheroots – which she would sell for a small profit. Moh Htoo are like a very rough cigar, with dry, flaky tobacco rolled up inside a long leaf. Often when people smoked them a glowing ember would fall out and land on their clothes or legs and burn them.

My mother used to rear pigs, ducks, turkeys and chickens. The duck and chicken eggs were to supplement our diet, but she sold some of the produce to earn extra income. If she killed a piglet, she'd earn around 300 Thai Baht, the equivalent of £4, from selling the meat. A fully grown pig might go for 2000 Baht. She used the money to pay our school fees and to buy school uniforms, or to buy things to sell on her stall – like the cheroots.

We had two lives now – our village one, and the weekends that we often spent in Manerplaw. I was seven years old when our Manerplaw life started to attain more importance for us. One evening my father came home with four Burmese students. He announced that they would be staying with us until they had managed to build a home of their own.

I had never met a Burman before, and it was very strange having them in the house, especially as my siblings and I couldn't talk to them, or they to us. They spoke Burmese and we spoke Karen. One evening one of the students explained to my parents exactly why they had come to join the resistance. My parents listened to his Burmese, and then explained to us what he was saying, in Karen. I didn't understand everything, but this was the gist of it.

At that time General Ne Win was the head of the military dictatorship in Burma. It was widely suspected that he was somewhat unbalanced. As if to prove this was so, he had suddenly announced that all banknotes except for the 45 and 90 Kyat notes were no longer valid. (The Kyat is the Burmese currency.) From now on, only denominations divisible by nine would be legal tender, because nine was a lucky number, General Ne Win declared.

Overnight, most people had their savings wiped out. It was the

last straw for a population that had been suffering under his dictatorship for years. People began protesting on the streets, and the
driving force behind the protests was the students. The marches
grew bigger and bigger, quickly spreading across the country,
until hundreds of thousands of protesters were marching in all the
major cities and towns. They were united in their call for an end
to the military dictatorship, and for the country to be returned to
democratic rule.

But on 8 August 1988 the military launched a bloody and horrific crackdown. Thousands of unarmed demonstrators were
gunned down in cold blood, and countless more arrested. Saffron-
robed Buddhist monks – who before now had always been
universally respected in Burma – were among those beaten,
arrested and killed. This became known as the 8/8/88 uprisings.

Many of those who had escaped the crackdown fled into the
Karen lands, ending up in Manerplaw – 'Victory Field'. They had
made their way to Victory Field by whatever means they could –
trekking across the mountains, or navigating the rivers that
snaked through the jungles. That's how the four students living in
our house had ended up here.

Upon hearing the students' story, I realized that the Karen were
not suffering alone. Other ethnic groups – including the Burmans
themselves – were suffering under the harsh rule of General Ne
Win and his junta. It was a surprise to learn that the Burmese junta
were oppressing their own people – fellow Burmans – as much as
they were ethnic groups like the Karen.

My father counselled the Karen National Union leadership to
welcome in the 8/8/88 refugees. One by one, offices of the democratic resistance groups sprung up around Manerplaw. Their
young men started to train to join the armed resistance, fighting
alongside our own Karen soldiers. My father was the perfect
candidate to help coordinate all these activities: he spoke fluent
Burmese; he was an animist, and so religiously 'neutral'; he had
been educated in Rangoon, and so he was familiar with the ways
in which the urban resistance functioned.

Manerplaw was transforming itself into the heartland of the democratic resistance movement in Burma, and my father was appointed as a Special Adviser to General Saw Bo Mya, the President of the Karen National Union, to help advise on the transformation.

None of this meant much to me at the time, apart from one glorious thing: with my father's new appointment he was pulled out of the front-line areas. As with my mother, he would henceforth spend the week working in Manerplaw, and most weekends he would be home with us in the village. In short, my father was coming home.

It was from this time that I really started to get to know my father, with his love of his flower gardens, and his belief that one day Burma would be free. The influx of the 8/8/88 refugees had instilled a new spirit of hope and resistance in Manerplaw. That spirit was all around us.

But it also had a darker side, for it would draw the attention of the junta ever closer to us.

Chapter Eight

THE RIVER SPIRITS

My parents didn't try to hide the truth of the war from us. But life went on largely as it had before, with laughter and with light.

I was eight years old by now, and I was looking forward to the end-of-term school picnic. But as the day approached my mother said I couldn't go. I was terribly disappointed.

'All my friends are going, so why can't I?' I objected. 'Why am I the odd one out?'

'I'm sorry, Little Daughter, but girls your age have to go with a parent,' my mother replied, 'and I can't take you.'

'But I can go with Bwa Bwa. She's old enough.'

'She's not your parent, is she? You'll just have to make the best of staying at home.'

The morning of the school picnic my mother was surprised to find me awake very early.

'Oh! This morning my Little Daughter is awake so soon. Why?'

I ignored her question, and smiled innocently. I had a secret plan to get me to the school picnic, and I certainly wasn't going to tell my mother about it. She prepared Bwa Bwa's picnic, wrapping the food in a big banana leaf and tying it with bamboo string. By the time Bwa Bwa was ready to leave, I had left the house and hidden myself well.

Bwa Bwa walked past the spot where I was hiding, and once she had gone a little way I started to follow her. I kept enough distance so she wouldn't see me, but close enough to not lose sight of her. She reached the school playing field, where there were already lots of children milling around. I managed to hide myself among them.

When I judged it was too late for her to send me back I ran up to her. 'Elder Sister! Elder Sister! I'm here now, and I'm coming with you.'

'No, no! You can't come,' Bwa Bwa replied, in surprise. 'Mummy won't let you. You have to go back home.'

'Please, Elder Sister. Please. It's a long way back, and you don't have time to walk me home.'

Bwa Bwa was annoyed, but she knew that I was right – there was no time to take me back. She agreed that I could come, but on one condition: I had to stick with her at all times. We set off and spent the next thirty minutes scaling Teak Mountain. We tumbled down the far side and ended up on a beautiful, sandy riverbank just upstream from Manerplaw. I had never been there before and it was such a lovely place for a picnic.

In no time we were in the river, playing and splashing about. In the back of my mind I knew that there was no packed lunch for me, but I hoped Bwa Bwa might share her food with me. Even if she didn't it was worth going hungry for such a lovely day out. Just as I was thinking these thoughts, I saw my mother hurrying out of the forest. I was so surprised to see her and I suddenly felt very worried.

I was called over. My mother explained to the teachers that I hadn't had permission to come. She had missed me at home and searched everywhere. She had asked Slone where I was, but he didn't know either. Eventually, she guessed that I must have followed Bwa Bwa. She knew where we were going, so she had followed. I was standing at my mother's side with my head hung low, feeling very guilty.

At the end of the story my teacher tried to tell me off, but she couldn't help laughing. As for my mother, she had brought an extra packed lunch so I wouldn't go hungry. My mother never once hit me or punished me for such naughty behaviour. She, Bwa Bwa and I spent a lovely day together. For once I had forced her out of the house and away from her chores, and it was good to see her enjoying herself. It had turned into the perfect day out!

In fact, the desire to be wilful and naughty seemed to run deep in the Phan family – or at least among the younger generation. One of our favourite games involved us 'borrowing' other people's boats and setting off on wild adventures. People used to leave their canoes lying on the riverbank moored to tree roots. No one ever locked anything as theft was unheard of. So we'd simply head down to the river, choose a dugout canoe that we fancied, and paddle off on an adventure.

Often, we'd have canoe races in the lagoon below our house. But one day we decided to paddle right across the river. The winner would be the first to reach the far side. I chose the biggest canoe I could find, and on the count of three we were off. We headed out through the calm water and in no time hit the powerful current of midstream. I had to paddle with all my might, as the rushing water tried to force the canoe around and arrow it off downstream.

We reached the calm of the far side with Bwa Bwa just ahead, and Slone and me in a dead heat. My sister and I grabbed an overhanging tree root and pulled our canoes into the side. It was time for a rest and to catch our breath. But Slone had to be just that little bit more adventurous. He jumped on to the beach, drove his paddle vertically into the sand and tied his canoe to it. He marched up the bank, telling us he was going exploring.

Barely had Slone disappeared among the trees when a long-tail boat went roaring past in midstream. The wash came riding in towards us, hitting the bank with a smacking slurp. As it receded it sucked at Slone's canoe, jerking the mooring paddle free. Slowly, the canoe was dragged further and further into the current. All of a sudden Slone came racing down the sandy beach and made a lunge for the boat. Bwa Bwa and I were killing ourselves laughing at his predicament.

He hit the river with a splash, came up gasping, and struck out after the canoe. He grabbed for the paddle, got hold of it, and pulled on the rope until he and the canoe were reunited. Bwa Bwa and I were laughing too much at our little brother to be able to help him, but finally he hauled himself back inside the canoe. Slone wasn't particularly annoyed with us for laughing at him: he knew he would have done the same if one of us had gone exploring and lost our boat.

All three of us were pretty wild and mischievous at around this time, and one of our key mischief-making tools was our homemade catapults. Each was made out of a length of thick rubber stretched around a Y-shaped stick. We'd carry them with us whenever we went into the forest, a bag over our shoulder stuffed full of clay marbles or small stones. Only boys were supposed to have them, but Bwa Bwa and I were determined to do whatever the boys did.

We'd go hunting in the forest. The catapult was very powerful and it could kill a bird outright. We'd take it home with us, pluck it, cover it in turmeric and other spices, and mount it on a stick to roast over the fire. Cooked like that the wild bird meat was delicious. Unfortunately, I was a useless shot. In fact, I don't think I ever managed to hit a single bird. Say Say was the best shot, followed by Slone. Luckily my brothers always shared whatever they had with us.

One day Slone came running up from the riverbank looking like he'd seen a ghost. It turned out that he'd been hunting with his catapult by the river. He'd failed to find any birds, and in his frustration he'd decided to take a pot shot at a passing long-tail boat. It was a hundred yards or more away, and he'd never for one moment thought he was going to hit it. He'd watched as the marble had streaked through the air, and hit the boatman bang on his thigh.

In an instant the boatman was searching for the culprit, red-faced with anger and pain. Slone had sneaked away and come running home. As he told me his story I was killing myself laughing, but Slone wasn't very happy. He was convinced the boatman had seen him and was going to come and search him out. From that moment on whenever we were told to go down to the river for a wash, Slone managed to make an excuse to get out of it. I kept telling Slone that no one had seen him, but he was very worried.

Eventually, my mother realized something was up. 'What's the matter, Little Son? You used to love playing by the river. What's happened?'

'I just don't feel like going, that's all,' Slone muttered in reply.

My mother came to ask me what was wrong. I decided to tell her what had happened, for I knew she would find a way to set Slone's mind at ease. When I related the catapulting incident, she laughed and laughed and laughed. She knew it was naughty of Slone, but she just couldn't help herself. She tried to be angry with him and to say that shooting people with catapults was wrong, but mostly she just wanted to reassure him that it was safe to go down to the river!

My independent, mischievous nature flourished in the freedom of the village. One rainy season the path that ran past our house became slippery. We decided it was great fun to use it as a slide, which made it even more slippery than ever. My mother hated us playing in the mud, as she feared we'd catch a chill, but it was far too much fun to stop. When we realized that people coming down the path were likely to slip up that was even more fun than ever!

We hid in the bushes and waited for someone to come. They'd hit the slope and go tumbling down, and we'd dissolve into fits of laughter. When my mother realized what we were up to she was angry with us. She warned us not to do it again. But Slone just couldn't be told. He waited until it was raining hard and then he repeatedly launched himself down the path on his backside, making it slick with a slushy mud. Then we hid and waited. People were hurrying along trying to escape the rains, which meant they hit our mudslide going apace.

They went tumbling down and ended in a muddy heap. It was hilarious to watch, and I had to put a hand over my mouth to stifle my laughter. Of course, that was all part of the thrill – the risk of getting caught! Eventually someone did see us, and they went straight to have words with my mother. When we went in for dinner she grabbed us each hard by the cheek, whilst warning us never to be so naughty again.

One day my father announced that his Little Daughter should have her hair cut short, like the rest of the children at school. I loved my long hair and didn't see why I had to cut it. When my father started readying the scissors I knew it was time to make myself scarce. Without a word to anyone I went and hid below the house. I crawled into a little gap underneath some firewood. It was barely big enough and I felt certain that no one would find me there.

I could hear my father searching for me. 'Little Daughter! Little Daughter! I'll only cut a little of your hair. Not a lot. Only a little tiny bit—'

There was no way that I was coming out. It was the dry season and the middle of the holidays so there was no school to go to. I stayed in my hiding place all morning. After he'd searched the house, my father went off to his gardens, checking behind the banana and pineapple groves. Still he couldn't find me. Eventually, everyone was called in to join the search. I was enjoying it enormously.

It wasn't until mid-afternoon that Bwa Bwa thought to check my hiding place. She bent down and peered in, and the surprise on her face at finding me was so funny to see. I put a finger to my lips and whispered for her to keep quiet. She did for a while, but by now my parents were getting worried, and she finally let on to my father where I was hiding. He came down and peered inside, breaking into a smile when he saw me. He wasn't angry at all.

He tried to coax me out by telling me he'd only cut a little, tiny bit of my hair. I decided that I must have shown him how important my hair was to me so I gave myself up. He sat me on his lap on the porch and began to snip away. But once he was finished I realized that he'd tricked me: he'd shorn my hair right up to my ear level. I was so angry I told him I wished I'd stayed in that hiding place for ever.

'You've made me look like a coconut!' I exclaimed. 'Look! Like a nasty old coconut that's been cut in half.'

'Little Daughter, you're young – and young girls have to have short hair,' my father tried to explain. 'Everyone else at school does, so why not you?'

'But I don't like this coconut style! Cutting it like a horrid coconut shape!'

'Little Daughter, when you're young you have to keep it short, then it's a lot easier to keep clean.'

I told him that it looked as if someone had got half a coconut and put it on top of my head and cut off all the hair sticking out the bottom. My father couldn't help but laugh at my description of my new hairstyle.

In my family my father was the one who showed his emotions more. Often, he saw terrible things with his work and it would really upset him. My mother was the opposite. Whatever she saw or whatever might happen, she generally kept it all bottled up inside.

If we played in the river, my father would worry that we'd get washed away and drown. He'd tell us we weren't allowed down there without him. But we didn't pay much attention to his warnings when he was away. One time he came home unexpectedly and caught all three of us diving in the river. He was really, really angry, but his anger masked his fear that one of us would get hurt or even drown.

My father took a bamboo cane and beat Bwa Bwa and me

around the legs. He didn't beat Slone as he reckoned Slone was too small to punish and that he'd just been following his big sisters' lead. It was really painful and it made our legs sting. But it wasn't *that* which was so distressing – it was the very fact that my father had raised a hand against us. I was upset and angry. I was in floods of tears.

My mother wasn't very happy, either. 'I gave birth to them and brought them up, and I never beat them,' she objected.

'But don't you know how you spoil the children?' my father countered. 'You'd spoil them rotten if you had your way. And playing in that river – it's so dangerous!'

'But I try to teach them to be good in a soft and gentle way.'

'Well, I didn't hit their heads. I hit them on their legs. Just their legs, that's all.'

My mother and father continued to argue, as Bwa Bwa and I went into a sulk. But, in fact, my father's fears were well founded. We quickly forgot his warnings and we were soon back to our old tricks. There was a new game that someone had invented – jumping out of a tree that overhung the river and landing in a huge splash. It was fantastic fun and we'd been playing this game for most of the day.

Eventually, we left our friends playing by the riverside and went home. But, from the window of our living room, all of a sudden we noticed that a crowd had gathered at the water's edge. We hurried down there, only to discover that one of the children was missing. Every Karen village has a headman, and ours was called Aung Ba. If there was a crisis in the village Aung Ba would ring the Moh – 'the call-the-people-together bell' – which hung by the village rice store.

On discovering the boy was missing, Aung Ba had called for volunteers to form a search line. As it was the dry season the water was low and it could be waded in all places. We watched aghast as the line of adults moved slowly up the river, feeling with their bare feet as they went. When they were almost at the overhanging tree one of them cried out that he'd found something. He reached under the water and emerged with the body of the missing boy cradled in his arms.

The boy must have been under the water for thirty minutes or so, but still they tried to save him. They carried him up the river-bank, held him upside down and tried to shake out the water. People gave mouth-to-mouth resuscitation, his father included. But finally it was obvious that the boy was dead and the village headman told everyone that it was time to give up. The father gave him one last desperate breath and then laid his son's head back on the wet earth. He let out a cry of loss and his wife burst into tears. It was a dark day for the village.

After that we took our father's warnings very seriously. We were so scared we stopped playing in the river for months on end. But by the next dry season we had all but forgotten about the boy who had drowned. The dry season was the best time for water games: the current wasn't so fast and the river was shallower and not so clouded with sediment.

Gradually, our childhood innocence was being tempered with a knowledge of the dangers of the world. First, I had seen grandpa die, and that had acquainted me with death through old age. Then, I had witnessed the horror of the dead body in the river, which had alerted me to the dangers of a faceless, and still distant, enemy. And now I had witnessed the death of my childhood playmate, which had shown me that none of us were ever too young to die.

One Christmas I decided I would follow Santa once he had finished doing his sweet-throwing routine. He disappeared into one of the houses and I hid myself where I could watch. He changed out of his Santa clothes, and suddenly he was the father of one of my school friends!

Some of my school friends had been saying that Santa wasn't 'for real', and now I knew they were right. We joked and laughed about it at school and tried to alert all the younger pupils to the fact that Santa was a fake. But they just got annoyed with us and told us not to be so stupid. If we kept saying such things Santa wouldn't bring us any presents next year, they warned.

It was around this time that I began to notice people with missing limbs in and around the village. The first time I saw a man with his leg ending in a stump at the knee I was so shocked. I asked my mother what had happened. Once again, it was one of those moments where she had to wrestle with a difficult decision – just how much did she tell a child about the horrors that were ravaging our people and our land?

My mother went on to explain that the Burmese regime planted landmines in Karen villages. These were like small bombs hidden in the earth. When people trod on them they exploded, injuring whoever might be near. Why would people hide things so as to blow other people's legs off, I wondered, especially when they didn't know who was going to get hurt? It was so cruel and senseless.

Sometimes, the Burmese soldiers forced Karen villagers to walk ahead of them, acting as 'human minesweepers', my mother said. They might have forgotten where they had planted their mines, and so they would force people to clear the way. Others just trod on the mines by accident, when they were going to and from their farms. This was all part of the Four Cuts policy, and the Burmese soldiers even planted mines in the doorways of people's homes and in the churches.

Bwa Bwa and I talked about it a lot. We felt so sorry for the victims of the landmines and wanted to know how we could help. The KNU had set up a workshop for the handicapped in Manerplaw and people came from all over Karen free state to have artificial limbs fitted. The prosthetics were made of plastic and wood, with a hinged steel cage providing leverage and support. The artificial legs had a fake foot, upon which people could wear a shoe to match that worn on their good leg.

Most of the amputees remained there until they had learned to use their artificial limb, and then they were able to return to their home village. But for the worst injured, the workshop and surrounding area became their permanent home. They and their families were given a place to live close to the workshop, where they could plant vegetables and rear some animals.

These families were the poorest of the poor. Their children started turning up at school, and they were often so sad. They knew their dads weren't like other fathers – they had parts of their bodies missing. That December our school put on a day of entertainment at the handicapped workshop, with singing and dancing to spread the Christmas cheer. In our culture December is the 'happy month', because it is the time for Christmas celebrations and present-giving.

Mostly, we had to make our own entertainment in the village. There was only the one television set, which was owned by Aung Ba, the village headman. No TV broadcasts could be picked up where we lived, and so all one could see was videos. Aung Ba was our neighbour, and if he was feeling in a generous mood he would invite us in to watch. But as soon as he let *us* in, all the children in the village would try to cram into his living room, followed by the adults.

I always managed to sneak to the very front, as I was small enough to squeeze between people's legs. But, eventually, Aung Ba got fed up with having so many people crammed into his house. After that he tried to keep people out, but it was never easy. We had no electricity in the village, and so he had to start a generator whenever he wanted to watch a video. As soon as we heard the roar of the generator, we'd know a movie was about to start and we'd rush over to his place.

We knew we weren't very welcome, so we'd wait outside to see what started playing. If a good movie came on, we'd sidle in pretending we were innocent children with no idea that we weren't wanted. For the adults it was more difficult, and our parents rarely if ever came to watch. Even if Aung Ba insisted on a 'private' viewing, we'd still stand outside and watch through the open windows.

At school the next day I'd announce: 'Guess what I saw at the village headman's house last night?'

Most of the children lived too far away and they couldn't get to see the movies. I'd talk about it all day long, repeating lines from the film that had stuck in my memory. The headman watched a lot of Burmese-made films, and one starred a man who kept flirting with the girls. His best line was: 'Lady, even though I am ugly, I do have a good heart.' We found this hilarious and would keep repeating that line over and over again.

One evening we watched a Burmese movie supposedly about the war between the Karen and the Burmese Army. In that movie the Karen soldiers burned villages, beat and killed civilians and raped women. By contrast, the Burmese soldiers were the nice guys, helping the villagers escape from the marauding Karen troops. It even showed Karen soldiers planting mines to blow off the limbs of innocent villagers.

That film was a travesty. It was a total reversal of reality. We were the ones being attacked. It was propaganda produced by the regime. We were very angry after watching it, for we knew the reality of what was happening out there in the remote Karen villages.

And all too soon, that terrible reality was going to become part of our own lives.

Chapter Nine

THE NAMING

One day my mother was taking us back to the village, after a weekend spent in Manerplaw. The river was low and difficult to navigate and so we decided to walk. It was a Sunday afternoon, and we began our lazy ascent of Teak Mountain. There was no hurry as long as we reached home before nightfall. It was thirty minutes or so by the time we reached the mountaintop. We paused to catch our breath, looking forward to an easy descent to the village.

Ten minutes later and we were at the foot of the mountain, from where the path followed a stream all the way home. My mother led the way as Slone, Bwa Bwa, Say Say and I chatted and larked about. But all of a sudden there was a massive spout of water just ahead of us. We knew instantly what it was, and it was terrifying. The deafening eruption could only come from an elephant, and we must have stumbled upon it as it was in the midst of having its bath.

I could see fear and shock written across my mother's features as she yelled at us to run. For an instant I turned to see what the elephant was doing, and there right next to us a whole herd was crashing about in the water. The last thing I saw was one turning its mighty head in our direction, and flaring its ears in anger, and then I ran. I pounded along the slippery path, my heart pumping fit to burst.

All of a sudden I saw my mother stumble and fall. She let out a muffled scream, before dragging herself to her feet and trying to stagger onwards. I cried out to her, but she told me to run and not to stop until I reached home. I did as she'd said, and ten minutes later I burst out of the forest into the village clearing. Bwa Bwa and Slone were just ahead of me, but my mother was nowhere in sight. Recently, we'd heard about an elephant turning on its keeper, killing him. The story – which I believed at the time – went that the elephant had eaten him. We were so worried.

I turned to search for my mother, anxiety eating away at me as I scanned the dark wall of trees. I told myself how strong and courageous she was, in an effort to calm my fears. It seemed like an age before finally a figure appeared, hobbling out of the forest shadows. It was my mother, and she was clearly having trouble walking.

As she emerged into the sunlight I could tell she was in great pain. We rushed up to her. She had blood pouring from a gash in her foot where she had fallen. We had no medicines as such, but we knew where to find the plant that my mother had used to heal my cut finger. Say Say went to fetch some and we bound up my mother's damaged foot with the leaves. Then we helped her home.

It took a month for my mother's wound to heal, and even then it left a painful and angry scar. Every day she had to re-dress the wound with fresh leaves. The sharp boulder that had cut her was showing only because the stream was so low, it being the height of the dry season. We worried that the dirty rocks had infected the wound. Our worries would prove well founded, for this was an injury that would come back to haunt my mother, and at the worst possible time.

Manerplaw was now the heartland of the entire Burmese resistance movement, and the military regime redoubled their efforts against us. I had started to notice lots of long-tail boats arriving below our house. Long green bundles were unloaded on the beach where we played and carried up past our house. At first I had no idea what a grim cargo those boats were carrying.

It turned out that each bundle contained a wounded, or dead, Karen soldier. Most were slung in a hammock from a single bamboo pole, forming a makeshift stretcher. I tried to hide whenever I saw those boats coming, but sometimes it was impossible to miss them. There would be two or three 'bundles' in each, and I had never seen so many of our soldiers so badly hurt, or killed.

I remember looking into one of those hammocks; I saw a face bloodied, swollen and pockmarked with shrapnel, the gentle brown eyes all but gummed shut with congealed blood. But worst of all was the young man's hands that ended in stumps wrapped in bloody rags. It was horrible.

None of us children had seen anything like this before. I went to ask my mother about it, and found her working in her vegetable garden.

'Mummy, where are all those soldiers coming from? And how have they got so horribly hurt?'

My mother paused and straightened her back. She seemed tired. She looked me directly in the face and tried to give me a reassuring smile.

'There's been a lot of fighting, Little Daughter. But it's far, far away from us. Those soldiers have been hurt, or killed, in the war. Their friends bring them back here to be treated in the hospital. And they bring back the dead to bury them.'

'But why is there so much fighting?' I asked. 'And where is it happening? It is *far away*, isn't it?'

Of course, I wanted the war to be far, far away. I imagined it to be so in my mind. The very idea that it might come to us, here, had never once occurred to me.

My mother put her arm around me. 'Little Daughter, it *is* far away, so don't you worry. It's at a place called Mae Ther Waw, and it's been going on for a long time. And Mae Ther Waw is a long way away from us.'

But the following week there was some terrible news. Moonlight's father was a Karen resistance fighter, and he'd been killed in the battle for Mae Ther Waw. My parents took us to pay our last respects at the funeral in Manerplaw. We were taken inside the soldiers' barracks to see the body. I stuck close to Bwa Bwa as we crept towards the coffin.

Moonlight's father's face stared up at us, ghostly white and gaunt. He looked so pale and pinched, as if all his blood had drained away. Moonlight was standing near the coffin, his face streaked with tears, to either side of him his distraught brothers and sisters. It was so sad seeing their father lying there dead, yet there was a part of me that was glad that it wasn't my father who'd been killed. As soon as that thought entered my head I felt so guilty.

Moonlight was crying; his brothers and sisters were crying; and their mother was crying. I wanted to cry with them, but somehow I couldn't. I didn't want to be consumed by emotion and to break down. I was trying to protect myself from the horror. The coffin was draped in a Karen flag, lifted up and carried to the graveside. A guard fired off a volley of shots and a bugle played the coffin into the ground. The sight of that dead body stayed with me for a very long time.

We began a relay with our neighbours in the village, as each took turns to keep Moonlight's family company. Each night for many nights there were ten or more people staying in Moonlight's house – providing solace to the mother, comforting the children, and helping with the cooking and other chores. We did this to give the family the proper time to grieve. I spent time with Moonlight and his sisters, but I tried to avoid talking about their father. Instead, I talked about school, or the games we played, or anything else that came into my mind.

Moonlight was one of eight children, and now his mother

would have to bring them up as a widow. It was a terrible thing to have happened. At school we tried to continue as before, but there was an unspoken, underlying sadness now, for everyone knew about Moonlight's loss. We were just children and we tried to put it behind us. We wanted to play and do well at school and forget all about the war. In our minds it was still a distant, invisible threat, and we wanted it to stay that way.

We didn't appreciate the fact, but Mae Ther Waw was a major defeat for the Karen resistance. For months our soldiers had been beating back attacks by the Burmese Army, who were trying to seize Mae Ther Waw – a high, rocky ridge that lay to the southwest of us further inside Burma. The Burmese Army had seized hundreds of Karen villagers as porters. As with the dead man in the river, those porters were being abused in terrible ways before being left for dead.

Our soldiers were finally forced to give up Mae Ther Waw and retreat to new positions. The fighters who came back from the front line looked exhausted. Many seemed relieved just to have survived a battle in which so many of their friends had died. We had lost hundreds of soldiers in the battle for Mae Ther Waw.

An early-morning parade was held for the returning troops. The Karen flag was hoisted and buglers played a fanfare as the soldiers lined up in their best uniforms. Young women and schoolgirls queued up to offer the soldiers garlands of bright yellow and orange flowers. Each had to step forward and bow his head so that the girl could place the flowers around his neck. As those young men turned away to march back into line, many had tears in their eyes.

I had been chosen as one of the flower girls, as had Bwa Bwa. It was a real honour and I was very nervous. I'd never done anything like this before. There was a soldier who looked to be in his early twenties, and he was really quite handsome. You were more or less free to choose who you gave your garland to, although the Karen Women's Organization was there in the background, making sure that no soldier was ever left out.

I chose that young, handsome soldier. I smiled at him, and he smiled at me. The drumming of the military band was so loud that we couldn't speak. Instead, I moved forward and offered him my garland. He removed his bush hat so that I could place the garland over his head. He had to bend low to receive it, and for one horrible moment it got stuck on his forehead. I wondered what on earth to do, and then he reached up and pulled it down himself.

In that parade we celebrated the fact that these soldiers had returned alive. That afternoon there was a memorial service to pay tribute to those who had fallen in the battle, and to honour their sacrifice. It wasn't something for children, and I didn't attend. Even so, their deaths brought home the reality of the war to us as never before.

Whilst trying not to scare us, my mother warned us in her own quiet way to be prepared in case there was an attack on the village. Here and there crude air-raid shelters were constructed, each consisting of a hole in the ground covered over with stout tree trunks and earth. My father set about constructing our own shelter. It was about the size of your average saloon car inside, so just big enough for us all to squeeze into. It was a big contrast to what my father usually liked to build – ornamental fishponds and beautiful flower gardens.

For several years now I'd known that my name had a special place in my father's heart. He used that name – Nant (Miss) Zoya Phan, *my name* – as his pen name when writing articles on the struggle for freedom in Burma. He was prolific in his writing, and he often used to show me what he'd published. I had never thought to ask him why he published under my name. I just felt so happy and proud that he and I shared the same name somehow.

Not long after the battle for Mae Ther Waw my father sat me down to explain exactly how significant my naming was to him. I was old enough and mature enough to listen properly now, and I hung on his every word. At the age of seventeen a Russian girl called Zoya Kosmodemyanskaya had joined the Second World War Soviet resistance. She had led sabotage and reconnaissance missions behind German lines, and her life story became one of the most enduring tales of heroism from that war.

In 1941, midway through a night mission in German-occupied territory, Zoya Kosmodemyanskaya was captured. She was tortured as her captors tried to extract information from her on the activities and membership of the resistance. But she refused to talk. Eventually, having failed to break her, the Nazis sent her to the gallows. As she stood with the noose around her neck, she turned to her captors and levelled a warning at them.

'There are two hundred million of us. You cannot hang us all!'

After the execution her body was left hanging from the gallows, as a warning to others.

When the war was over Zoya Kosmodemyanskaya was declared a 'Hero of the Soviet Union'. She was the first woman ever to receive that distinction. Zoya's brother, Shura, had also perished in the war, in the battle for Koenigsberg. Zoya's mother went on to write the story of her children's war exploits, in a book entitled *The Story of Zoya and Shura*. My father had found a copy of that book whilst at university in Rangoon, and Zoya's story had struck a powerful chord with him.

He was moved by the similarities he saw between Zoya's struggle and that of the resistance in Burma. The Nazi regime had been a brutal, totalitarian one – just as the Burmese junta was. Its efforts to exterminate the Jews and other minorities mirrored the junta's efforts to exterminate the Karen and other ethnic groups. And the struggle to resist the Nazis had been a long and costly one in terms of lives, just as it had proved to be in Burma.

Of course, I'd heard snippets of this story before, especially when visitors asked my father why I had such a strange name. But my father had never given me such a direct and personal explanation as to why he had chosen to name me 'Zoya'. He went on to explain that the name originates from the Greek *zoy*, which means 'life', and this was another reason he chose it. But mainly, he hoped that I, like the original Zoya, might fight for the survival of my people.

Perhaps it was due to my mother's problems giving birth to Bwa Bwa that my father had been so determined to be present at my birth. My sister had been born the wrong way round – feet first – and it was a very difficult time for my mother. Sometime after that Bwa Bwa had fallen ill with hepatitis. The only way in which to save her was a blood transfusion, but my sister had a rare blood group and she needed a donor with the same blood type.

The first time she had needed a transfusion a family friend, Mahn Sha Htoo Ghaw, donated his blood. But then she needed a second transfusion and my father could find no suitable donor. Eventually, he tried the prison, which was situated in central Manerplaw. He went around all the inmates searching for someone who might save his daughter's life. Finally, he found a man whose blood matched, and out of the goodness of his heart that man agreed to provide it. In an effort to say thank you, my father took him fruit, vegetables and fresh eggs from our chickens.

Two years after Bwa Bwa's birth my mother had fallen pregnant for a second time. Once again my father was away, and my mother was working in the office. One day when she was six months into the pregnancy a boat carrying rice supplies docked at the riverside. My mother didn't hesitate in helping to unload the forty-kilogram rice sacks.

She picked up one of the sacks and started to carry it up to the office. It took her longer than usual, because of the pregnancy, and that night she felt a terrible pain in her stomach. She was taken to the clinic, but her baby miscarried and she lost it. She never even knew which sex it was. It was a horrible time for her, especially as she was alone.

Once my father had explained to me the full significance of his naming me Zoya, my childhood aspirations to become a teacher seemed somehow so inappropriate. In my father's hopes for my future – that I might struggle for the survival of my people – I felt there lay my true calling.

I was doing better and better at school. Recently, I had won a Karen scholarship of 20 Thai Baht a month – the equivalent of 30p – with which to buy notebooks, pens and other school materials. In fact, I often found myself competing with Bwa Bwa to be the best student in the school.

Bwa Bwa was twelve years old and she had just sat the exams that all Karen students had to take in order to get a place at secondary school. The results were compared across the whole of the Karen free state and Bwa Bwa was declared the top pupil overall. Bwa Bwa was given a scholarship and publicly congratulated by the Karen education minister, Padoh Shwe Ya Heh.

It was such an honour and I felt so proud of my sister, as did my parents. Both she and I were showing great academic promise and we had dreams of getting a further education.

Chapter Ten

PARADISE LOST

By the time of my last year of primary school I was studying science, maths, geography, Burmese, English, Karen and basic politics. That last subject included lessons on democracy – what it was and why it was worth fighting for, and what it would mean for us if Burma became a free and democratic country.

The Karen have no single word for democracy and so we call it *ka mler a tar bah tha* – 'the will of the people'. We were taught that in a democratic country the government is elected by the majority of the people; and we were told about self-determination, which we called *naw ka sar ta per law tha*.

Whilst I was taught about such things, I didn't always *understand* them. The Karen education system was one in which you learned by rote. It wasn't designed to make you *think* – it was designed to make you learn. I just memorized our basic politics lessons, learning the words and definitions off by heart, in order to pass the exams.

My favourite subject was maths and I was least fond of science.

I liked English, especially as we were taught that this was the language of international communication. I knew that if I wanted to go on to further education I needed to do well in English.

I had a dream of going to university after completing my Karen education, which could go no further than secondary school. That dream was inspired in part by my father, for I knew that he had studied for a degree in Rangoon. I wanted to follow in his footsteps, although I had no idea how I was going to achieve this. But I lived in hope that I would manage somehow.

It was at around this time that my father brought my mother a special gift – a tiny long-wave radio. It was only a cheap thing, but to us it was a precious possession. One day we were listening to the Karen language radio – a Karen-run service that broadcasts out of the Karen free state. A famous Karen singer called Julia Pan Bun – Julia Flower Bud – came on the air. She sang a song about students going to university and the joys of learning.

It was a catchy song, with guitar and drums, and Bwa Bwa and I sang along to the lyrics. Hearing it made us even more determined to get to university. We knew that we couldn't do so in the Karen areas, and as children of the resistance we couldn't go to study inside Burma, either. So the only option had to be going to study overseas, but we had absolutely no idea how we might manage that!

Many of my school friends shared this dream of education and a bright future. But the gulf between our situation and where we hoped to end up was so enormous. We had practically nothing in our village: no way to earn an income, a very basic education system, and all but non-existent healthcare. We had little or no appreciation of the obstacles – financial, educational, geographical and political – that lay in the way of our dreams.

The sheer business of daily survival was more than enough of a challenge. One day Naw Paw – Miss Flower – fell ill with fever and was sent home from school. It wasn't uncommon for children to fall sick with terrible fever, and more often than not the cause would be malaria. Most of us recovered with time, even though there were few or no medicines available.

Naw Paw's father was a famous resistance fighter, but he had been captured by the Burmese Army and was languishing in jail. Her mother was also in the resistance, and she happened to be away. Naw Paw was left at home to recuperate, whilst her brothers and sisters continued with their school studies.

But one afternoon they returned home to discover that poor Naw Paw had died. It had been such a horrible death. Her swollen tongue was clamped between her teeth, and her skin was lacerated and bruised from where she had thrashed around in her fever and cut herself on the sharp edges of the bamboo floor.

Naw Paw and I used to share our lunches at school, and we were very close, but I decided that I just couldn't go to her funeral. I was too scared of how my friend had died, the image of which seemed seared into my mind. But the night after her funeral Naw Paw came to me anyway, in my dreams. She appeared as a ghostly white form standing over my bed.

She stared at me. 'Zoya, I have come to live with you,' she declared.

In my dream I was terrified. 'No, Naw Paw, you can't live with me,' I told her. 'Don't you know you're dead?'

Naw Paw insisted that she had to come to live with me. I kept telling her she couldn't. 'No, it's not possible – you're dead, Naw Paw, you're dead!'

For ages I kept arguing with her like this, until I suddenly woke up. I gazed all around me in the darkness. I couldn't see anything, but at least there was no sign of Naw Paw's ghost. My mother and father were away, and I couldn't get back to sleep again. I was too afraid of having that same dream.

I didn't sleep properly for months after that. My fear was that Naw Paw's restless spirit had decided to come to live with me in my world, and that it would never leave. It was an irrational fear, a fear of the unknown and of death, but it haunted me all the same.

My father was away on a special mission at the time. He'd been sent to negotiate an alliance with the Wa, a tribe that have, like us, been fighting the Burmese junta for decades. The Wa inhabit an area far to the north of the Karen, on the border with China. As with us, their territory straddles the border line: some of the Wa live in China proper, in Yunnan state, whilst others are in Burma.

The Wa were once known as the 'Wild Wa', because of their tradition of head-hunting, and their United Wa State Army (UWSA) was a force to be reckoned with. My father's mission was to draw the Wa into an alliance with the wider democratic resistance. Whilst he was visiting Wa state my father was asked to adopt a young Wa boy. He was an orphan, and as with Say Say, the reason behind the request was to get the boy an education.

At first my father had resisted. The return journey from Wa state promised to be as challenging as the journey there had been. My father had trekked through the Karen jungle and hills, crossed large tracts of Thailand, and then travelled on foot and horseback into the remote Wa highlands. He feared the journey back would prove even more difficult with a young Wa boy in tow.

But my father believed absolutely in the value of education. Eventually, he agreed to take the Wa boy – that's how Ah Sai came to join our family, and he would stay with us for a year or so before returning to his village. Ah Sai is a traditional name in the Wa language of the Wa tribe. Ah Sai was around twelve years old when he came to live with us, and he spoke not a word of Karen.

None of us could understand the Wa language, and so at first Ah Sai could only communicate with my parents in basic Burmese. He called my father Poe-Poe – Burmese for 'grandfather'; my mother was Pwa-Pwa – Burmese for 'grandmother'. And with us Ah Sai had to use sign language, plus the odd bit of Burmese that we had learned at school.

Ah Sai started his education in Year One at junior school. He was a big, strong boy in any case, and his complexion was much darker than that of the Karen students. He was like a giant in the class, towering over the other pupils. But Ah Sai took it all in his stride. As far as he was concerned he was getting an education, and that was worth just about any sacrifice.

One day we decided to go swimming in the river. We wanted Ah Sai to come with us, but we didn't know how to tell him. Bwa Bwa went to him and told him, gently, 'la-lay' – which is 'come' in Burmese. It was one of the few phrases that we knew. She beckoned for him to follow. Soon, Ah Sai was splashing and larking around in the river with the rest of us.

Ah Sai quickly learned to speak Karen. Whenever he did his Karen homework he would read it out loud in a powerful, booming voice. It would echo around the village of an evening, and we knew that all the neighbours could hear. But we didn't mind. We were proud of his efforts, and by now Ah Sai had become like another brother to us.

Ah Sai came to join us just as the year was coming to an end. On 31 January 1993 we celebrated Karen Resistance Day, a yearly festival that marked the founding of the resistance. One of the biggest attractions of the day was Ta Ker Met Su – our martial art.

The famous Karen fighter Joe Ruby was going to fight. He was the overall champion at Ta Ker Met Su. Before the fight started, Joe Ruby and his opponent squared up to each other. They flexed their bulging muscles and performed their finest moves. Joe Ruby was famed for his skill in dodging and feinting to fox his opponent. I was certain that he was going to win. As the drumming and the crashing of cymbals built to a crescendo, each fighter lifted his legs and bent his body into contorted shapes, to show how flexible he was.

The fight began in a flurry of punches to the head and stomach and kicks from the legs. It was fast and furious. Soon the fighters were lost in a cloud of dust. If either fighter fell the bout would have to be stopped, for no one was allowed to hit someone on the ground. I couldn't help but thrill at the spectacle, and I could tell that my mother and sister and brothers were as gripped as I was.

But all of a sudden I felt the earth shake and the horror of a distant rumble cut the air. All around me people stiffened as they strained their ears. And then it happened again: the faint boom-crash, muffled by distance and the thick jungle. And then the first cry went up from the crowd as someone spotted the black shape of aircraft arrowing through the air. Instantly panic took hold in the crowd, with people running in all directions.

My mother grabbed me by the arm and called to my brothers and sister. 'Quick! Run! Run! Back to the house as fast as you can!'

She had never forgotten the lessons she had learned as a soldier – the most important of which was to get into cover as quickly as possible. We ran as if our lives depended on it and hid in the underground shelter that my father had built for us. As we crouched there in terror, we could see the glint of the aircraft diving down on to the distant mountaintop, and the tiny plumes of smoke below as their bombs hit.

The enemy had launched an attack on Twee Pah Wee Kyoe – Sleeping Dog Mountain – a high ridge lying to the west of our area. In profile it looks like a giant dog lying fast asleep, hence the name. All along the ridge we had trenches and bunker systems as Twee Pah Wee Kyoe was a key line of defence against the enemy. As the aircraft repeatedly dive-bombed the positions, the enemy started up a booming mortar barrage that crashed into the jungle all around the ridgeline.

For the first time in my life I could actually see the enemy with my own eyes and hear them attacking us. I could see and hear their might – their sleek, shiny aircraft and their big, booming guns. For the first time in my life I felt small and scared and vulnerable in the face of their power, and it was terrifying. I held tight to my mother's hand, and hoped and prayed that they would go away and leave us all alone.

My mother's fear was that the regime would know that we had gathered for Karen Resistance Day and send their aircraft in to attack us. We crouched in the shelter for hours on end until the light was gone and the noise of the bombing faded away into the darkening silence. Little did we know that this was just the start of the enemy assault on Twee Pah Wee Kyoe, an epic battle that would signal the beginning of the end of happier times.

After that attack we tried as best we could to continue with our lives as before. Two months later I had to sit my final junior school exams. My mother would criticize me for being lazy, and my teachers used to complain that I never really applied myself, yet I always seemed to be lucky in my exams. The result placed me second in the entire Karen area. A boy from another school had beaten me to first place, but I was really pleased with my mark, especially as I was awarded a scholarship to take with me to secondary school.

Secondary school lay across the Mu Yu Klo River, at Pway Baw Lu village. Bwa Bwa was already going to that school, and now I would be joining her. In the rainy season the route to school was by canoe across the river, and then we would race through the jungle to see who could be first into class. I loved it, especially as there was always stiff competition to get a head start on the others. In the dry season we could wade the river by sticking to the shallow parts, and then the race would be on!

Bwa Bwa was pushing sixteen now, and she felt herself to be too much of a young lady to go racing through the jungle with me and my classmates. Instead, she would walk to school in a sedate manner, chatting with her friends. In their minds this was the way to act properly and in a lady-like fashion.

One morning at school assembly we had a special presentation from one of the teachers, Zipporah Sein, who would go on to become leader of the Karen National Union. She told us the story of a former pupil called Paw Paw – Flower Flower. Paw Paw had travelled overseas, to a country called Canada, and there she had won a place at university. Those of us who studied really hard might be able to do the same, the teacher told us.

Bwa Bwa and I talked about this, and we decided that we were going to do as Paw Paw had done and try to study overseas, but instead of Canada we decided we would go to England. We knew that England was where Saw Ba U Gyi, founder of the Karen resistance movement, had been to university, and we wanted to follow in his footsteps.

Meanwhile Say Say's education was already over. He had grown into a kind and strong young man. One day he announced his plans to become a resistance fighter. He was inspired in part by my mother's war stories, and in part by what he had witnessed growing up in his home village. I was proud of my elder brother when he joined the Karen Army. He qualified as a special forces soldier, joining an elite unit that carried out missions behind enemy lines.

I knew it was dangerous, and I knew that one day my elder brother mightn't come back alive from one of those missions. But there was no stopping Say Say. The fight was strong in our family, but the time of darkness was almost upon us.

The battle for Sleeping Dog Mountain was intensifying and two family friends were killed in the fighting. One was called Thaw Htoo – New Gold, and the other was Ta Eh Soe – First Love. After the initial attack, the distant rumbling of the battle had become a daily backdrop to our lives. At the funerals for Thaw Htoo and Ta Eh Soe I couldn't fail to see how horribly torn apart their bodies were. The faces, legs and arms of the two men were wrapped in torn, bloody bandages.

I worried more than ever about my brother, Say Say. My mother kept telling him that she wanted him to give up soldiering, but ever since high school he had wanted to fight. My mother and Say Say had cut a deal: if he would agree to complete his secondary education, then she would allow him to join the Karen resistance. Solemn promises had been made on both sides so there was no way that she could go back on her word and stop him.

I continued to do well at secondary school, but there was a real sense of worry in our lives now. My parents were increasingly edgy and uneasy. The war was drawing closer, as the massive might of the Burmese Army tried to crush our resistance, destroying villages and forcing hundreds of thousands to flee. By now everyone knew someone whose father or brother had been lost to the fighting.

Every day more and more Karen soldiers were passing back and forth through our area. In spite of this, I never for one moment believed that we were in any real danger.

Chapter Eleven

SLEEPING DOG MOUNTAIN

No one told us, but the battle for Sleeping Dog Mountain was a crucial one. If the ridgeline was taken then little would stand between us and the might of the Burmese military machine. Even so, we knew the situation was serious. Villagers were being asked to help with the defence of Sleeping Dog Mountain, the main task being to carry food and ammunition up to the mountaintop positions.

It was a voluntary thing, and we all wanted to help. Much to Slone's annoyance he wasn't allowed to, because he was still in primary school. But Bwa Bwa was a strapping sixteen-year-old, and she volunteered right away. I wanted to go with her, but I doubted whether my mother would let me.

'Are you certain you want to?' my mother asked Bwa Bwa, for the umpteenth time.

'Yes, I am,' Bwa Bwa replied.

'You really, really want to do this?' my mother queried.

'Of course! My friends are going and so should I.'

Eventually, my mother gave in, but there was no convincing her when it came to me.

'You're too small, Little Daughter,' she said. 'If anything happens you won't be able to run away.'

'But Bwa Bwa can go, so why not me?'

'Bwa Bwa is older and bigger, and she can look after herself. But you, my Little Daughter, you're too small.'

I didn't think it was very fair, but there was no way around my mother. I was worried for Bwa Bwa, but I was still annoyed that I couldn't go myself. The students were divided into those who would carry the food to the ridgeline, and those who would cook for the Karen soldiers lower down the mountain.

Bwa Bwa took the more dangerous job. She would be carrying food parcels wrapped in banana leaves to the front-line troops. Most of the men in the village volunteered to fight.

On her first mission Bwa Bwa was away for several days. My mother was eaten up with worry, especially as we could hear the faint boom of explosions from up on the ridge and see the occasional enemy aircraft. My father told me that the Burmese military had launched a major offensive, bombing from the air and shelling from the ground. Karen villagers were fleeing from the area, as the military were targeting civilians. Most hid in the jungle without food or shelter, but a good number were forced across the border into Thailand as refugees.

Despite what my father told me, I still thought that the fighting was a long way away and that it would never reach us. I overheard my parents talking about foreign oil companies propping up the regime, by investing in Burma. The military leaders purchased new weapons and funded their war against us using money provided by these investors. By contrast our weapons were old and worn; some even dating back to the Second World War. When I heard my parents talking about such things I didn't fully understand. This was adults' business and I was still a schoolchild.

Bwa Bwa found her volunteer mission exhausting. It took a day to walk up to the ridgeline, and almost as long to come back again. She returned hot and dirty and tired, and with her head full of horrific images of the war. It was so high on that ridgeline that she had to gasp for air, and was only ever able to carry a small load. She had been so thirsty during the climb, but was determined to get the food to the soldiers, for she knew they were defending our very lives.

She returned from a subsequent food-carrying mission with very sad news. Saw Happy (Mr Happy) – a young man from our village who had volunteered to fight – had been killed. He had taken up his gun in a position on the front line of the battle. It seemed impossible to us – he had only been up there a matter of weeks – but Saw Happy was dead. His was one of the many lives snuffed out in the battle for Sleeping Dog Mountain.

Not long after that the war lurched ever closer, becoming a very real part of our lives. It was September 1994, and one Sunday the church pastor gave an unusually impassioned sermon. His name was Pu Ghay Dweh – Grandfather Handsome – but he was a very stern figure. His house was right next to the school playing field, yet he hated children playing there. Bwa Bwa used to joke that we only ever went to church out of fear of the pastor!

He urged us all to pray as hard as we could, for the Karen faced a severe challenge. The military junta was trying to use religion to divide us, he said, and we had to pray for unity. Religion was the one thing that might split the resistance asunder. Bwa Bwa and I didn't really understand what he was going on about. As far as we could see the greatest challenge we faced was to defend Sleeping Dog Mountain.

But unbeknown to us, tensions between Buddhists and Christians within the Karen resistance were rising. The first most people knew about it was when some Karen soldiers started attacking boats at the confluence of the Salween and Moei rivers, at Thu Mwe Hta village. It was about an hour's boat ride from us so not that far away at all. Things quickly escalated. The group declared themselves to be a splinter movement, and gave themselves the name Democratic Karen Buddhist Army – the DKBA. They allied themselves with the State Law and Order Restoration Council (SLORC) junta.

We children knew little about this at the time, and understood even less. All we did know was that our father was one of those allocated the task of meeting the DKBA, to try to defuse the problem. We were used to him going off to front-line areas on various missions, so we thought little of it when he disappeared this time.

My father had been away for two weeks when my mother started to sicken. The injury caused to her foot when we had fled from the elephants had never really healed properly. Now it flared up again, the old wound looking angry and inflamed. In fact, my mother was worried sick for my father, and her health was suffering with it. He was only supposed to have been gone a couple of days. She'd kept it from us, but the negotiating team – my father included – had been taken captive.

For the first time ever I witnessed my mother sitting around listlessly and doing nothing. It wasn't like her at all, and I put it down to her sickness. I made her hot Burmese tea and placed a large stone in the cooking fire to warm. When it was nice and hot, I wrapped it in a cloth and gave it to her so she could hold it under her blanket and keep warm. My mother appreciated these gestures, but nothing seemed to lift her spirits.

She became feverish with worry. Gradually, she was no longer able to hide her fears. We seemed to have a constant string of visitors to the house, and she kept asking if any had news of my father. Our neighbours started coming to spend the night with us, during which time they prayed with us for our father's well-being. In fact, they were acting exactly as they would have done if a family member had died, and as we had done when Moonlight's father was killed.

As the days passed we learned fragments of the truth ourselves: our father had been captured along with his fellow negotiators; he was being held in a prison beneath the monastery at Thu Mwe Hta; our own soldiers might have to go in and rescue them. My mother tried to convince us that he would be fine, even as she was sitting there looking so drawn and consumed by worry.

It was my brother Say Say's unit that had been sent into the jungles around Thu Mwe Hta to launch a rescue, should one be necessary. They were in position to assault the monastery where my father was being held. But the DKBA had forced local people to move into the area surrounding the monastery, using them as a human shield against attack. The KNU commander decided that the risk of killing so many innocent people in an assault on the monastery would be too great. It was such a difficult and dark time for us: my mother was ill and plagued by worry; my father was being held captive; and my brother was in a unit tasked with the rescue assault. No one could find the courage to tell my mother, but word had gone around the village that my father had been executed. This seemed quite likely, as the DKBA often executed KNU leaders.

Eventually, one member of the negotiating team was released. They hadn't all been killed after all. My mother went to see him. My father was alive, he told her, and being held captive in an underground prison. There was still hope.

A few days later, a boat docked at the riverside below the village. All of a sudden I caught sight of my father walking up the path towards us. I screamed out to everyone that Daddy was home, and we all went rushing down to meet him.

'Daddy! Daddy! Daddy!' I yelled, as I threw myself into his arms. 'You're home! You're home!'

My father smiled at me, weakly, and ruffled my hair. We were surrounded by people talking all at once, as half the village seemed to have gathered to greet him. Whatever he had been through over the past few weeks what struck me most was how weak and exhausted he was looking. People crammed into our living room as my father sat cross-legged on the bamboo floor. I may have been a 13-year-old girl, but I still sat right on his lap as he went about telling his story.

'We went to listen to their demands and see how we could

settle things amicably,' my father began. 'There was a monk who, although not a formal leader of the DKBA, was the mastermind behind them. We soon realized that he had been sent by the regime to cause trouble. He had been up to the front-line areas asking the Buddhist Karen soldiers why there was no pagoda there. He said they needed to build a big white pagoda to worship at, right where they were.

'Obviously they couldn't do that, as it would have given their position away,' my father continued. 'But the monk told the soldiers that this was religious prejudice, and proved that only Christians mattered to the Karen leaders. You know how people respect the monks, and this was the start of all the trouble. Underneath the monastery at Thu Mwe Hta they'd built up a secret arms store. The monk called on the soldiers to revolt, and some of them joined him—'

My father paused for a second. 'When we arrived they arrested us, and placed us in an underground dungeon, beneath the monastery. I tried to talk to the DKBA leaders, but they just told me they were going to do whatever the monk told them to. Most of those in the DKBA were just innocents – simple soldiers who believed every word the monk told them.'

My father was kept in the pitch black of the dungeon as his captors took away his fellow KNU leaders and executed them. At one point they had put a gun to his head and acted as if they were going to kill him. My father was certain that this was an operation engineered by the junta's military intelligence. In Burma Buddhist monks were universally revered, so using a monk as an agent was a clever move.

'The regime has a big and active intelligence service, and they had set this up well,' my father concluded. 'But we hope that the innocents – the easily led soldiers and villagers – will see that they've been misled and come back to us. The resistance – Christian, Buddhist and animist – has to be united, for only in unity can there be victory.'

My father had tried to end his story with a touch of hope, to give the villagers something to feel happier about. In spite of what he had been through, he tried to give them something to believe in. But he looked drained and fatigued as I had never seen him before. As I sat on his lap listening to him I was worried and angry at what had happened.

As I cuddled up to him I realized that I wasn't quite as small as I used to be. I could tell that I was tiring him, and eventually I got down and sat at his feet gazing up at his tired features. I realized then how much I loved him and how good it was to have him back with us alive and reasonably well.

And for the first time I realized how special he was to others, as well. For me he had always just been Daddy, but now I could see how widely he was loved and respected. He was not just my father, he was a leader that people looked to for hope and inspiration. I was so proud of him.

During the weeks that he had been kept from us it was as if my heart was breaking. On the day that my father returned to us it was like sunshine flooding back into my life. It was a miracle that his life had been spared, and for the first time in ages I saw my mother smile again. But there was to be little respite; the war was closing in fast now.

A few days after my father's return the village headman rang the alarm on the village square. He announced that schools were to be closed immediately and until further notice. Everyone was being put on a war footing. People were advised not to go out after dark, and if they spotted anyone moving around at night then they were to report it to him immediately.

Because we couldn't go to school any more it made sense to go and stay with our parents in the Manerplaw house. Sleeping Dog Mountain was clearly visible from there, and on some days we could see the eerie spectacle of the enemy aircraft launching their attacks. I felt fear gripping my heart.

Ever since the attack on Karen Resistance Day our mother had made us stay in the shelter whenever we could hear or see the planes. Sometimes we were stuck in the shelter all day long, wishing we could be playing out in the sunshine. We'd play our games but most of the time we were very bored, remembering the days when we could climb trees and splash in the river. Life would be like this for the rest of our time in Manerplaw, which, unknown to us, was rapidly running out.

They would come several at a time, circling above the ridge like sleek black hawks. Then they would dive and release their bombs, and there would be the tiny puffs of the explosions below. I'd always ask my mother which area it was they were attacking. Often it was the positions right on the ridgeline itself, but some-times it would be Karen villages. I couldn't imagine what it must be like to be a villager being dive-bombed like that – yet I was soon to find out.

The first time the aircraft came to drop their bombs on us I was in the loo. It was in the afternoon, and by now we were used to hearing the drone of the enemy bombers circling in the sky. But all of a sudden there was a series of horrible, piercing screaming noises right above us, and the aircraft dived to attack. Each scream ended in the massive boom of an explosion – so close that the air shook and the bamboo walls of the toilet rattled with the shock waves.

As the terrible noise died away, it was replaced by my mother's screaming. 'In the shelter! Everyone in the shelter, now!'

I bolted from the loo and sprinted for the shelter, which was on the far side of the house. I was the last to reach it – Slone, Bwa Bwa and my mother were there before me – and I could hear my mother desperately calling for me.

'Pomu Sit! Pomu Sit! Little Daughter!' she was crying. 'Where are you?!'

We stayed in the shelter all that afternoon, as the aircraft roared around in the skies above. I wasn't crying: I was more struck dumb with fear. I was so scared I wouldn't even venture out for a pee and had to bottle it up inside. As dusk descended over Manerplaw the sinister drone of the aircraft died away and we decided it was safe to venture out. My mother had left already to prepare the evening meal, and we were bored with crouching in the darkness trying to play the stone game.

When my father came home that evening he told us how he had been walking on one of the paths through Manerplaw when the planes had attacked. He had no choice but to dive into a nearby patch of 'water bush' – thick reeds that grow in the riverbeds – to take cover. When the bombing was over he'd emerged covered in mud from head to toe. He told us this story in an effort to lighten the mood, but we could tell that he was worried.

After eating a subdued meal my father told my mother how worried he had been. Bombs had fallen all around Manerplaw, and no one doubted that the aircraft would return to attack us again. My father urged my mother to be careful, and for us all to get in the shelter at the first hint of an attack.

'The situation just keeps getting worse and worse,' my father remarked, quietly. 'You must take good care of the children. Who knows where it will all end.'

A few days later I had a wonderful and unexpected surprise: Say Say came home on leave, together with one of his friends. I had missed him so much and I was so happy to see him. We were sitting as a family having lunch, when suddenly the heart-stopping scream of a diving aircraft drowned out our chatting and laughter. Before we could even move the first bomb exploded with a massive boom!

In an instant Bwa Bwa and I were dashing through a door in the side of the house and had dived into the safety of the dark shelter. Say Say was the last to reach the shelter, but by then it was full. My mother kept trying to drag him in, but there was no way he could fit. Meanwhile the aircraft kept circling overhead and howling down upon us, each bomb shaking the ground terribly.

Finally, the noise of the aircraft died away to silence. It was then that we started to tease Say Say about only ever getting his head inside the shelter.

'What's Elder Brother thinking of?' Bwa Bwa demanded. 'He

thinks that even if a bomb falls on his bum he'll be okay, 'cause his head's inside!'

In spite of our fear, we all laughed. I poked my head outside, and the first thing I caught sight of was a smoking crater on the beach below the house. There was another just up the hill, right in the midst of my father's flower garden. No wonder the explosions had sounded so close – they had been!

We had seen war movies featuring bombing, on the video at the village headman's house, but this was completely different. The scream of the diving aircraft had crashed into my ears, possessing my head, and piercing right to my heart.

When my father came home that evening he was angered by the indiscriminate nature of the attack. The pilots weren't even trying to hit military targets; they were trying to kill and maim civilians, and by doing so spread their terror. As my mother and father discussed the day's events, Say Say and his friend went out to inspect the bomb craters.

A few minutes later they returned with the tail fins of two bombs. Each was bright red in colour and about the size of an adult's hand, with four fins splayed out from the centre. They had a horrible, burning smell about them. As we inspected them I became more and more fearful. Seeing these carefully engineered steel bomb parts really brought it home somehow.

I suddenly thought: 'This is real; it is really happening to us for real.'

My parents spoke long into the evening in hushed tones. The following morning my mother sat us down for a talk. She told us that we had to pack a bag with some clothes and our important possessions, in case we had to run. She tried to reassure us that it was only 'in case'. My brothers and sisters and I loved our home, and we just tried to convince ourselves that we would never have to run away.

I had a little black rucksack and into this I packed my two good dresses, one blanket, a small mirror that I used for applying the Tha Na Kah cream, and my school pens and notebooks. I grabbed my few family photos: one of me at four months old; another of me with Bwa Bwa, standing in front of our house; and one or two group photos of the family. And that was it; my bag was packed. I just hoped and prayed I would never need to use it.

After I had packed my bag I told my mother how scared I was. 'Why do we have to be ready to run? Is that really what's going to happen to us?'

My mother tried to reassure me. 'Little Daughter, we'll be all right. I understand why you're scared, but we will get through this. Whatever happens, we'll be together and we'll get through it.'

Her words were a comfort to me. I still didn't understand how serious things were for us. But that night I had a horrible dream. I was coming home from school and as I walked towards the village I saw a huge fire. As I got closer I realized it was our house that was burning. I ran and ran to try to get to the house, but I could never reach it. The harder I tried the more it seemed to keep moving away from me.

I woke up with a start. I sat bolt upright in fear. It was so vivid that I wondered for a second if our house was burning for real. First thing in the morning I told my mother about it. She told me not to worry. It was only a dream and nothing like that would ever happen to us.

But we Karen believe in foresight and the prescience of dreams. And despite my mother's comforting words, the atmosphere in our house was tense now. Everyone was worried. Even the trees, the river and the very earth seemed worried. When we went into the forest we found it quiet and brooding, as if the trees were waiting for something bad to happen.

It was the calm before the storm.

Chapter Twelve

THE RIVER OF BURNING TEARS

Because we had now been attacked, I was more curious as to why the enemy were trying to get us. What had we done? Why us? Why our home?

My mother told me that the regime wanted to capture Manerplaw, because it was the headquarters of the Karen resistance and the wider democratic resistance in Burma.

After the uprising in 1988, a new and even more brutal dictatorship had taken power. It called itself the State Law and Order Restoration Council (SLORC). (In 1997 it changed its name to the State Peace and Development Council, after being advised by an American public relations firm.) Democracy activists had formed the National League for Democracy (NLD), led by Aung San Suu Kyi, daughter of General Aung San, who had led Burma's independence movement. They continued the campaigns for democracy and this, combined with international pressure, led to the regime being forced to agree to elections, which were held in 1990.

Despite the SLORC trying to rig the elections by setting up lots of political parties as a front, using state media for propaganda, and detaining opposition leaders, including putting Aung San Suu Kyi under house arrest, the NLD won 82 per cent of seats in Parliament. Instead of handing over power the SLORC launched a new wave of repression, arresting and torturing newly elected MPs.

Some of the MPs fled to Manerplaw and established a government in exile. This further infuriated the SLORC Generals, and with their new planes and other weapons, paid for by increasing foreign trade and investment, they were determined to wipe us all out.

I was proud that the Karen had given sanctuary to the democracy activists, but also I was worried about the escalation of the attacks on us. I heard people talking about Aung San Suu Kyi, but I was just a child and no one explained to me who she was.

In January 1995 the word that I had been dreading finally came. My father was home early, and he and my mother closeted themselves in the bedroom. They talked for ages, and finally my mother announced that we had to leave. My father helped her pack some food, before we each of us took up our backpacks and headed down to the river, where Karen soldiers were helping families to escape. At the water's edge there were lots of people, each waiting in turn for a boat.

As we waited in line my mother suddenly turned and hurried back to our house. After a few minutes we saw her emerge with some coriander seedlings, and she started planting them. Bwa Bwa, Slone and I stared at each other in confusion: if we were leaving, why was our mother bothering to plant coriander? And what a time to choose! My father motioned for us to get into a waiting boat, and then he hurried up the hill to our mother.

'Look, you have to leave,' he urged her. 'The boat's waiting for you.'

'I'm just planting a little coriander—'

'Look, we don't have much time, and you're wasting it planting coriander!'

'But when we come back it'll be ready for us—'

My mother shrugged and gave up what she was doing and
allowed my father to lead her down to the river. I glanced around
at the other families in our boat. It was full of women and children
and old people. They were staring at my mother as if she was
crazy. My father bundled her into the boat and stood back to see
us off.

'Hurry!' he urged us. 'When you reach the other side climb the
mountain and head for the village. I'll catch up with you later.
And remember to hurry—'

His last words were lost in the snarl of the engine, as the boat
driver gunned the throttle and backed us out into the current. As
we pulled further into midstream I could see that the riverbank
was lined with crowds of people, all of them laden down with
possessions and intent on leaving. Everything looked so sad: the
people, the river, the beach, the trees and the mountains beyond.

The evacuation of Manerplaw – Victory Field – was under way;
the day that I never thought I would see had come.

The boat driver got to his feet, leaned his weight on the engine
and steered the boat around. As it turned into the current I saw
my father hurry off. Apart from what we carried on our backs we
had left everything: our chickens, ducks and pigs; our house and
our flower garden.

As we powered across the river I was thinking about the newly
hatched chicks and who was going to feed them. I adored them,
and I was more worried about them than I was for my father. He
had promised to catch us up, and I had no doubt that he would do
so.

In a way the only spark of hope came from my mother's ges-
ture with the coriander. If she had been so intent on planting it,
surely she believed we would be back again?

As we disembarked from the boat, I heard the unmistakable
boom of an explosion behind us, and then there was the muffled

chatter of gunfire ringing out from the forests to the north. Minute by minute, the noise of the fighting seemed to grow ever nearer. The final assault on the heartland of the democratic resistance had begun.

We were all scared now. I could see the worry on my mother's features. Never before had we heard the crackle of gunfire so clear or so close. Slone set off on the path towards the village, striding ahead as if he were an adult and urging my mother to hurry after. I have to confess that I was the most afraid. I felt as if life itself was being torn apart. But Slone marched ahead, always the little warrior, and ordered his older sisters to follow.

'I'm scared,' I breathed as I caught up with my mother. 'And where's Daddy? Isn't he coming?'

The thought of him staying behind to face that gunfire was unbearable, but my mother's answer was drowned out by an almighty explosion as the first big mortar round slammed into the centre of Manerplaw. We rushed onwards, too afraid of the bombs and bullets at our back to linger or to talk. As we climbed, the trees filtered out the noise, but the odd booming explosion still echoed around us. At each I would jump and hurry on as if something horrid and fearful was creeping up behind me.

We joined a stream of people heading towards the village, and everyone appeared worried and panicky. Parents kept urging their children to walk more quickly and to keep up. By the time we reached the village it was dark. Normally, people would light oil lanterns at dusk, but tonight there were few, if any, alight. A blackout had been imposed on the village, so as not to give away our position to the enemy.

We made our way along darkened paths to our house. My mother set about boiling some rice, all the while calling out to our neighbours for any news they might have. In the back of my mind was the fear that my father had been caught in the fighting. We were all so exhausted from the shock of the evacuation that we went to sleep almost immediately after eating. But as for my mother, she stayed awake and watched over us all night long.

It was not a good night. Every few minutes I'd waken with a start, as the boom of an explosion went echoing through the forest. Then it would be quiet for a while before the next crash. In the morning my mother fixed breakfast, and then she told us that we would have to move on. The village wasn't safe for us any more. We would have to move further towards Thailand to try to escape the Burmese soldiers.

I had no toys or any special mementos to take from the house. I had no make-up or toiletries. In fact, the only 'make-up' I had ever worn was lipstick that Bwa Bwa and I had improvised, by smearing some old vitamin tablets across our lips. Even then I'd used the black ones by accident, instead of red, and ended up with black lips – much to Bwa Bwa's amusement.

My mother loaded each of us with as much rice, fish paste and salt as we could carry, and then it was time to leave. We headed for the river, which we could follow south-east into Thailand. The route was all but impassable on foot, for the water was channelled between several, steep-sided gorges. But there were so many people waiting for the boats – thousands and thousands of them – and by the evening we knew that none was coming for us. We had to return to spend another fearful night in the house.

This time it was even worse. Once it was dark we could see the sky on the far side of Teak Mountain lit up an unearthly, fiery orange, and we knew that Manerplaw was burning. The forces of the SLORC had taken and laid waste to Victory Field, the heartland of the resistance. Clouds of smoke coloured an angry red by the flames billowed skywards. It was heartbreaking.

The village was gripped by an echoing silence. Everyone stared at the vision of the inferno. As my mother gazed at the fiery sky, I wondered what thoughts were going through her mind. There were no words for this. I thought of my father, who had promised to catch us up, and whether he had been caught in the fiery hell that was Manerplaw. The noise of the fighting hadn't stopped completely, but it was more sporadic now. And we could smell the reek of burning.

Deep down in my heart I felt so sad. I knew that our homeland was burning, and I was so angry. I tried not to think about it. Bwa Bwa and Slone were deathly quiet, as they watched that eerie glow spreading across the night sky. We were so traumatized that we couldn't even talk. It was only in the early hours of the morning that we drifted off into troubled sleep.

In the morning we were down at the river again, waiting. It wasn't until late afternoon that a boat finally came for us, and even then people started panicking, worrying that there wasn't enough space for everyone. Luckily, the village headman intervened, establishing some order: women and small children went first; then women with teenage children; and finally the old and infirm.

Our turn came and we got into the long-tail boat. It was already laden down with people, sacks of rice and piles of possessions. By now the boat was dangerously full, and the able-bodied adults were told to walk. The way through the forest was difficult, but it was doable. Finally, we set off up the river, the boat low in the water and the powerful engine straining to carry its heavy load.

As we drew away from my beloved village I gazed back at it longingly. Eventually, it was lost from sight around a bend in the river. I couldn't believe that we were leaving. I told myself that we would be back. We had to be – the coconuts on our trees were just about ripe now, and we would have to come back to harvest them. My sister had become an expert at climbing them and plucking the coconuts so we could drink the delicious milk.

After two hours' journey up stream the boat reached the limit of its travel; any further and the river became too dangerous to navigate. We stopped in a high-walled, rocky gorge, within which the water was funnelled in a series of angry rapids. In the forests to either side there were crowds of people, all of them like us fleeing from the attacks. They carried heavy loads in woven baskets strapped to their heads, pots, plates and foodstuffs all wrapped up in cloth bundles.

The grey-blue smoke of cooking fires drifted through the trees as people boiled a little rice to sustain them on their journey. The boat pulled over, we unloaded our possessions and went to join them. Mostly, they were women and children scattered in family groups. Each had its own sad bundle of possessions, and each had the same bewildered air about it – as if people were unable to comprehend how dark and uncertain their lives had suddenly become.

We threaded our way through the trees, searching for a spot where we could rest. As we did so, I heard a voice cry out my name. It was Moonlight, and he was able to give me some hurried news of our friends. Tee Ser Paw and Lily Flower had both passed through this place the day before, but they had moved further towards Thailand and the promise of possible safety.

My mother told us that we would camp here for a little while. I presumed we were waiting for news of my father. My mother began work on a temporary shelter. She was an expert at building such things, for she had spent years living in the jungle as a soldier. There was no shortage of people to help us, for those who had already made their own shelters were happy to lend a hand.

Four bamboo posts were driven into the ground, to support a raised bamboo floor. A bamboo roof frame was built above, and sheeted over with a length of plastic that my mother had carried with her. Outside the front entrance she made a cooking hearth from three large stones. The shelter had no walls, but there was room enough inside for us all to sleep in the dry.

It was the cold season right then, and the night air would be laden with a heavy fog that crept up from the river. That first night we had to share someone else's shelter, as ours was unfinished. It was crowded, but no one seemed to mind. We cuddled up together in an effort to keep warm.

There was little sign of the war any more. Apart from the roar of the river, the forest all around us was deathly quiet. We were in the midst of dense jungle, and if the fighting was still going on we couldn't hear it. Instead, there was a subdued, fearful atmosphere and people communicated mostly in whispers. It was a tough and hostile environment in which to try to make even a temporary home.

For two weeks we stayed in this place-with-no-name, living like ghosts in the forest. Each day we ate the rice, salt and fish paste that we had carried with us. It was never enough, as my mother was rationing our food, and we were always hungry. But at least we were alive and there was something in our bellies.

At this time my mother never ceased to amaze me with her strength and resourcefulness. She was so strong; she was like a hero to us all. She knew how to survive in a place such as this; she could fell her own bamboo as well as any man, construct her own shelter, keep the fire going and the meals coming.

She went about trying to create a sense of structure and security out of our fractured lives. She built a temporary loo next to our shelter. A hole was dug in the ground and walled around with bamboo, interwoven with banana leaves. My mother advised other families to do the same, for if we used the river as a toilet it would be too dirty to drink from.

As the eldest and strongest child, Bwa Bwa acted as my mother's aid. When we weren't helping them, Slone and I stayed in the shelter. My mother didn't want us to go far; she wanted us always to stay within her sight. She was worried that the Burmese Army would track and follow us as had happened in her past life when she was a soldier. If that happened, she wanted us near at hand.

Everyone was talking about the same thing: what were we going to do now? Some said there was a place of safety where people were heading. It was called a 'refugee camp', and everyone there became 'refugees'. In the past I'd heard my parents talking about refugees, but I didn't understand the concept. We talked among ourselves about what a refugee camp might be like: was it like the village; was there a school and a church; did people there look after their neighbours?

My mother took on an informal leadership role in this place-of-no-name. People would come to her seeking advice. If they were tired, she would counsel them to rest for a few days, to rebuild their strength. Once they had slept and eaten, they could continue the journey with their heavy loads. Otherwise, they might press on and be overcome with exhaustion in the deep jungle. And she told the young mothers to try to stop their babies from crying, by keeping them on the breast the whole time – for a baby's cries might attract the enemy.

As for me, I was at an age where I was changing from being a child to a young adult. I knew my body was going through changes. I was becoming a woman, and here in this place-with-no-name was the worst place to be doing so. The total lack of any privacy was horribly embarrassing. I was shy about my body. When I went to bathe I would wait until it was almost dark and ask my mother or sister to come with me. We would slip into the cold river wrapped in longyis and try as best we could to wash the day's grime from our bodies.

Day by day our friends and neighbours from the village left this place-with-no-name, until there were few remaining. Bwa Bwa was tearful at seeing all her childhood friends leaving. She wondered if she would ever see them again. But I found myself unable to cry. I was crying inside, but I felt as if I should try to be strong. So I kept the trauma bottled up inside me.

As those we knew from the village left, strangers kept arriving. Sometimes there was a young mother with five or six children. The mother and the eldest children had to carry the toddlers and baby, and so they had little strength or space for food. Some were starving. I had never seen children crying with hunger, but I did now. It was heartbreaking. Invariably, my mother would insist on them having some of our food, even though we didn't have enough ourselves.

She would press them with a blanket, or some other precious possession, and they would be so grateful for her generosity. My mother was so very kind, even in the midst of our own suffering.

She would happily give away whatever she had if she felt it would help others.

We had been in this place-with-no-name for two weeks and had just sat down to a lunch of boiled rice, when all of a sudden my father stepped out of the forest shadows. It was like a miracle. The last we had seen of him was a lone figure by the riverside at Manerplaw, which since then had been burned to the ground in a massive battle, whilst we had been forced to flee. Yet now we had been reunited, and he was safe and well. He was covered in dirt and grime from the forest, and he looked totally exhausted, but at least he was alive!

He sat down with us to eat, and as he did so he told us his story. After we had left him he had prepared to evacuate with the KNU leader, General Saw Bo Mya. It was in part my father's responsibility to see that the general was safe and avoided capture or death at the hands of the enemy. My father had taken him on a long and difficult journey through the jungle, to a new location where the resistance could establish a makeshift headquarters.

My father couldn't tell us where that place was, for obvious reasons. If we were captured and tortured by the enemy, we might reveal where it was, with catastrophic consequences for the resistance. Once my father was certain that the new location was safe and secure, he had set off again to find us. He had asked for news of us on the way, and one of the long-tail boat drivers had been able to give him our exact whereabouts. And that's how he had found us.

I hadn't wanted to think about what might have happened to my father in the weeks that he had been away from us. I had convinced myself that he was all right. If I thought about the dangers I worried for him, so I tried to blank them from my mind.

My father was only able to stay with us for an hour or so. Knowing that we would need help with our onward journey, he had brought two young men with him. Tu Chin and Eh Moo were both in their early twenties, and they were Karen soldiers and friends of the family. Eh Moo had been injured, and Tu Chin was very sick, so neither could be on the front line fighting right now.

Before leaving, my father told us how much he trusted in our mother's ability to look after us. He told us to trust in her and support her on the journey that lay ahead. Our only option was to follow the countless others who had headed into Thailand and the refugee camps. Eh Moo and Tu Chin would accompany us on that journey. My father told us he would catch up with us there and see us again soon.

As he readied himself to leave, it struck me how gaunt and troubled he seemed. He was borne down by the weight of responsibility he was carrying on his shoulders. He hugged and kissed each of us goodbye, kissed my mother farewell, and was gone.

The following morning at first light we set off. I wasn't sad to be leaving the place-of-no-name, I was just uncertain about what lay ahead. Having seen my father had lifted my spirits enormously. And having Eh Moo and Tu Chin with us was a real blessing. They hefted the heaviest loads as we set off into the deep jungle.

The path snaked through the dawn mists, sticking to the eastern riverbank and climbing steadily out of the gorge. A few minutes into the jungle and it was rocky and slippery underfoot. To the left a near-vertical slope fell to the crashing waters of the rapids below. One slip and it would likely be our last. We followed the footsteps of those who had gone before, trusting that if they had made it so could we. We talked only in whispers, for in silence lay our greatest safety.

By the end of that first day we had reached an area that was dominated by enormous trees. The forest canopy was high above, and little light filtered down to the forest floor, which was all but devoid of vegetation. There were plenty of places where we could rest for the night.

Beneath one of the largest forest giants we spotted a group of people in a makeshift camp. It turned out to be our friend from the village, Winston Churchill, together with his parents and sisters and brother.

They welcomed us with brave smiles, and we settled down to join them for our first night in the deep jungle.

Chapter Thirteen

UNDER THE BIG TREE

That first night we slept on a plastic sheet laid on the ground. My mother was very careful about where exactly we should sleep, for the tree above us was as ancient as the hills and some of the branches looked as if they might fall. We made our bed beneath one of the firmest-looking boughs. The night-dark forest canopy was sprinkled with bright sparks – the stars high above. It would have been a magical place to spend the night, had we not been fleeing our village and on the run.

Winston Churchill's family had built a temporary shelter under the big tree, and my mother decided that we would do the same, with the help of Eh Moo and Tu Chin. We would remain in this place for a few days, she said, resting and rebuilding our strength for the onward journey. For two weeks we'd eaten nothing but small portions of rice, salt and fish paste. Nearby was a stream of sweet fresh water, and the forest was sure to be full of wild foods.

As the adults went about constructing the shelter, Bwa Bwa and

I went to the stream, hunting for crabs and prawns. We could not find enough for a proper meal, so when we'd caught enough for a soup, we went scavenging for bush food instead. We found wild vegetables, and banana pith and shoots (the flesh of the banana trees), to add to the prawn and crabmeat. The vegetables were not what we'd normally eat, with little nutrition, and banana pith was only ever eaten as a last resort, but after the past two weeks even this watery soup seemed like a treat.

We were all of us physically and emotionally exhausted – but especially my mother. Her exertions at the place-with-no-name had drained her terribly. Under the big tree was a good place to rest, and we could scavenge for wild food. And after under-the-big-tree none of us knew what lay ahead. Moving on was a daunting prospect.

A week after our arrival Winston's parents decided they had recovered their strength enough to continue their journey. With all their children it was difficult for them to travel quickly. They planned to follow the river upstream, which was the direction travelled by those who had gone before. None of us had ever been this way previously so we didn't know what lay ahead. It led deeper into Thailand, which meant possible safety, but also uncertainty.

As more and more refugees arrived in the forest around us it became harder to find food. So one early morning we took up our loads and set off walking, leaving the big tree behind us. The path through the forest was very faint, and all we could do was follow the tracks made by others. The route led along the riverbank, sometimes on the rocky beach right next to the water where there were few footsteps visible, at other times snaking high up the steep valley sides.

As we walked my mind wandered. I thought about school: would I ever be able to restart my studies? I had just been moved up a year at Pway Baw Lu school, because I was doing so well. I wasn't far away from taking the equivalent of my GCSEs. But with each footstep we were leaving school further and further behind. Where might we settle, how might we end up living, and how might I study? I just didn't know.

That evening we stopped on a sandy riverbank, right next to the waters of the Mu Yu Klo. It was the dry season so we weren't too worried about the river rising overnight and drowning us. We lay out on the sand under an open sky, the noise of the rushing river loud in our ears.

As I lay there staring up at the starlit heavens, I wondered how such a beautiful land could be full of so much evil. We had named our land Kaw Thoo Lei – Land of No Evil. But now the SLORC had sent their soldiers to lay waste to that land. All of our hopes and our dreams and our visions of the future seemed lost. Manerplaw lay in ruins, and we were running for our lives.

We spent a week on the banks of the Mu Yu Klo, gathering our strength. Each time we spent a day struggling through the jungle it seemed to take so much out of my mother. I was beginning to realize that she was not as young, or as invincible, as she once had seemed. Every day more and more people came to join us on the riverbank, as they fled from the soldiers who were rampaging through the villages to the north of us – and with each came the same story of fleeing from the killing and the burning and the terror.

The murder and mayhem was spreading outwards from Manerplaw. Each family told their story of how they had had to flee and which villages were now under attack. More often than not after a few whispered words people lapsed into a silence – a silence informed by the shock and trauma of the past few weeks and days. Mostly, they were caught up in their own trauma: where to run to escape; how to save their families; how to survive the journey that lay ahead.

One morning I plucked up courage to ask my mother the one thing that was preying on my mind: when would we be able to go home?

'Moe, when can we go back to the village?' I asked her. 'Will it be long?'

Bwa Bwa and Slone pricked up their ears. It was the one question that we had all been dreading to ask, but to which we all wanted an answer. *When could we go home?*

My mother glanced at me with tired eyes. 'I'm sorry, Pomu Sit, we can't go back. Everyone has left—'

I was silent for a moment with the shock of it all. 'Never? We'll never go home?'

My mother shook her head. 'Pomu Sit, the Burmese soldiers have taken over our area. We *can't* go home. There's no home to go back to—'

I stared at the sand, tears pricking at my eyes. I could hardly believe it, but that was what my mother had said. *We weren't ever going to go home.* It was the first time my mother had told us the grim reality of our situation, and I felt devastated.

'But Moe, we just want to go home,' I heard Bwa Bwa whisper. 'What's so wrong with that? Why can't we?'

'There's nothing there for us any more,' my mother answered. She was on the brink of tears herself. 'I'm sorry, I'm sorry – but the village is gone.'

Tears trickled down Bwa Bwa's face. 'We'll never see it again? Never?'

My mother gave Bwa Bwa a hug, and held out her free arm to me. 'We'll have to go to Thailand, to become refugees. But we'll still be together, we'll still have each other, won't we?'

'But I don't want to be a refugee,' I told her. 'Refugees are people who need help. People who can't survive on their own. We're not like that, are we?'

'No, Pomu Sit, we're not like that,' my mother agreed. She gazed into my eyes. 'But now we have no choice. We have to go to Thailand. There's nowhere else we can go.'

At the end of that week we had our first concrete news of what might lie ahead. Some of the adults from our village had travelled back the way they had come, to tell us that they had found a little uncertain sanctuary. They had reached a place called Mae Ra Moe, where a temporary refugee camp had been established.

Thousands of Karen were there already, and people were clearing the jungle to build huts for themselves.

The Thai authorities had agreed that this could be a 'temporary settlement' – which meant that for now at least people wouldn't be declared illegal immigrants and pushed back into Burma. The Karen Refugee Committee – a group set up by the KNU to try to deal with the influx of refugees into Thailand – was trying to get the United Nations to recognize Mae Ra Moe as a refugee camp, and to give it formal protection.

I had no idea what the United Nations was at this time, and only the vaguest concept of the life and status of a 'refugee'. But one thing I did understand: Mae Ra Moe was a Karen area. All the villages around there were Karen, albeit ones situated within Thailand. So we would be in a Karen area, surrounded by Karen people – those who spoke the same language as us. This was the one bright light on an otherwise dark and stormy horizon.

And so I began to nurture a new hope – a hope that once we got to Mae Ra Moe we could rebuild our lives pretty much as before. If we couldn't go back to our village, we would build a new one, just like the old one, and we would surround ourselves once more with our neighbours and friends. We would build a new school better than before, and lessons would start up again. And we would rear our ducks and chickens and pigs, and replant our vegetable and flower gardens.

We spent a few more days on that riverbank, and the very process of living consumed our every waking moment. There was so much to do just staying alive. We hunted for *kaw soe dot* – water spinach – which grew by the riverbank. From the shadowy places in the forest we plucked the young shoots of ferns, which we boiled up as a green vegetable. We sought out the distinctive *ka thay kaw may dot* – the horse-hoof plant – whose leaves resemble a shiny, curved hoof. Even the emerald grass that grew by the river – *ta ka dot*, 'bitter leaves' – could be boiled up to make a spicy stew.

My mother urged us to be up before the dawn, to eat breakfast in the half-light, and to be always on the lookout and to be ready to run at the first hint of trouble. She was fearful that the enemy would track, find and attack us.

'Eat quickly,' my mother urged. 'Don't speak – just eat! If the enemy comes and you're in the middle of eating you'll be left behind. Always be ready to run.'

I glanced around at the forest fearfully. Ever since fleeing the village we had heard nothing more of the war. No gunfire in the forest, no booming explosions and no aircraft overhead. It was hard to imagine in the peace and serenity of this beach by the river in its secret valley that such horror was still going on.

'Are they still after us, Moe?' I asked.

'I don't know. There's no way of telling. But we have to be careful, just in case.'

In spite of her physical exhaustion, it was now that I really saw some of the fierce resistance fighter that my mother had once been. She knew so much about the ways of the enemy, and of soldier-craft. She knew that darkness was our friend, for it cloaked our presence in shadows. But it was also a potential foe, for the enemy might creep up on us unnoticed. She was forever listening and trying to sense a threat. She knew that just when the forest was at its most silent might well be when the enemy was near.

She knew that smoke from a cooking fire signalled danger, for it could be seen from a distance, but that cooked food was vital if we were to rebuild our strength. She knew to cook at night, for then smoke was more or less invisible against the dark sky. But if there was a bright moon the silhouette of the rising smoke could be a giveaway. She knew that the glowing coals of a cooking fire would be highly visible at night, and so to shield our fire from prying eyes.

She knew for us to always keep our bags packed and be ready to move at a moment's notice.

Eventually, my mother decided that we were ready to continue the journey. We pushed onwards through the forest, following the river further and further towards its source. We came across scores of other villagers on the way, and all of them were moving in the same direction as us. The worst were the families with old people or very young children. The old and the young were unable to manage the steep, jungle-clad hills, and so the able-bodied adults had to carry them piggyback style.

We made our way along the side of a steep gorge, where one slip would carry us into the river. It was hundreds of feet below, with thick bush lining the rocky, boulder-strewn banks. The water was smooth and dark where it was deep, but rough and white in the shallow areas. We clung to trees and bushes as we felt our way along the steep path, our flip-flops trying to find a grip as we did so.

When the going got most difficult we took it in relays. Bwa Bwa, Slone and I would wait quietly in the forest as my mother and the two men went back to fetch one bag at a time. It was too difficult and dangerous to carry more. Once all the bags were with us, we would move on and establish a new muster point for the next stage of the relay. In this way we neared Mae Ra Moe.

Eh Moo and Tu Chin went forward to scout out the ground ahead. This was the first time in four weeks that we would be coming out of hiding, and we had to be careful. They found a place where we could make a camp for the night, and came back and fetched us. As we trudged exhaustedly into Mae Ra Moe, it seemed to me like a vast version of the place-with-no-name. As far as I could see, makeshift shelters were strung out under the trees, and a haze of grey wood smoke hung over everything.

We made our way through the camp, following the river to our chosen spot. Some families were living under little more than a plastic sheet hung from the trees. Others had made temporary shelters, just as we had done in the place-with-no-name and under-the-big-tree. Some families had even started to build proper bamboo houses, similar to those back in the village – itself an indicator of how long they planned on being here.

Eh Moo and Tu Chin had chosen a spot next to a small stream, at the far end of the camp. The two families closest to us were from our village. My mother knew them by name, and she went and greeted them as cheerfully as she could. With Eh Moo and Tu Chin's help, we made the simplest of shelters by stringing up our plastic sheet. Then we cooked and ate some rice and bedded down for an exhausted sleep.

Our neighbours had told us that no one was to show any lights in the camp. This meant no oil lanterns or torches. If lights were shown then they might lead the enemy to us. This was a harsh reminder that we still weren't safe, even here. Although we were in Thailand, in a semi-official camp, there was little to stop the enemy from sneaking across the border and attacking us.

My mother had warned us to keep our bags packed with essential items, in case we suddenly had to run. A camp committee had been established, and the able-bodied men had set up a twenty-four-hour security watch. Volunteers patrolled the camp perimeter, but the only weapons they carried were sticks. If there was an attack they were to raise the alarm so that we might have the chance to escape.

It wasn't the best of situations in which to prepare for my first night's rest in Mae Ra Moe camp. I lay there, searching the dark wall of forest all around me for the enemy. My mind churned with unwelcome thoughts. Although there was a sense of security in numbers, the very fact that there were so many of us here might draw the enemy to us.

Eventually, my exhaustion got the better of me and I fell asleep. The next morning I awoke feeling rested. Bwa Bwa and I set off for a walk to the river, to see if we could find somewhere to wash. The dirt and grime of the jungle was still thick upon us. We'd barely reached the water's edge when I spotted the familiar form of Lily Flower just across the way from us.

'Lily Flower! Lily Flower! Hi! Hi! Over here! It's us! Bwa Bwa and Zoya!'

We ran over and hugged. It was so good to see her! Lily Flower had always been big and solid and strong, and that was something so reassuring about finding her here.

She had so many questions for us. 'When did you get here? Are you staying nearby? Where are you? Where?'

'We're just there by the little stream, on the hillside,' I said, pointing. 'There – that's where we're staying. Where're you?'

'Down by the riverside. Look, you can see our place from here. So, we're almost neighbours!'

'And all your family are here?' I asked.

'Everyone's fine—'

Lily Flower, Bwa Bwa and I did our best not to discuss the darkness that had engulfed our lives during the past few weeks. In our culture people try to avoid talking about such horrors wherever possible. And if we ever did have to mention such sadness and tragedy and loss, we would often do so by trying to make light of it, making jokes to cheer each other up.

Lily Flower's family had constructed a temporary shelter five places away from our own, so she was practically on our doorstep. And it turned out that Moonlight's family was only a few spots away from her.

That same day we discovered that Ter Pay Pay and his mother – our 'grandma' – had arrived in the camp. Grandma must have been approaching eighty years old, and it was a miracle that she had made the journey alive. Ter Pay Pay had been a resistance fighter in his youth, and he was still fit and strong. At points on the journey he had had to carry grandma on his back. I was really happy to find them here, especially when they suggested that they come and live with us.

Eh Moo and Tu Chin would soon be returning to rejoin the resistance. Ter Pay Pay would be a great help to my mother as she set about trying to rebuild our lives. Like Say Say, Ter Pay Pay was a man of the forest. He knew how to cut bamboo, build shelters and survive better than most. And grandma would be great company, as we tried to keep our spirits up in the face of becoming 'refugees'.

Ter Pay Pay was deaf and dumb, and he was also illiterate. But he managed to communicate using sign language. He would indicate my mother by rubbing his cheek in a circular fashion, signifying the Tha Na Kah cream that she wore. He would run his palm over his forehead to signify my balding father. And he would indicate each of us children by showing our height above the ground with his hand.

Ter Pay Pay was single, and although he liked some of the girls in the village he was rarely able to communicate his affection for them. The best he might manage was to give a girl a gift of fruit or vegetables. Then she might realize that Ter Pay Pay was fond of her. But still it had proved hard for him to find one that would accept him.

Ter Pay Pay, Eh Moo and Tu Chin set about building us a proper shelter, of the type we had had at the place-with-no-name and under-the-big-tree. Whilst they cut bamboo in the forest, Bwa Bwa, Slone and I set about crushing it, to make bamboo flats. Together, we constructed two sleeping platforms side by side – a larger one for us, and a smaller one for Ter Pay Pay and grandma. The split bamboo floor and wall gave us a bit of privacy.

Ter Pay Pay had even managed to bring some chickens with him. He'd tied their feet together and slung them upside down on a pole. And there was a little bamboo cage full of chicks. At times he'd been trekking through the jungle carrying his possessions, his mother on his back and the chickens. What a journey they must have had!

That first day in the camp I made it my job to look after the chickens, making sure they didn't run off. By the end of the day our shelter was ready. As my mother cooked some rice I gazed out over the camp. Everywhere there were families doing the same as us – cutting and carrying bamboo and building shelters. As I watched all this activity, I told myself that it must be only temporary. Surely there had to be a way back to the village. But in my heart I knew that this was it. My mother had told us the truth: there was no going back.

The following morning a buzz of excitement went around the camp. A group of white people had arrived, and they were giving out emergency materials. The elders – grandma among them –

started talking about how this was the 'youngest brother' coming back to help the Karen, just as our legends predicted. As the old poems foretold, he was coming in our hour of need to make amends for stealing the golden book. I wasn't really interested in what they were saying. I was interested in what these white people might have brought for us.

My mother set off for the far end of the camp. An hour or so later she returned with an enormous tarpaulin, which was a stripy sky blue. The white people were giving one to each family, as roofing material. It was far better than our thin plastic sheet, and Ter Pay Pay soon had it rigged up to cover the entire shelter and cooking area. As we sat beneath our new roof, my mother told us more of what she'd learned during her journey to the far end of the camp.

That part was furthest into Thailand, and a gate led out on to a dirt track that in turn led to the nearest town. It was also the location of the camp headquarters, plus a clinic staffed by Karen nurses. That clinic had been set up by a non-governmental organization (NGO). This was the first time that I had heard mention of an NGO, but all that I understood was that this was 'white people helping us'.

There was another group – the Burma Border Consortium – giving out food rations. But these were limited to those truly in need, which meant families whose own food supplies were exhausted. After four weeks living in the forest we were pretty much out of rice, so we fitted that category. In order to get the rations we would have to register with the Karen Refugee Committee. Once we had done so we could collect a rice ration, and a little salt and fish paste. I was starting to get a sense of what it was going to be like living as a refugee.

There was a small spring in the undergrowth beside our shelter, and this we decided to make our washroom. We rigged up a split bamboo pipe on stilts, which funnelled the water downhill. You could crouch under the free end and splash in the falling water. Bwa Bwa and I would go there at dusk and wash in relative privacy.

As our new home took shape the hope grew in my heart that we might rebuild the village here in Mae Ra Moe. The shelters were crammed far closer together than was normal, but I didn't see why Mae Ra Moe couldn't be made in the image of Per He Lu village, only much bigger. Sadly, things could never be that simple.

Mae Ra Moe had been divided into sections. We had ended up in Section Seven, which was at the far western end and nearest the border with Burma. We were situated on a hill overlooking the Mu Yu Klo River, which had been our constant companion ever since fleeing the village. At the opposite end were Sections One to Five, situated on a tributary of the Mu Yu Klo.

Once settled in a section, it was pretty much established that that was where one would stay. That first week I discovered that Sweet Water Flower was living in Section Six, so down the riverbank a good way from us. And Winston Churchill and his family were also living in that section.

Nightingale was also living in Section Six, but she was across the river from us. A few days after our arrival, she crossed the river on a bamboo raft and came to look for us. It was great to be reunited with her, but it was now a real journey to get to her house. Whilst most of my friends from the village were in the camp, we were spread over a far greater distance.

But the biggest drawback of the camp was that we were trapped. As non-official refugees we were told that we had no status in Thailand. Whilst the Thais would tolerate our presence *inside* the camp, there was to be no leaving it. This sense of being imprisoned just added to the feeling that here we had no future, and that our lives had come to a dead end.

A few months after our arrival at Mae Ra Moe the Thai authorities issued orders that we were to assist with building a fence around the entire camp. Each section had to construct its own part of the fence, and barbed wire was provided for the purpose. If there wasn't enough barbed wire we were supposed to cut bamboo stakes to make a stout palisade.

When that barrier went up it sent out a clear message to us: at all times we were supposed to remain within the confines of the fencing. Of all the hardships we were to suffer in the camp, this was the one we hated most. For a people long accustomed to wandering free, this entrapment was like death to us. The very idea that we couldn't just wander at will in the forest was unbearable.

If the Thai police caught anyone outside the camp, then they would be treated as a 'non-person'. Such non-people would either be imprisoned, or shipped back to where they had come from – which meant Burma. We would be handed into the custody of those from whom we had fled – the SLORC regime's border police or their security agents.

We would be handed back to those who had spent decades trying to wipe us off the face of the earth. And that would be a death sentence.

Chapter Fourteen

NO REFUGE

From the camp entrance a dirt track led through the jungle to Mae Sa Lit, the nearest Thai town. It was a thirty-minute journey by jeep, but it may as well have been a whole universe away. As non-people, there was no way that any of us were ever going to go there.

I didn't really mind. I'd seen a real town, and I had no desire to do so now. I just hated being trapped in the camp.

During the first few days I noticed groups of Thai soldiers on patrol around the camp. I was amazed at how well equipped they were: each had a pair of shiny leather boots, a smart uniform and a sleek, modern-looking gun. It made me so sad to think of our own resistance fighters, many of whom wore flip-flops and carried weapons that were decades old and held together in places with wire. I realized then that we Karen were so poor that we couldn't even equip our army properly.

We couldn't speak Thai, and it was highly unlikely that any of the Thai soldiers could speak Karen. No one was certain if they were there to protect us, or to police the camp boundary and keep us in. But one thing was clear: they were a very professional-looking army. I imagined how our resistance fighters would have fared in recent battles, if they had had such equipment. But I was soon to learn that with the Thai soldiers, appearance wasn't everything.

Life in the camp settled into a rhythm, as we set about building a proper house for ourselves, Ter Pay Pay and grandma. In the early morning the adults would go to cut bamboo from a nearby grove. By lunchtime they would be back for a snack, usually some leftover rice from breakfast. In the afternoon we'd help our mother clear a little land around our plot, to plant vegetables. Once the cut undergrowth was dry, we would burn it so the ashes would fertilize the soil. This was the daily pattern of our lives for that first month in the camp.

My main responsibilities were to look after the chickens and to fetch water from the spring. There were families living around the spring, and it was a slippery, muddy slope to get there. People washed in the spring, and the water bubbled up into a dirty brown pool. I had to take it back and boil it over the fire. We tried only to drink boiled water, for there was a risk of catching cholera. I'd keep a pot of Karen tea brewing over the fire, so that those doing the hard work could come and refresh themselves.

We built a toilet set apart from the house and modelled on the one we had back in the village. A bamboo frame sat over a deep pit, with a bamboo pipe poking out to let the smelly gasses escape. Whenever we children had a spare moment, we'd go scavenging for wood in the forest. We'd cut it into short pieces with a machete, tie them into a bundle using vines, and jam the machete in the middle. We'd carry those bundles home on our heads, with a longyi scrunched into a doughnut shape cushioning the load. But with so many people gathered together in the camp, firewood soon became in short supply. The temptation to go searching outside the camp borders was always there.

During the weeks when we were trying to rebuild our shattered

155

lives there was no time to play. It was so different from life back in the village, yet there was little opportunity to ponder how life had changed.

At one time people must have farmed in the area of the camp. We could tell where fields had once been cleared from the bush. Our house was in an open area, but it backed on to a steep hill that was covered in forest. Tall trees and bamboo groves led up to a mountaintop far behind us. To the front we looked out over the river and to a cluster of shelters set among jungle and bush on the far side.

Just as soon as we had cleared and burned a patch of land, my mother planted her vegetable garden. In a sense she had prepared well before fleeing the village: she'd brought with her chilli, aubergine and bean seeds. Most families had had to flee so suddenly that they had practically nothing with them. My mother would share around what little she had, and it struck me again how kind and caring she was to others, disregarding our own privations.

My mother even gave away one of Bwa Bwa's few items of clothing – her favourite pink top. Bwa Bwa loved that top very much, and she was so upset to see it go. But my mother said that we should be happy to give such things away. She gave it to a young mother who had a tiny baby and whose husband had lost a leg in the war. Their need was greater than ours, she said, and in that she was right.

Each section in the camp formed its own committee, and each group of ten households elected a team leader to sit on that committee. My mother was chosen to represent our area. She would go to the committee meetings and raise any concerns that the households she represented might have, and report back to them afterwards. During those first months in the camp everyone was plagued by the fear of an attack, and this was our overriding worry.

In response to such fears the camp committee instituted a strict security regime. By nine o'clock in the evening all candles and torches had to be out, so that the enemy would find it harder to target us in the darkness. And from then until morning we had to speak in hushed whispers.

But my mother remained convinced that the enemy were going to attack. The time she feared most was daylight. That was when the enemy could better see us to kill us. Often, she sent us off to the furthest end of the camp to hide in the forest. We'd take a packed lunch of rice, and we were not to return before dusk. We hated hiding in the forest like that. All you could do was sit still and keep quiet, whereas if we were working at least we were keeping ourselves occupied.

It was now more than a year since the first time that I had run from the enemy aircraft. Ever since that day I had lived with fear as a constant companion. Even now, the camp didn't seem like a sanctuary. The sudden sound of the wind in the trees was enough to make my heart thump in my chest. Fear began to take over my life. It ate away at me.

There were daily rumours that an attack on the camp was imminent. One day the Karen resistance were able to send us concrete news of the danger we were in: the enemy had crossed the Moei and Salween rivers and were heading for the camp. We were warned to be constantly on the lookout. If we saw the enemy we were to raise the alarm. Then the camp organizers would tell us in which direction to run.

One day Bwa Bwa, Slone and I were out cutting firewood. It was bright and sunny, with slender beams of light streaming down through the leafy bamboo. All of a sudden we heard screams from below us, followed by the pounding of running feet. As we turned to stare in the direction of the camp, we caught sight of a crowd of people charging in our direction, children clutched in the adults' arms.

An instant later my mother was standing outside our hut, crying out to us: 'Quick! Quick! The camp is being attacked! Run! Run! Deeper into the forest!'

We darted down to the house and grabbed our bags: our

mother had drilled into us that we were *never* to leave without them. Then we helped grandma to her feet, as she was almost too old to walk, and with Ter Pay Pay hurried her into the forest.

As we did so, we heard that awful, hated sound once again – the crackle of gunfire ringing out from behind us. It was two months since we had last heard that fearful noise, and now we were refugees and it was all happening again.

We headed deeper and deeper into the forest, climbing on to the high ground. Eventually, the noise of the attack faded away behind us. It seemed that we had escaped, for now at least. We crouched in the dark shadows of the densest bamboo thicket, straining our ears.

I felt like a terrified rabbit as a fox stalks it through the trees. We were tense and fearful, as we watched and listened for signs that the enemy was coming after us. We spent the entire day hiding. Eventually, one of the camp organizers came to find us. The enemy had swept into the camp from the east, attacking Sections One and Two, which had been completely burned to the ground. The soldiers had opened fire indiscriminately and people had fled for their lives. Dozens had been captured and marched away into the jungle.

The Thai soldiers had a guard post by the refugee camp's main gate, but when the enemy attacked they were nowhere to be found. Those Thai soldiers who had struck me as being so well armed and fierce-looking had run away. They had stayed away for several hours, in which time the enemy had burned down part of the camp and kidnapped people. My mother was convinced that the Thai soldiers had *allowed* the enemy in to attack us. What else could explain their actions?

She was so angry. The Thai soldiers were supposed to provide security, but they had failed to do any such thing. They faced the might of a battle-hardened Burmese Army controlled by a ruthless junta. With some 400,000 troops, Burma's army is far larger than those of most developed nations. The last thing the Thais wanted to do was pick a fight with them over a bunch of Karen refugees.

We didn't go down to Sections One and Two. We were too scared to do so. We didn't want to see the burning remains of the refugees' newly built huts, but we could see the plume of white smoke billowing over the camp. At any moment there could be another attack, and we wondered if we wouldn't be better camping out in the forest. Eventually, we bedded down in our hut, but using our bags as pillows and with Ter Pay Pay and my mother watching over us.

There were no more scares that night, and the next day we received word that the enemy had withdrawn into Burma. For now at least, the danger seemed to be past. A week later some of the women who had been kidnapped found their way back into the camp. We had been so worried for them, especially as some were my mother's friends. The soldiers had taken them to use as human shields. They had forced them to march ahead, in case there were any minefields.

By now our own supplies of food were utterly exhausted, and so we had to survive on handouts from the camp charities. As Mae Ra Moe wasn't an official refugee camp, there were no UN food rations. Instead, a makeshift group of NGOs tried as best they could to feed us. The food supply was irregular, but at least it kept us alive. The rice was 'broken rice' – the dusty remains of the husking process – and it was gluey and gritty when cooked.

We were doing all we could in the camp to help ourselves, but imprisoned in such a small space, we just could not survive without more help. More foreign agencies started to arrive, and gradually our rations improved, but they were still only barely enough to survive on. Each person would get roughly the equivalent of a mugful of rice every day, and each month every family would get a small pack of salt, a two-litre bottle of cooking oil, a kilo per person of yellow beans and a kilo of fish paste per person. We never got meat or fresh vegetables.

The fish paste consisted of small fish in salt water. The fish were mostly broken, sometimes so much that they were already like a paste. Each month we would look forward to getting the fish paste ration, searching excitedly to see if we could find a whole or almost whole fish, but this would happen maybe only once a year. Every day we would pound some of the fish into a paste which we would mix with the rice to give it some flavour. Later we would be able to grow garlic, chillies and onions, which we would mix into the pounded fish paste.

We stuffed the jar with a special leaf that we found in the jungle, which stopped the fish paste from going off completely. But however careful one might be, flies always seemed to get into the jar and lay their eggs. The eggs would hatch into maggots, and in no time we'd find ourselves with a jar full of maggoty fish paste. If we didn't have anything else to eat, it would be boiled-up maggoty fish paste for lunch or supper. Of course, we did our best to pick out the maggots.

As a family we had always been so self-reliant. My mother was used to working hard and relying on her own wits to look after her family. Accepting handouts like this felt so abnormal. But we had no choice. In the camp you either took the handouts, or you starved.

My mother was working so hard that she started having migraines. They would start in the evening and prevent her from sleeping. And with the poor-quality food she started to lose weight. All we could supplement our daily rations with were the few vegetables we could grow around the house. We weren't allowed to leave the camp to search for wild food. I was a growing teenager with an appetite to match. I was often hungry, as there was rarely enough to eat.

Ter Pay Pay's chickens were too valuable to kill to eat. Their eggs were a precious source of extra protein. I made it my mission to feed them up and raise new broods of chicks. I used to take the broken rice, spread it out on a woven bamboo tray, and sift out any inedible bits. Those I fed to the chickens, and that's how I tried to encourage them to hatch out their eggs.

With life being so tough my mother started to have a short temper. She'd make us hide in the forest, but we'd get bored and sneak back into camp. Then she'd scold us for disobeying her orders. She'd get very angry, more so than was normal, and I wished then that my father was there to cool her temper. The constant insecurity and tension was really getting to her.

I wanted to make life a little easier for her. By now we had a good crop of aubergines, ladies' fingers and water spinach. I helped my mother earn a little income by selling our produce. With her assistance I priced a bunch of ten ladies' fingers at 3 Thai Baht – around 5p. A nice bunch of water spinach was a similar price. And three aubergines were 5 Baht.

I went from hut to hut, asking if anyone wanted to buy. It was a hard sell. People had precious little money and everyone was trying to grow their own food. In a good day I might make 40–50 Thai Baht. But I was better at making sales than my sister or little brother. I think it was because I was so utterly determined.

I gave the money to my mother. When she had saved up enough, she would go to buy whatever basic essentials we needed. Thai traders had set up a makeshift marketplace at the far end of the camp. There were around 15,000 refugees in Mae Ra Moe by now – a big captive population to sell to. Every family had tried to grab what little money they had before fleeing their village, so there was custom to be done. The little money my mother had she would spend on cooking pots, plates, clothes or some extra food.

Sometimes my mother would buy us a little treat, like prawn crackers, or a bag of boiled sweets, but only if she could afford it. Or she might buy half a kilogram of sugar, which was a real extravagance. Some of the refugees made rice flour bread, and my mother might buy some of that. It was sweetened with sugar, and we'd eat it right away.

None of us had any idea where our father was at this time. I was worried for him. I wondered where he might be and how he was surviving. Occasionally, I wondered whether he thought of us at all. I missed him so much. I told myself that he was still alive, but I didn't know for sure. We had no way of communicating with him, wherever he might be.

Sometimes I'd ask my mother about him. 'Moe, where's Daddy d'you think? D'you think he's okay?'

'I'm sure he's all right, Pomu Sit,' my mother would reply. 'He's off doing his duty, and we have to trust him in that.'

'But where is he?'

'I don't know. No one does. When he can he'll come and find us.'

In my mind my father was off doing heroic work deep inside Burma. He was doing as Zoya the Russian partisan had done, and operating behind enemy lines. He was preparing a counter-attack by our resistance fighters. And as they had done in the Second World War, the forces of freedom in Burma would defeat a seemingly invincible enemy. In time we would be able to go back to our land and our homes.

I lived in that hope. It kept me going amidst the fear and hopelessness of the camp.

It was my dream of the future.

Chapter Fifteen

A TIME OF DARKNESS

We had arrived in the refugee camp in February 1995. By April most people had finished building their homes, and we turned our minds to other things. 'Summer schools' were set up for the camp children and staffed by volunteers. Each camp section had one, with lessons held in the open in the sunshine. Their theme was simple: how to maintain hygiene in the refugee camp. With thousands of people crammed into such a small area, the potential for disease was high.

We were told we had to wash our hands before eating. Before going to bed we were supposed to wash our feet, as invariably they would be covered in mud from the day's activities. Rubbish – plastic bags, paper, food tins – had to be thrown into a pit and burned. Prior to arriving in the camp we'd rarely had rubbish to dispose of, for there were few such throwaway items back in the village. So we didn't know not to throw such things into the spring where we collected water, or into the river.

One of the NGOs gave us proper toothbrushes and toothpaste,

and we were taught how to brush our teeth morning and night. We were given soap and shampoo with which to wash our bodies and our hair, and we were each given a little bag in which to keep our toiletries. We hung these from the bamboo wall of the bathroom that we had constructed at the back of the house.

After the hygiene lessons we had a sewing course, in which we were taught to repair our clothes, for we wouldn't be getting any new ones any time soon. We were taught to keep our clothes clean, even if they were old and worn. My father had been a stickler for cleanliness, so I took all of this very seriously. I really enjoyed these classes because I was learning new and useful things, but most of all I was happy to be getting some schooling once again.

Summer school lasted the whole of April, with lessons in the morning and workshops in the afternoon. One of my classmates was Lily Flower. We were given cloth, needles and thread by an NGO that worked with the Karen Women's Organization. It was good to be learning again and feeding my head, instead of hiding in the forest, or doing the daily grind of the chores.

By June of that year a new secondary school had been built. It was situated in Section Five, which meant I would have to cross the river to reach it. Even so, I was determined to attend lessons. But the journey across the river was too difficult and dangerous, especially when using a bamboo raft in the rainy season. So my mother proposed that a high school be built for our section of the camp.

The camp committee called for volunteers to help, and a building was put up made of a bamboo frame and a roof thatched with leaves. An old rice farm to one side of the school was converted into the playing field. The teachers were all volunteers from within the camp. The classroom walls were only of thin bamboo, so we could overhear the goings-on in other lessons. Slone was in Year Five, and I could listen in on his class if I wanted.

The school had opened in the midst of the rainy season. It was only a short walk from our house, but even so we would get soaking wet. So my mother saved up and purchased two umbrellas from the marketplace, one for Bwa Bwa and one for me. She couldn't afford to buy one for Slone, so he had to walk to school wrapped in a plastic sheet – the one that we had used as our makeshift shelter when fleeing from the village.

The outer walls of our school were only waist high. During the worst storms rain would drive through the sides, preventing us from continuing with the lessons. We'd have to huddle together on the far side from the storm, until the worst had blown over.

In the refugee school I enrolled in Year Eight, and chose to sit right at the front of the class. I volunteered to sit there, for I knew it would prevent me from messing around too much. Having jumped a year back in the village school, I knew I would have to work extra hard now if I was to do well. I wanted to make my parents proud of me.

My favourite subjects were English and maths, but we had precious few resources with which to learn. We had no textbooks of our own. The teacher would write out the section of the textbook we were to study on the blackboard, and we would copy it down. Often, the entire lesson would consist of little more than this. There would be little or no explanation and discussion.

I often had little real understanding of what I was 'learning'. We had a young Karen man teaching us English; another teaching us Burmese and Karen language; a maths teacher; a geography and science teacher, and another for history. But many were not trained teachers at all. Before fleeing to the refugee camp they had been office workers or housewives. They had volunteered to help and were trying their best. In the refugee camp it was all about making do.

Our geography and science lessons turned into English lessons by default, because the textbooks were all in English. The teacher came from Rangoon, and he spoke English with a Burmese accent, which we found hard to understand. One day he was trying to teach us a new word. It sounded like 'choochooba'. He kept repeating that word: 'choochooba'. None of us had heard an

English word like that before. Eventually, we realized what he was trying to say: it was *cucumber*. We did learn some English in those lessons, but not a lot of geography or science!

In spite of the deficiencies of the school, we weren't ungrateful – far from it. We knew the teachers were volunteers and that they were giving up much to try to give us an education. We were relieved to be learning, whatever the shortcomings of our teaching staff and their facilities, and I applied myself 100 per cent to my studies.

By now I knew that I was a refugee and what that entailed. I had always wanted to be a free person living freely in my own country and relying on myself. But here in the camp we were helpless, and totally reliant upon the charity of others. I hated being a refugee and the stigma that came with it.

With the start of school my spirits began to recover. At least this was something we were doing for ourselves. But I worried about the future. Would I continue to live as a refugee? I wondered. And if so, for how long? And would we ever get to go home and establish the village anew?

As for my big sister, her situation was far worse than my own. Bwa Bwa had just finished high school, and she was eager to continue her education. She had been hoping to train to be a doctor. Instead, all they could offer her in the refugee camp was a course on palm reading and fortune-telling. It was a 'further study' course set up by one of the refugee volunteers. It was either that, or nothing.

The lessons just seemed to drive her crazy. She would come home and grab my palm and gaze at it, before rolling her eyes and telling me I was going to have two husbands when I grew up, both so ugly! By the end we would be killing ourselves with laughter. Or she'd come home with what looked like a map, but was actually a star chart. Bwa Bwa would use it to predict what sort of person I was, and what bizarre things the future held in store for me.

It wasn't the fault of the camp organizers that Bwa Bwa

couldn't go on to further study. In a camp as large as Mae Ra Moh, where 10,000 people were seeking refuge, there were bound to be people qualified to teach her medicine. And the NGOs would have helped us by donating facilities. The problem was the Thai authorities. They had decreed that no further study was permissible in the refugee camps, and that no refugees were allowed to leave the camps to seek further education opportunities in Thailand.

Those of Bwa Bwa's age and older were trapped. For the whole of that first year in the camp Bwa Bwa seemed lost. Slone and I were continuing with our studies as best we could, but Bwa Bwa's life had reached a dead end. Not surprisingly, Bwa Bwa was often depressed and confused, as were many of the people her age. And I knew that once my own high school studies were done, I'd be in the same situation as her.

Occasionally, reports filtered into the camp concerning the resistance, but our best source of news was my mother's tiny long-wave radio. It was our most precious possession, and my mother had been determined to salvage it when we fled the village. She carried it with her wherever she went in a little bag slung over her shoulder. It was tuned to the BBC Burmese Service, or the Voice of America, or the Democratic Voice of Burma – a 'free Burma' radio station that broadcast out of Norway. Until Manerplaw fell it had been based there, and my mother had worked for it.

Each evening our camp neighbours would gather at our house to listen to the radio. My understanding of Burmese was still very basic, and all the stations broadcast in Burmese, so I had to keep asking my mother what was being said. This was our one link to the world outside the camp, and although I was only given snippets of information I could tell that things were going badly for the resistance. It seemed highly unlikely that we would get to go home soon.

The more that possibility receded, the more we had to try to make a life for ourselves in the camp. I was chosen to be on the school volleyball team, and we competed against the other sections in a camp league. Considering I was small and not very good, I was proud to have been selected! My position was a pusher-upper. When the opposing team served I had to receive the ball on my cupped hands and throw it up high, so one of our strikers could smash it over the net. We never made it into the final, but we had a great time trying!

At school I had learned about Saw Ba U Gyi, the founder and hero of the Karen resistance. In the years prior to the Second World War, Saw Ba U Gyi had travelled to Britain to study at Cambridge University. He had taken law and qualified as a barrister. He had practised in the United Kingdom for eight years, before returning to Burma and serving in the government. He had gone on to found the Karen National Union, becoming its first president.

It was Saw Ba U Gyi's story that had in part inspired me with the idea of studying overseas. As he had done, I wanted to go to the United Kingdom to take a degree and go on to help my people. But in the refugee camp I had never felt further from achieving that dream. I had no connection with anyone abroad, and I wasn't even free to leave the confines of Mae Ra Moh camp. To the gate and the fences was as far as I could go. I worried that my hope would die, and that I would never leave.

Five months after our arrival in the camp we finally had news of our father. Early one morning a friend of the family came to find us. His name was Mahn Nyeigh Maung, and he and my father had been friends since their youth. He told us that our father was fine, and that he had sent us a message. He wanted us to know that he missed us, and that we should look after ourselves and especially our mother.

I had so many questions I wanted to ask Mahn Nyeigh Maung. 'But where is he?' I blurted out. 'And what's he doing?'

Mahn Nyeigh Maung smiled. 'He's somewhere safe, so you don't need to worry about him at all.'

'When can he come to see us?' I asked.

'He'll come as soon as he can. Trust me, he misses you all terribly, and he'll come.'

I was so happy to hear this. Of course, it would have been better to see my father in person, but this was the next best thing. He was fine, and he was coming to see us – that was good enough for me. As for my mother, in spite of her tough life she supported my father and backed him in what he was doing. Without the resistance, there was no hope that any of us could ever go home and live in peace.

Before leaving Mahn Nyeigh Maung took my mother to one side to have a private word. From where we were sitting we were able to hear most of what was said. My father had been unwell, he explained. Recently, he had addressed a big meeting of the resistance. Halfway through his speech he had collapsed with exhaustion. He was recovering, but he had been pushing himself too hard, and he could only come to see us when he was able.

I could tell from my mother's reaction that she was worried for my father. As for Slone, Bwa Bwa and I, we were devastated. It was almost impossible to think of my father getting ill. He had always been the picture of good health, and I couldn't imagine what had happened to make him so unwell that he collapsed.

My mother asked Mahn Nyeigh Maung for any news of Say Say. But he knew nothing of him, and neither did my father. Presumably he was off fighting with the Karen resistance some-where towards the front line. Attacks on our villages were escalating, and the Karen soldiers were under more pressure than ever. But that was the lot of the resistance fighter, and that was the lot of Say Say.

My mother had been a soldier in her time, and she tried to be pragmatic about this lack of news. But still she was worried sick for Say Say. She had brought some of his things to the camp – a few clothes and his school photos. And she had salvaged my father's most precious possessions. But when she might get to give them to either Say Say or my father was anybody's guess.

Life went on in the camp as it had before. More refugees kept arriving. Mostly, they were Karen villagers who had been trapped in the jungle for months on end and had taken an age to get there. The new arrivals described how the Burmese Army were setting up outposts in the jungle, to block the routes leading to the refugee camp. They had been forced to make long detours to avoid them, playing a deadly game of cat and mouse with the enemy.

Several months after our arrival in the camp a young man called Saw Nyi Nyi – Mr Younger Brother – came to visit. He was a close friend of my parents. A number of the younger generation had left their parents behind when they came to join the resistance, and my mother and father were like surrogate parents. Many of them found my father someone they could look up to and learn from.

Saw Nyi Nyi worked for Burma Issues, an NGO that documented human rights abuses in Burma. One night he organized a special treat for our section of the camp. He borrowed a video player and a TV set so he could show a film in the school. Hundreds of people gathered to watch. The film was called *Beyond Rangoon*. It told the story of an American woman journalist who got caught up in pro-democracy demonstrations on the streets of Rangoon. The SLORC ordered the soldiers to open fire, and she fled with survivors to the border region.

But the trouble with the film was that it was in English. Even those of us who were studying English at secondary school found it hard to follow. For most of the audience it made no sense at all, for they didn't speak any English. It was made all the more difficult by having a small TV set and a giant crowd trying to watch. I was little in any case, so I had to push right to the front to see. But I would have preferred to see an action movie – like James Bond or Rambo – something to take our mind off all our troubles.

Saw Nyi Nyi realized that the film showing was a bit of a disaster. We talked about it afterwards, and we all agreed that a Rambo film would have been much better. For some reason the Karen loved Rambo. Rambo was very tough and good at defeating his enemy, which was something resistance fighters and their families could relate to.

And to us the Rambo films were inspirational – for the message seemed to be that no matter what the odds one brave warrior could win the day. When faced as we were with the massive might of the SLORC that was a message we Karen needed to hear. Their armed forces outnumbered ours some 30:1, and unlike them we had no sophisticated aircraft and big guns.

Being forced into the life of a refugee had taken away some of my innocence and my faith in the world. I was growing up quickly. Suffering, fear, hunger, separation and relentless attacks – all of these had become a part of my life over the last year. I had had to grow up fast.

I had to leave my bright, magical childhood behind me, as did my friends.

Chapter Sixteen

THE JOURNEY HOME

My mother had been getting more and more irritable and bad-tempered because life was so hard for her in the camp. Sometimes she upset me with her anger. If I lost track of one of the chickens, she would yell at me.

'Don't you see there is a chicken missing! Go and look for it – now!'

She had never been like this before, and I knew it was due to the stress. She was over fifty years old now, and in fleeing the village and ending up in the camp she had aged so much. Compared to other people's parents she looked old, and she had stopped worrying about her appearance. She never bothered to apply the Tha Na Kah cream to her face any more. She didn't have the time to make it and she knew that my father would love her, whatever she looked like.

In March 1996 I had my Year Eight exams. If I passed I would go on to Years Nine and Ten, my final years of high school. I sat exams in seven subjects: maths, science, English, Karen, history,

172

geography, Burmese. I had studied as never before that year, and in each of the monthly tests I had been doing well. I found I could answer most of the questions in the exams, and I was convinced that I had done okay.

With the exams finished school was declared over, and it was time for the summer holidays. The following day was a hot and sunny Saturday. Bwa Bwa and I had just finished lunch, and we were sitting on the bamboo steps of our house, gazing out over the camp. On the bottom step was a scattering of flip-flops, for we considered it rude to wear our shoes inside the house.

All of a sudden Bwa Bwa let out a cry. 'Oh my God! Pah-Pah! He's back! He's here!'

In a flash she had jumped to her feet and was dancing around on one leg as she shoved on her flip-flops, and then she raced off down the hill. I followed her as fast as I could, but Bwa Bwa was quicker. She reached him a little ahead of me and flung herself into his arms, almost knocking him over. An instant later I was upon him, throwing myself into the free arm that he held out to me.

'How are you? How are you?' he asked, smiling, as he tried to hug us both tight. 'Such big girls! When did you get so big?'

For a few seconds I just buried my head in the warm, familiar smell of my father. I couldn't believe that it was really him, that he had come home to us. I nuzzled into his checked shirt as he hugged the two of us tight.

'Come on, girls! I'm about to collapse!' my father laughed. 'So, tell me – how are you?'

'I'm fine, Pah, just fine,' I smiled. And then the words started to tumble out. 'I'm just so happy to see you because we all missed you so much and I've just done my Year Eight exams but your friend said you were ill—'

My father took Bwa Bwa and me by the hand and led us up to the house as I burbled away happily. My mother was at the entrance, smiling down at us. It was so good to see her looking happy.

We sat in the living room and drank Karen tea as our father told us about his journey to the camp. Bwa Bwa, Slone and I were so overjoyed to see him, and we each kept giving him the biggest of hugs. I was hanging on his every word.

But hardly had he been with us for ten minutes when he went to have a private word with my mother. We were left sitting in the living room, wondering what was happening. We didn't have long to wait to find out. Soon my mother announced that it was time to leave. We had to pack our things and leave the camp right now. We were going to live with my father in his village!

There was barely time to take on board what she had said. A car was waiting for us, my mother explained, and if we missed it then that was the end of going to my father's village. It was too far and difficult and dangerous to make it on foot. We began throwing things into bags in a fevered rush. As we packed, a crowd gathered at the house. Each person was greeting my father and asking for news of the resistance.

As they chatted to my father we hurried to finish our packing. A lot of what we had accumulated in that house we could leave, for Ter Pay Pay and grandma would not be coming with us. Grandma was too old and frail to be going anywhere now. As before, we each restricted ourselves to one bag. We didn't have much to pack anyway.

I chose to take my washing things and my precious photos, including some new ones that Saw Nyi Nyi had taken. Each of us had taken a few of the photos to keep for ourselves. If it was chiefly me in the photo, then I had claimed it. But if it was me and Bwa Bwa, I'd usually let her have it. A couple of skirts and pairs of shorts, a pair of jeans and a towel, plus my little mirror, and then I was done.

I asked my mother where exactly we were going.

'Where is Pah's village? And how long will it take to get there?'

'It's not too far,' she replied, but her mind seemed elsewhere. 'We'll just go and visit, then come back here. A few weeks are all we'll be away.'

It did seem strange that my mother thought we could come into and out of the camp at will. I knew how difficult it was for refugees to do so. But in reality, my mother knew we wouldn't be coming back here again. She had only said what she had said to make it easier on us, and to hurry us in our packing. Every minute counted in terms of catching that vehicle and getting out of there.

I could hear my mother going around our neighbours in a rush, telling them that we were leaving and saying her farewells. She was wishing people good luck, and it didn't sound like a temporary leaving to me. I was confused.

'Are we really leaving for good?' I asked her. 'Or is it just a visit. You said it was just a visit—'

It was important to me to know, for if we were leaving the camp for ever I wanted to say goodbye to my friends.

'It's just for a short while, you'll see,' my mother tried to reassure me. 'It's just to visit the village, that's all.'

Neither Bwa Bwa nor I were convinced. As Ter Pay Pay helped my mother parcel up the last of her things, I talked about it with my big sister.

'If we're leaving for good we'll lose all of our friends,' I said.

Bwa Bwa nodded. 'I know. And we don't know what this new place is like. Is there a school there even?'

'I don't know. Let's try to ask Moe. Pah's too busy with all these people.'

The more we tried to enquire what was happening, the more our mother insisted it was just a visit. My father was surrounded by a crowd of visitors, so we couldn't ask him. I noticed how exhausted and tired he looked. He clearly hadn't recovered fully from his illness. At least if we were going to live with him for good he could be cooked for and pampered and properly looked after.

Finally we were ready to go. We were leaving just about everything with Ter Pay Pay and grandma – the chickens and pigs we had reared, our pots and pans, our vegetable gardens. Ter Pay Pay and grandma acted as if they thought we were going away for a short visit and would be back soon. We said a rushed and confused farewell, lifted our packs and set off for the far end of the camp.

As we made our way through the camp people were calling out their goodbyes. Some of my friends were there, and they were crying. They knew in their hearts that we were going for good, especially as my mother had said her farewells to their parents. And by now I was more or less convinced myself that we would never be coming back, but I couldn't cry.

I was sad to be leaving my friends, but I was excited at the thought of getting out of there. Wherever I was going I would be with my father, and I would no longer be a refugee. I was sad, but happy all at the same time. I told myself that one day I would see them all again. One day, I'd come back to find Nightingale, Sweet Water Flower, Lily Flower and all my other childhood friends. Whatever happened to me now, I wouldn't forget them.

The car had driven as far as Section Five, where the river blocked the way. It was a smart, open pickup truck, and I had no idea how my father had managed to get the use of it. We climbed into the back, and sat wherever we could – either perched on the sides and tailgate, or squatting on our bags. Once we were settled, my father got into the front and we were off. A short drive through the camp and we reached the gate. It consisted of two wooden posts, with a long pole suspended between.

We pulled up, and I heard the driver speaking with the guards in Thai. The guards glanced at us, asked the driver a few questions, nodded and then the pole began to rise. My heart was in my mouth as it crept slowly upwards, and then accelerated to the vertical as the weight took hold. The guards stood back and waved us through. For the first time in over a year we were leaving Mae Ra Moh camp!

We rumbled through the gate and on to the dirt track. I glanced all around me. Thick jungle stretched away in every direction. The track snaked through the trees, a thin, red, dusty scar amidst the shadowy green of the forest. It was little wonder that so few people knew the camp existed. It was so well hidden. Most

Thais – even those local to the area – didn't know that there was a refugee camp there.

As the pickup bounced and bucked along the rough track we hung on for dear life. It was too noisy and dusty to talk much, and I reflected on what had happened. We had done our best to rebuild the village in Mae Ra Moh camp, and I was sad to be leaving our neighbours and friends behind. In spite of all the shortcomings, in the camp we had a certain, ill-defined status as refugees. But now that we had ventured out we were nothing but a group of illegal immigrants in Thailand.

We had begun a new adventure. But I had no idea where it might end, and it was a daunting and frightening one.

For what seemed like an age we weaved our way through the dense forest. Finally, we emerged on to a smooth black road surface – tarmac. Suddenly, I found myself surrounded by hooting cars and tall, shiny buildings, and metal lamp posts towering over us like animals pouncing to strike. It was the first time in my life that I had seen a 'proper' town. I had never imagined buildings could be so big, or so numerous!

Everywhere I looked there were crowds of people dressed in clean, smart clothes. We drove past a school, and all the children were in neat white-and-blue uniforms. What a contrast it was to our own rickety bamboo school, peopled by malnourished refugee children with no equipment or smart uniforms. I stared at everything in amazement. To me it was like watching a scene from a movie.

The jungle quickly gave way to shimmering green rice paddies, which stretched away to the flat horizon. I had never seen a landscape like it. It was dusk by the time we reached the town of Mae Sariang. Street lamps came on as if by magic, and windows were illuminated by a warm yellow glow.

It was dark by the time we reached our destination, a house on the far side of the town. We were introduced to the owner of the house, who was a friend of my father's, and given a delicious dinner of real rice – as opposed to broken rice! – and chicken curry. I couldn't remember the last time I'd eaten anything that tasted so wonderful.

That night we bedded down on the floor of my father's friend's house, and in no time at all I had fallen into a deep sleep. It had been a day of untold surprises and change, and it had quite exhausted me. The first thing I thought of when I awoke the following morning was my father. I had fallen asleep without even saying 'night-night' to him. I was so disappointed when my mother told me that he was gone. He had woken early and headed off on some mission connected to his resistance work. I felt let down.

After a hurried breakfast we set off again in the car – only now we were without my father. Slone and I sat in the front squeezed on to the seat next to the driver. We had asked our mother where we were going, and she had told us it was a place called Mae Sot. We knew Mae Sot was another town in Thailand, but we had no idea what it would be like.

The road followed a river that ran through a high-walled gorge. It twisted and turned alarmingly, and before long Slone and I were feeling sick. We didn't know what to say to the driver, but luckily he stopped for a rest. We jumped out and ran into the bush and promptly vomited up our breakfast. All the rice, vegetables and fish paste ended up in the bushes.

'Oh my Little Son and my Little Daughter – you're sick!' my mother exclaimed. 'I'm so sorry—'

Neither Slone nor I could respond; we were still heaving into the bushes, although there was nothing left to come out. We'd never been in the hot, airless interior of a vehicle before, and it had made us feel awful.

'Sit in the back,' my mother suggested. 'That way the air will be in your face, and you'll soon feel better.'

She was right. Though far less comfortable, the back of the pickup was the place for us. Bwa Bwa had taken our place in the front, and Slone and I lay down to try to sleep. We were exhausted from all the travelling and the vomiting, and we dozed on and off as the hot sun climbed into the sky. We stayed that second night in Mae Sot, a town which seemed even bigger than Mae Sariang. Again, we were put up in a house owned by a friend of my father's.

On the third day we headed out of Mae Sot, on a journey that lasted some five or six hours. We passed through several Thai police checkpoints. At each the driver spoke a few words in Thai, and we were let through. I had no idea what he was saying, but whatever it was it seemed to do the trick. But at each checkpoint I saw groups of scared-looking Karen sitting by the roadside. The Thai police had arrested them as illegal immigrants, and the same might happen to us at any time.

Eventually, we left the plains of Thailand and headed into the cover of the forested hills that run along the border with Burma. As we did so I began to feel a little more at home again. Finally we reached the border, at a place called Klaw Htaw. There we found a Karen vehicle waiting for us. It was such a relief when we discovered that the driver was someone we knew. It was Joseph – who we called 'Uncle Joe' – a friend of the family from our days in the village.

We threw our bags into the back of Uncle Joe's pickup, and set off into the deep jungle. Uncle Joe took us on a rough and little-used dirt track, and in that way we sneaked our way back into Burma. An hour later we reached Ther Waw Thaw – The New Village. This was where my father had his home. As I glanced around me I suddenly spotted a familiar figure. It was Nightingale!

I cried out to her, waving excitedly from the back of the pickup. 'Hi! Nightingale! Nightingale! It's me – Zoya!'

She ran over and we hugged each other tearfully. It turned out that she had left Mae Ra Moh camp a few months before. I'd been unaware of it, because she was living in a different section from me and going to a different school, and we'd practically lost touch with each other. We were both so happy to be reunited with a childhood friend in a Karen village once again. I asked her where she lived, and she pointed out her house to me. It was just nearby.

Ther Waw Thaw was surrounded by jungle-clad mountains. If I forgot for a moment where we were, it could quite easily have been any area around Per He Lu village or Manerplaw. As I looked around me I felt as if we had been living in an alien country, but now we were back in our homeland.

I suddenly felt as if I really had come home.

Chapter Seventeen

THE NEW VILLAGE

Uncle Joe took us directly to my father's house. The dirt road passed through the village marketplace and petered out at the edge of a beautiful lake. We unloaded our bags and followed a path along the water's edge to the far side. There my father had built a small bamboo-framed house on a vantage point overlooking the water.

On three sides the beautiful expanse of the lake was fringed with houses, whilst the rest was thick forest. The lake was fed by freshwater springs, and one bubbled out next to our house to form a tiny stream. It was there that my father had built the bathroom.

The lake was the hub of village life. It was where the village elephants would come to bathe, and where the village children would swim. From the house we could watch the elephants lumbering in, guided by their mahouts. They'd suck up gallons of water in their trunks and spray it all over themselves. After the elephants had been the lake looked like a muddy soup. Until it settled, it wasn't very inviting to go swimming.

At the front of our little bamboo house running down to the lakeside my father had planted a flower garden. There were tiny roses, and big purple lily flowers, and bright yellow bushes that were cut into neat borders. The flower garden was reflected in the placid waters of the lake, and it was magical. My father truly had an eye for what was beautiful and uplifting for the soul.

Uncle Joe and Nightingale helped us move in. The house consisted of a one-roomed bamboo structure, even smaller than the one we had been living in at Mae Ra Moe camp. But we didn't mind. It was where my father had lived for the past year and it was our home. The weather was noticeably colder here, for the village was situated in the highlands.

Planting a flower garden wasn't perhaps the most practical way to prepare for our arrival in the village. But it was always my mother who was the more pragmatic one of my parents. The day after our arrival she set about clearing land above the house, where she could plant her vegetables. Below that she wanted a duck house and a place to keep pigs. Both the ducks and the pigs would love it there, she declared. They could go down to the lake to dabble about in the muddy shallows.

My father returned from Thailand, but he went straight to Htee Ker Plur – Very Muddy Pond – village, the new headquarters of the Karen resistance. I knew my father did something very important within the KNU, but I didn't know what exactly. Whenever my friends at the refugee camp had asked me why he was away, I just told them he was in the resistance.

He could only come to visit us in The New Village when he was free from his work. Most of the children had fathers who were farmers, teachers or businessmen, but a few like us had parents in the resistance. On the one hand, it made me feel proud: I knew Karen people were being attacked and forced to flee their villages, and I knew we had to resist.

Yet at the same time I knew the resistance deprived me of my father – and so part of me resented it. Children with 'normal' fathers had them living at home all the time. I had experienced some of the horrors directly, so I tried my best to understand my father, and why his work took him away always. I missed my father and I wanted him to be with us.

Shortly after our arrival in The New Village my mother found out she had friends in a nearby village, and we went to visit. Once there we learned that a summer camp was taking place and we were invited to join in.

The theme of the camp was learning English, and our teacher was a white Canadian woman called Emma Ghost. At least her surname sounded like 'ghost' to Bwa Bwa and me. It was actually Gorst! Emma was young, tall, pretty and blonde. She had volunteered to come to Burma to teach the Karen English, and I thought it was very brave of her to have done so.

Bwa Bwa and I were both in her class. I was closer to Bwa Bwa at this time, as she was a girl and we were growing up and getting into girly things. Slone was too young to attend the summer camp, so he stayed with our mother. After the experience of fleeing from our village to the refugee camp, Slone had changed; the angry young man had become a shy and quiet boy.

I was very shy with Emma at first, especially as I couldn't speak much English, and she had no Karen. We had to communicate in sign language, or in broken English. At first she taught us very basic stuff: my name is Zoya; I am fifteen years old; I have one sister and two brothers. But from the very first lessons I realized she had a different way of teaching, one that I really enjoyed.

There was no copying down verbatim in Emma's lessons, and there were to be no tests or exams. It quickly became apparent that with Emma the idea was to enjoy ourselves as we learned. She was the first teacher to really try to make me think, as opposed to learning by rote. She wouldn't tell us answers; she would make us discover them for ourselves.

Emma would hand out sheets of paper photocopied from textbooks. On the handouts there were blank spaces, and we had to fill in the gap in the sentence or paragraph. Emma tried to make us understand what a noun, or verb, or tense was, not just to learn each of the words. At times she'd divide the class into groups, and we would have to go away and work on a subject and then come back and present it to the class.

For the first time I felt a new language really coming alive. It was so different from copying from a blackboard and learning by rote, with little explanation. We had to learn to reason for ourselves and develop basic critical thinking skills. I loved the way she involved us in the learning process, and I found her way of teaching captivating and challenging, and full of laughter.

Over the month of summer school Emma became our friend. She loved to play the guitar and sing. Her favourite were romantic numbers, sung by the likes of Rod Stewart. She'd strum her guitar, and once we'd learned the words we would sing along with her. It was a novel way to learn English, and often we made the most hilarious mistakes.

One day we were sitting out on the grass singing, when Emma put down her guitar and fetched some photos. First, she showed us ones of her family, and then her boyfriend. He looked like one of the famous white actors I'd seen in the movies – but not Rambo! We giggled shyly at the picture, especially as he had such a funny goatee beard. It made him look like my mother's goat, and no Karen man would ever wear a beard like that.

After our year in the refugee camp it felt so good to be free. I was happy just to do simple things: walking from one village to another; making friends; playing the guitar and singing at the tops of our voices; laughing freely long into the evening. None of this had been possible in the refugee camp. But the best thing of all was the freedom – freedom to go where we wanted when we wanted, and not being fenced in.

I felt safe where we were. There was no sense of a war going on, or of a horrible threat coming closer and closer. It was like a little slice of paradise compared to the refugee camp. We ended up telling Emma all about life as a refugee, and she in turn told us about growing up in Canada. It sounded like a place of such free-dom and opportunity.

At the end of the summer camp there was no formal gradu-ation or passing out. Instead we ate a meal together. There was a coconut milk, sugar and water sauce, into which we dunked little balls of boiled rice flour. We call this meal *ko ber baw*, and it is one of my favourites. Then we went to the village water festival and we threw water at Emma, and she did her best to soak us. It was such fun!

Emma travelled back with us to The New Village, and stayed the night in our little house. The following morning she went into my father's flower garden and smelled every single flower that was in bloom. Later, Uncle Joe brought the car for her, and Emma left for Thailand and her long journey home to Canada. We had an emotional parting, and promised to write to each other if we could.

A week after Emma left my father returned to The New Village. We went rushing down to greet him by the lakeside with cries of 'Pah-Pah, you're back! You're back!'

My father gave us all a hug, and a warm smile like sunshine lit up his features when he saw my mother.

'I'm so proud of you,' he told her. 'You're so strong. You brought them out of the refugee camp, through Thailand to here. And now you've taken them to the summer camp. And look at all the useful things you've been doing to this house! You are stronger than I ever imagined you could be!'

My mother smiled at him shyly. I knew she felt proud, but she was lost for words.

Later, my mother sat us down for a chat. She'd spoken to my father, she explained, and they'd decided we were going to stay in the village, and not return to Mae Ra Moe camp. Well, we did still miss our friends, and we had left a few things behind. But we were hardly going to worry about that. Anything, rather than having to return to the life of a refugee in that prison-like camp!

The one thing I really did regret was leaving my school exercise books behind. But my mother told me that there was an excellent missionary school in The New Village. It was far better than anything on offer at Mae Ra Moh camp. Just as soon as the holidays were over we would enrol for lessons.

My father had brought us a present. It was a small, battery-operated tape player, with a selection of English pop songs on cassette. It was to help us learn English. One of the bands was a Canadian Country/pop group called The Moffats. We decided that our favourite Moffats song was 'I Miss U Like Crazy', which pretty much summed up our feelings towards our father.

And there was a tape by the Danish band Michael Learns To Rock. They sang slow rock ballads that were easy to listen to and learn English from. They were hugely popular in Karen areas. Our favourite track was 'Twenty-Five Minutes'. It tells the story of a guy who leaves his girlfriend, but then realizes she is his true love after all. He tries to find her, but when he does he is twenty-five minutes too late as she's already gone ahead and married another man.

With Michael Learns To Rock we could follow the words printed on the cassette cover as we tried to sing along. Bwa Bwa had an English–Karen dictionary, in case there were any that we didn't understand. We were so happy with my father's gift. We loved music, and we loved learning English. And it was the first cassette player that we had ever owned as a family.

The only drawback was that the tape player needed batteries. You could buy them in the village marketplace, but we rarely had the money. We learned instead that once a battery appeared exhausted, you could bite it all over until it was covered in teeth marks, and that would give it a little extra life.

Sadly, my father was home for one day only. He would be leaving for work the following morning. We sat out in front of the house at a low bamboo tea table my father had built. The house had a view over his flower garden down to the lake. For a while we chatted and laughed – a happy family back together again at home.

I was wedged firmly on my father's lap, and I intended to stay right where I was. My sister and little brother felt they were too grown up to sit on his lap, but not me. My father put his arms around me and hugged me tight.

'Little Daughter, you're too big to sit on Daddy's lap,' my mother objected. 'You're a big girl now. Don't you feel embarrassed?'

'No,' I replied. 'I like it this way. I like it just the way it is!'

My father laughed. 'Oh, my Little Daughter! My Little Daughter!'

My father knew there was no embarrassing me where he was concerned.

After a while my father declared: 'Okay, who's going to help me in my flower garden?'

I jumped to my feet. 'I will! I will!'

Slone and Bwa Bwa followed suit. 'We'll help too!'

My mother rolled her eyes. 'You've just got home and all you want to do is tend to your flowers! Well then – you can go and eat your flowers too!'

We burst out laughing. When my mother was play-acting angry she could be very funny.

When I was a small child my father used to carry me everywhere. I decided I wanted him to do so again and take me into the garden.

'Pah, put me up on your shoulders like you did when I was little,' I said. 'Go on. Please!'

My father went as if to pick me up, but my mother stopped him. 'You have got to be joking! A big girl like her!'

My father shrugged. 'You're probably right . . . Little Daughter, I can't carry you. Your mum won't let me, and anyway you're too big. But come—'

My father held out his hand to me. As he did so I had an image in my mind of when I was little. I used to follow my father and jump on his back when he was least expecting it. I'd cling on for dear life and force him to carry me. But I had grown up, and there had been precious little time to enjoy my childhood with my father. Now I was fifteen years old and it was all but over.

Bwa Bwa, Slone and I set to clearing the vines and weeds that were choking my father's flowers. As we worked, he told us the name of each, and what made it particularly unique. My father seemed happy and relaxed as he tended his blooms. It was amazing how his garden always had this effect; it seemed to take all the stress and strain away from him.

Of course Bwa Bwa, Slone and I competed to see who could weed the garden the best, so as to please my father the most. During the weeks he had been away none of us had shown much interest in the garden. In fact, I was more like my mother. I could see a practical benefit in growing vegetables, or raising pigs, chickens and ducks, for they gave us food to put on the table.

But helping my father in his flower garden was the best way to spend time with him. Now and then he would break off from his weeding and give me an affectionate kiss. He would announce what a great job I had done arranging some stones to make a little wall or pulling up the vines to clear the path.

That day in the flower garden flew past. In no time the sun was dipping behind the mountains, and our little house was thrown into cold shadow. School was about to start, and I wondered if my father might take me to the village market to buy some exercise books. I knew with my father I could get anything I wanted, if I tried hard enough. It would be a real treat to go shopping with him.

'Pah, will you take us to the market?' I asked. 'We're about to start at the new school, and we left everything behind in the refugee camp.'

My father paused for a second, before answering: 'Little Daughter, I have to leave for work early in the morning. But I'll make sure your mother takes you instead.'

I felt so disappointed. It wasn't so much the shopping that mattered – it was that *he* would take us shopping. I felt as if he'd missed the point.

'All right, well, if you won't take us to the market why not take

Dewsbury Library

Tel: (01484) 414 868
Email: Dewsbury.lic@kirklees.gov.uk

Customer ID: *****2223

Items that you have borrowed

Title: Little daughter : a memoir of survival in
      Burma and the West
ID: 800209876
Due: 05 August 2023

Title: Saladin : the life, the legend and the
      Islamic empire
ID: 800574425
Due: 05 August 2023

Total items: 2
Checked out: 6
Overdue: 0
Hold requests: 2
15/07/2023 15:03

Thank you for using the bibliotheca SelfCheck
System.
We hope to see you soon.

www.kirklees.gov.uk/community/libraries

us with you?' I persisted. 'The least you can do is take us to Htee Ker Plur and show us where you work. If it's not to be the market, you can show us your place instead!'

My father laughed. He liked it when I challenged him like this. 'Oh, now, this really is my Little Daughter!'

He thought for a moment. 'All right, Little Daughter, I will try and take you to my place. But I'll have to arrange transport, which means asking someone else for a car. But I'll try.'

I was happier now. At least it was a promise of something to come.

My mother had prepared an evening feast to welcome home my father. There was chicken and vegetable soup, followed by yellow bean curry with rice, and the obligatory fish paste pounded with chilli. We didn't often eat this well, but there was never any inedible, broken rice or rancid, maggoty fish paste. What a change it was from the refugee camp.

Over dinner I tried to sit on my father's lap, but he pushed me off with a gentle laugh.

'Eat your dinner, Little Daughter . . . And give me some space to eat mine!'

My father took the ladle and spooned out some chicken soup for Slone, Bwa Bwa and me. But he stopped short of my mother's bowl. I could see her waiting for him to serve, but this was his way of teasing her.

'This is ridiculous!' she announced. 'You serve all the children but not your wife!'

We laughed and laughed at my mother as she acted all annoyed. Everyone seemed so happy that evening. We were back together as a family, and we cherished those few precious hours. My mother seemed especially happy. It was as if a radiant light was shining out of her.

After dinner my father drank green tea, and listened to the BBC Burmese Service on my mother's tiny radio. We gathered around but I couldn't understand much of what was said. My parents talked in Burmese for a while, and I knew they were discussing the news. Eventually my father snapped off the radio and announced that there was nothing of interest to report.

He turned instead to family matters, and in particular schooling. My situation was straightforward. I was going to enrol in Year Nine at the local mission school. And Slone would be enrolling in Year Six. The big issue was Bwa Bwa. The only option seemed to be to see what the school might have to offer in terms of further education. She hoped it wouldn't be more palm reading!

It was cold in The New Village, especially at night. Bwa Bwa and I had found our skin cracking and drying with the cold. We shared one bedroom, whilst Slone and my mother shared another. My mother was always complaining that Slone used her as a pillow!

Bwa Bwa and I had got into a habit of play-fighting before we went to sleep. We'd do Karen boxing, kicking and hitting each other until we were warm from the exertion, and then we'd dive under the blankets. It had become more and more competitive, until Bwa Bwa had to knock me down to win. She was bigger than me, and her best move was to catch hold of me and squeeze me tight in a bear hug until I begged her to stop.

By then we'd be breathless from the exertion and the laughter. My mother and Slone would hear everything, as the walls were bamboo-flat thin.

'What're you doing in there!?' my mother would shout. 'Stop it! We can't sleep!'

We'd just ignore her and carry on fighting. It was the only way to get warm. But that evening with my father home we didn't fight at all as we didn't want to do anything to spoil things. Bwa Bwa and I went to bed with our tummies stuffed full of all that good food, and hugged each other for warmth.

In the morning my father was gone. But at least there was something to cheer our spirits – a letter delivery care of Nightingale. A man had come to our village bringing mail from Mae Ra Moh camp. I had letters from just about all of my friends. They hoped that I was happy and that life in the village was good. But things in the refugee camp were as bad as ever, it seemed.

I became tearful as I read their letters, each of which was scribbled on the old pages of an exercise book. I wanted to write and let them know how sweet and good it was to be free, and to urge them to try to get out of the camp. I realized then how much I missed my friends. Apart from Nightingale, we hadn't made many friends in The New Village.

Bwa Bwa and I talked, and we decided that we had to go back to the camp just so we could see our friends. We went and told my mother what we had decided to do. She told us not to be so silly. It was impossible. We had no transport; it was a long way and dangerous; and we might get trapped in the refugee camp. In any case, school was about to start here in the village.

But Bwa Bwa was adamant that she wanted to visit the camp. She kept going on at my mother about it. I supported Bwa Bwa, in part because we were so close and I looked up to my big sister. Yet my mother had no time for it. She pointed out that we were enjoying the freedom of being in our homeland, living free – yet we wanted to go back to the prison-like camp! It was madness.

The more we insisted the more she told us to stop being so stupid. Here we were free. Here we were living on our own land in our own home. Here we weren't forced to beg and take charity from others, which was the life of a refugee. Slone backed my mother. He told her that wherever she was, then that was where he wanted to be. Of course, my mother was correct and Slone was right to support her. It was the letters from our friends that had so unsettled us.

Once our mother had convinced us I wrote a letter to each of my friends. I told them how much I had loved getting word from them. I told them that I wanted to see them, but that it was impossible. I told them how we couldn't risk travelling through Thailand with dozens of checkpoints. And I told them that I knew I would see them again one day.

For a couple of days Bwa Bwa and I moped about, but we soon got over it. And then we got a message from my father. He was inviting us to go and visit him in his workplace, and Uncle Joe had volunteered to drive us. We were so excited, and it was certainly something to do to take our minds off our missing friends.

It was a two-hour drive to Htee Ker Plur. When we got there we found that my father was billeted in a tiny bamboo hut. I couldn't imagine him being anywhere without a flower garden. But here there was only a small vegetable patch, and that was it. It was pretty grim.

My father took us to visit friends, and to see the local KNLA base. KNLA stands for the Karen National Liberation Army, and it is the armed wing of the Karen resistance. The soldiers seemed relaxed and easy-going, and there was little sign of the ongoing war. But it was the rainy season, and there wasn't much fighting during the rains. Roads and rivers were impassable, and the SLORC found it impossible to resupply their troops.

Being in that base made me think of Say Say. I asked my father if there was any news of him. As far as he knew Say Say was alive and well, and his unit had moved into an area to the far north of us. I missed Say Say enormously, and I worried about him. The area he was operating in was deep inside Burma, and I feared that he might be captured or killed.

Htee Ker Plur was where the KNU was rebuilding its head-quarters. It was the new location of the democratic resistance after the fall of Manerplaw. It was a place for soldiers, democratic opposition leaders and administration people. There were few children and no schools. It was also plagued by mosquitoes, which screamed around our heads all night long. The only way to deal with them was to build a fire, throw green leaves on to it, and sleep the night in a smoky fog.

I didn't like this place very much. In fact, I felt sorry for my father having to stay here. In this place his priorities had changed. For the first time in his life he had prioritized food ahead of flowers. His hut was on a hilltop, and he had to carry water from a stream below – but he was doing so to water his vegetables, not flowers.

In each of his flower gardens he'd invested much emotional

energy, but here it was physical energy only that he'd put into his vegetables. One he did out of necessity; the other out of love. The enemy had destroyed his flower gardens at Manerplaw, and in the village, and that must have pained my father.

For if someone destroys your love it really hurts.

Chapter Eighteen

THE MISSION SONG

A week after our return to the village, school started. Just as my father had promised, my mother took us to the village market to buy us some school things. Bwa Bwa and I got a brand-new white blouse and blue skirt each, and Slone got the boy's version of the uniform. It was the first time we had been bought any new clothes since fleeing our village.

Bwa Bwa and I also got a tube of lipstick each. It had a bottom you twisted up, and it turned our lips bright red. It was far better than smearing our lips with old vitamin pills! I decided my lipstick was very precious and that I would keep it for special occasions.

Near the market was a Buddhist monastery perched atop a hill. It was built of a rich, dark red wood, and it exuded warmth and a deep peacefulness. Each morning the monks would walk around the village with their clay begging bowls. A novice monk would walk ahead, ringing a flat little bell suspended on a string. Whenever we heard that sound we knew the monks were coming seeking alms.

I'd been up to that monastery a few times for the Lah Pweh – Full Moon – ceremony. Each month the village would gather at the monastery under the full moon. There would be chanting and prayers, and lovely food. There was sweet rice porridge, spicy chicken curry and sticky rice with fresh coconut.

I loved Lah Pweh, for the whole village would be bathed in silvery moonlight. We could walk wherever we wanted without even needing a torch. Sometimes, the dogs would be barking at the moon. We would tease each other that they had been spooked by ghosts, and we'd end up scaring ourselves!

Recently, my parents had started to encourage Slone to become a novice monk, and they wanted Bwa Bwa and I to become nuns. It wasn't uncommon for Karen children to serve a short period as an initiate. Usually it would be for a few months during the summer holiday, after which they would return to their studies. Although they weren't Buddhist themselves, my parents respected the Buddhist way of self-reflection and humility, and they wanted to instil such values in us.

The village was mixed Buddhist, Christian and animist, although Buddhism was the predominant religion. The school was a Christian mission school. It was one of the best in the area, and no one seemed to mind very much about its religious affiliation – my parents included. As for becoming nuns, Bwa Bwa and I knew that they had to shave their heads. We didn't want that, and so we refused point blank!

The day I started at the new school I had to explain to the headmaster – *thera* Tha Wah – teacher White Heart – why I didn't have my Year Eight exam results. I had left the refugee camp before they were released. He checked with my mother, and she told him that I was very dedicated to my studies and had always done well. I got accepted into Year Nine on her word. As for Bwa Bwa, she was accepted on to a course of further education in English and Bible study.

That first day at school I realized that I knew some of the students. One was a girl called Mular Moo – Hope Life – and I recognized her from Per He Lu village. She was older than me, and we hadn't been in the same class, but we knew each other from around the village. And there was a boy from the village called Sah Moo Daw – Star In The Sky. The rest of the class were totally new to me.

We each had to introduce ourselves to the other pupils, telling them where we were from and who our family was. I felt embarrassed to say that I came from a refugee camp, so I thought about telling them I'd come from Per He Lu village only. But I had to say where I'd done my Year Eight, which meant that I had to talk about the camp. I felt like a second-class citizen admitting that I had been a refugee.

No one seemed to mind though, and I quickly made friends. One of the most beautiful girls in the whole school was called Eh Phyo Paw – Collective Love Flower. Eh Phyo Paw is considered a very lovely name in Karen, for it means you are loved by everyone and as beautiful as a flower. Collective Love Flower was in my class and we quickly became the best of friends.

It was a big school compared to the one I had attended in the refugee camp, with some thirty teachers. There was a teacher from England, called *thera* Tom – teacher Tom – and he was unbelievably tall. We nicknamed him Grandfather Long Legs, after Major Seagrim, but not to his face, of course. Plus there was James, another tall teacher from England. And there was an Australian called Jacob who turned out to be my English teacher.

Fairly quickly Jacob proved himself to be something of a disciplinarian. One day some pupils had been messing around in class. *Thera* Jacob decided to punish us all by making us walk back to our dormitory, and then race back to the school. The problem was his face had gone bright red with anger, and as we were running someone made a joke that it was the same colour as the Ta Aut Ghaw Kee – 'the monkey with the red bottom'. We all laughed so much we could barely run any more, and he got even crosser, and more red-faced, and that made us laugh even more.

Thera Jacob introduced a new way of marking us called 'continuous assessment'. Under this system exams were replaced by the marks we got in our coursework. It seemed like a good idea to me, and I redoubled my efforts in English. Our first continuous assessment task involved filling in the blanks in English sentences, and marking certain phrases as 'true' or 'false'. I handed in my homework certain that I had done well.

I couldn't believe it when our marks were handed out, and I had been given zero out of 100. I sat at my desk feeling stunned. Zero? How could I possibly have got zero? Something had to be wrong. Other students had got over ninety, and they were beaming happily. As I sat there staring at that 'zero', I felt tears trickling down my face.

My tutor was a kind and gentle Karen woman called *theramu* Paw Lah Soe.

'Zoya, what's wrong?' she asked me.

'Well, I did my homework very well and I expected to get a high mark,' I blurted out. 'But instead *thera* Jacob gave me a zero and I'm so unhappy.'

My emotions were all mixed up. Half of me was upset, the other half so angry. I told her I couldn't have got zero. There had to be a mistake. She said she would go and check, and was back a few minutes later. *Thera* Jacob had told her that he hadn't seen any homework from me. That wasn't possible, I objected. I had put my name on my work and he had given it zero. How could he have given it a zero if I hadn't done any!

My tutor didn't know what to say. 'Well, I'm going to see *thera* Jacob myself,' I announced.

It was unheard of for a pupil to challenge a teacher, especially a foreigner. But I was so annoyed that I marched over to his office. The door was half open and I could see him sitting at his desk. He looked up and didn't appear that surprised to see me. I had tearful eyes and a flushed face. He on the other hand looked completely unperturbed.

'*Thera* Jacob, you told my tutor I didn't do my homework,' I announced. 'But you know I did. You marked it. You gave it a zero.'

He shook his head. 'I didn't see any homework by you.'

'But how could you mark it if I didn't do any?' I persisted.

'All I said was – *I didn't see any homework by you.*'

'But why not? I submitted it with my name clearly written on it. How could you not see it?'

'I'm just saying I didn't see any work done by *you*.'

I couldn't for the life of me grasp what he was driving at. 'Look, I'm not happy. You gave me a zero. How can you give someone a zero if you didn't see their homework?'

Thera Jacob sighed. 'Okay, I'll look into it. I'll let you know what I decide.'

That night I couldn't sleep properly, I was so angry. The next day *thera* Jacob explained that he had found my homework after all. He handed it to me with a mark of 96 per cent. I didn't say anything. I was just so happy that I had gone from zero to the highest mark in the class.

But I had learned something, too. I had learned that in spite of the odds, in spite of tradition and in spite of power, if I believed something was wrong or right and pushed for the truth I would eventually get there. And whenever someone tried to really put you down you just had to redouble your efforts and you would win through in the end.

I made another school friend called Moo Moo – Life Life. She was in the year above and was always coming top of her class. We struck up a friendship walking home from school one day as her house was on the lakeside. I loved going around to her place. Her brother had a guitar, and in the evenings we'd gather at Moo Moo's home, and sing along at the tops of our voices as the boys strummed.

Moo Moo's brother had a favourite Karen song called 'Ta Eh Hsoe' – 'First Love'. It was sung by a famous Karen pop star called Naw Ler Htoo – Miss Golden Stone. It went like this:

Oh my very first love,
Whom I love the most,
I would like to be with you.
You are my only hope,
Higher than the sky,
Deeper than the ocean.
I love you more than anyone.

Oh my very first love,
Whom I love the most,
Please come and rest in my heart,
You are my only hope,
And you are my strength.
I open my love door for you,
Come, come into my heart,
I'll keep all my love for you.

When I sang that song, I wasn't thinking of anyone in particular –
I was just happy to enjoy the singing and the company of friends.
Singing and laughing together – that's how we spent our evenings
at Moo Moo's house. We sang long into the night, gazing out over
the starlit lake. No one told us to shut up. People enjoyed hearing
our happy songs. After we'd sung our hearts out, we'd cook some
food and eat, and then we'd wander home in the velvety darkness.

More often than not Collective Love Flower was with us. She
had a special reason to come, for she was going out with Moo
Moo's brother. He was called Eh Ker Ter – Loved The Most. It was
no wonder Collective Love Flower had a boyfriend. All the boys
were after her, but she only had eyes for Loved The Most.

When Loved The Most sang 'First Love' Collective Love Flower
gazed into his eyes. I had no one's eyes to gaze into, but I didn't
feel left out. There was one guy who liked me, and he was in the
same class as my sister. One day he wrote me a letter asking if I
felt the same for him. The letter had been delivered by one of his
friends as he'd been too shy to bring it himself.

I wrote back saying that I wouldn't mind being his friend, but at the moment I didn't want a boyfriend. In my letter I mentioned the fact that his father had a garden full of durian. Durian is a tree with a foul-smelling but delicious fruit, which I adored. I told him that I would like to visit him to get some of his father's durian – which more or less implied I wanted the durian, but not to go out with him. I mentioned this to Moo Moo and Collective Love Flower, and we laughed and laughed and laughed.

After that love letter I received ones from other boys, but I rejected them all. For some reason I just wasn't interested in having a boyfriend. Collective Love Flower was great. She supported me wholeheartedly in this. She said if I didn't like anyone, then I should stay single. It was my choice.

In our age group everyone wanted to marry freely, for love. However, in the past parents had chosen who their children should marry. A girl still wasn't supposed to say that she liked a boy, for then she would be looked upon as being 'easy'. A boy could tell a girl he liked her, via a letter, but if a girl tried to do the same that would be seen as forward and wrong. So all a girl could ever do was wait for a man to somehow miraculously realize that she liked him.

Back in Per He Lu village a girl in Bwa Bwa's class had got into trouble for being 'forward'. She was around sixteen years old, and one day she had failed to turn up at school. After a week of this the teacher had decided to investigate. It turned out that the girl was pregnant. She was instantly expelled from school. She had to marry the boy who had made her pregnant, but even then the burden of scandal fell on her far more than on him. She didn't go out of her house until the baby was born, and it would take years to live down the scandal.

I had a new subject at my new school, which was Bible study. *Thera* Doh Moe – teacher Big Life – was our Bible teacher. He had a fuzz of dark curly hair, which was unusual for a Karen, who mostly have dead-straight hair like my own. We had to memorize verses from the Bible and the stories of the different characters. We had Bible study tests, although these didn't contribute to our overall mark for the year. But if we did well we would get a prize, which was an incentive for me to study hard. I always wanted to win the prizes!

Some of the Bible verses stuck in my mind. There was the story of Queen Esther. She was married to a king who kept many slaves. Queen Esther's cousin was arrested and accused of being a rebel. He was about to be executed when she learned of his fate. She organized a great feast for the king, during which she broached the subject of her cousin and the slaves. Wise rulers always showed lenience, she counselled. The king was moved by what she said, and he freed her cousin and the slaves.

I liked this story. I saw it as a morality tale of one woman relying on the courage of her convictions to help her people. I had seen and experienced how we Karen were suffering, and I hoped, like Queen Esther, I would have the courage to help them if the opportunity arose.

There was the story of Joseph, who went from being a house-slave in Egypt to being the adviser to the king, and who saved the Egyptian nation from famine. The lesson I took from that story was that if you behaved in a good, honest way your life would be happier and more fulfilled. Honesty and forgiveness were paramount in the story, which was a good lesson to learn in life.

Halfway through that first year at the new school I became very ill. It might have been because of bad food or water, but I had something wrong with my insides. My stomach was in agony. I couldn't eat anything. I couldn't go to the toilet properly. I could barely walk. I started to get weaker and weaker. Next to the school was a clinic set up by Dr Cynthia Maung, a Karen doctor who had fled the August 1988 military crackdown in Rangoon.

Dr Cynthia had set up a series of clinics in the border region. She also ran mobile 'backpack' clinics – similar to that which the French couple had brought to our village when I was little. She was a humble, gentle person, but she also projected a real presence. As I grew weaker and weaker my mother's concern mushroomed. Finally, she decided I had to go to Dr Cynthia's clinic.

I was immediately put on a drip, which contained a clear liquid. It had some writing on it in English, but I was too ill to pay much attention to it. Day after day I was kept on that drip. After school Collective Love Flower, Moo Moo and Nightingale would come to visit me, to see if I was okay. And Bwa Bwa and Slone looked after me as best they could. As I couldn't eat solid foods I was given rice and chicken soup, but even that often caused me to vomit.

The medics had explained to my mother what was wrong. I had gastroenteritis, which causes abdominal pain, cramps, fever, diarrhoea and the inability to eat. It was only the drip that was keeping me alive. I had no idea just how sick I was until I was all but recovered. It was then that my mother explained things to me. Gastroenteritis is a killer. It was Dr Cynthia's clinic – one that is funded by charities and foundations from all over the world – that had saved me from almost certain death.

I didn't know it then, but this would not be the last time that one of Dr Cynthia's clinics would save my young life.

Chapter Nineteen

RUNNING FROM BULLETS

Every month my father would come home for a weekend's leave. I looked forward to his visits very much. One evening he returned home to tell us that he was holding a big press conference in the village the following day. Which of us would like to come? We didn't know what a 'press conference' was exactly, but any chance to do something with our father was something to be grabbed at. We all wanted to go.

Early the following morning we set out together for the village green. Every few moments someone would stop and greet our father.

'Padoh, good morning,' they'd say. Padoh means 'respected leader' in Karen.

My father would return the greeting, and ask them how they were, and how their children and families were. Mostly, he'd never met these people before. They knew him from hearing him on the BBC World Service, or Voice of America, or reading his articles. I felt proud to walk beside him and to be his Little Daughter, for my father seemed to be someone very special.

When we arrived at the village green there were hundreds of people gathered. My father joined some speakers on the stage, and we sat on the ground in the audience. General Saw Bo Mya, the leader of the KNU, said a few words. He explained that the Burmese Army were continuing to wage war against the resistance, Karen villages and civilians. The KNU were trying to solve the problem by political means, whilst doing their best to defend the people.

One of the leaders of the democracy movement, who was also a good friend of my father's, spoke next. But he gave his address in Burmese, which I couldn't understand. I could hear people clapping, so I presumed it was good stuff. There were several video journalists there, mostly from the Thai and Burmese media.

My father spoke last. He was a great orator, and he really knew how to engage his audience. He made two main points, and each really touched my heart. The first was that we had to defend our people by force of arms, for the SLORC were waging a brutal war against us. In this we had no choice. The second was that we had to work with everyone in the country who believed in democracy, no matter what their ethnic background. We had to be united against a common enemy – the military dictatorship.

People were clapping and cheering what my father said. This was the first time that I had ever seen him speaking in public, and I was suddenly seeing a new and amazing side of my father. He went on to talk about a recent peace delegation that he had led. Their aim was to speak directly with the SLORC Generals, to try to reason with them and negotiate peace. Four times they had travelled for talks, and each time the Generals had demanded what amounted to an unconditional surrender.

My father had reasoned that the SLORC must first remove their troops from Karen areas, and stop burning our villages, raping our women and killing our children. That was the minimum required from our side to reach a ceasefire. But the Generals demanded that the resistance first give up their arms. This was a de facto surrender, and it would leave us at their mercy. The

SLORC had no interest in dialogue. They refused to discuss a political solution, or any form of compromise.

'How can we have genuine dialogue with the Generals when they refuse to stop shooting our farmers and raping and killing innocents?' my father said. 'How can we lay down our arms, to allow them to continue to burn our villages? How can there be genuine negotiations, when they even refuse to stop doing these things?'

After the conference my father was mobbed by the media, for interviews.

I turned to my sister. 'Wow, wasn't it amazing? I really liked what Pah said. Did you hear him? He's so strong when he speaks like that! I never realized.'

Bwa Bwa and I had always known that he did important work in the resistance, but we had never really understood what exactly. Now we knew. He had gone to Rangoon to risk meeting the Generals face to face, and he had refused to be bullied or to back down. This was the first time we had heard things of this kind. My father never talked about such stuff at home. Perhaps that was because he didn't want to tell us what to think; he wanted to leave us free to make up our own minds.

That evening I really wanted to tell my father how proud I was of him. I wanted to tell him that he was my hero. But there were too many visitors for me to do so. I never got the chance to sit with him for a few minutes alone to speak with him, and the next day he was gone, returning to his work.

A few days later I was coming home from school when I spotted a familiar figure wandering along the path towards me. My heart missed a beat! I couldn't believe it! It was Say Say!

I rushed up and jumped on him, almost knocking him over. I was so happy. Bwa Bwa was with us and she was crying with happiness at Say Say's return. When we reached home my mother started fussing over him, and she declared that she would cook a special feast of welcome. But Say Say said he couldn't wait. There was some cold, leftover rice and he just took it and started to wolf it down.

Poor Say Say was so hungry. He was practically starving. He ate every last grain of that leftover rice, and then he licked the bowl clean. He placed it on the bamboo floor and glanced up at us.

'You should never waste any food. *Never*,' he said. 'I've learned never to throw even a grain of rice away.'

Over the years that he'd been away Say Say had changed. The war had aged him way beyond his years. He had seen untold horrors out there on the front line. Say Say had been stationed in Papun, an area far to the north of us. At first he had been fighting the enemy, but increasingly he had been tasked with helping the victims. Thousands of civilians had fled and Say Say had been given the job of guiding them through the jungle so that they might escape.

So many of those people had been starving, he told us. Men, women and children had nothing to eat. He'd been forced to witness people die, even as he tried to save them. Mostly, it was the old and young who perished, for they were always the most vulnerable. My mother told him that she was sorry for what he had been through, but Say Say insisted he was glad to have seen such things, for only that way could he know the truth of what was happening.

That evening we sat down to a proper meal. Say Say told us that he hadn't eaten like this for a very, very long time. In Papun he had been forever on the move. If he and those he was protecting stayed in one place for any time, the SLORC soldiers would find them and attack. He told us about such terrible things: Karen women who had been gang-raped and killed in the most disgusting ways imaginable; farmers shot in the stomach for no reason, and left to die in their fields; villagers working as porter-slaves and left to a slow and lingering death.

Whole villages had been set on fire and entire families burned alive in their houses. Children died of malaria, cholera or simple hunger – that's if the enemy soldiers didn't get to kill them first. It was like a vision from hell.

I asked Say Say how far Papun was from us. I was so relieved when he told us that it was a long way away. We were safe for now, he said. The village wasn't in any immediate danger.

'How did you find us?' my mother asked him. 'How did you know where we were?'

'It was Pah,' Say Say answered. 'He told me. He sent a message to the commander of my unit. It took me a whole month to find my way here.'

Say Say stayed with us for a week. He spent his time helping my mother in the garden and eating the hearty meals she prepared. He was so thin he was like a skeleton. His stomach had shrunk to nothing, for he'd never had enough food to put in it. In the past he had always been healthy and strong. I couldn't believe what those years on the front line of the war had done to him.

Aunty Black had also come to stay with us. She was not an aunty by blood, but was almost as close to my mother as a sister. We had known her in Manerplaw. She had no family, and so when we all ended up in Mae Ra Moe refugee camp we had taken her in. Now she had come from the camp to be with us again, and we were all so pleased to see her.

I was so happy to have Say Say back again, but he had changed so much. He seemed quiet and subdued, and I wondered how he was dealing with the terrible horrors that he had witnessed. I feared he was traumatized by what he had been through, and who wouldn't be? My father came home at the end of that week, and told us that Say Say would be returning with him to his place of work. For now at least he wouldn't be going back to the front line.

The visits from my father and Say Say lifted all of our spirits. My mother especially seemed a lot happier after the lows of Mae Ra Moe camp. We were happy with our life in The New Village, and things had almost gone back to how they were before. But hearing Say Say's stories was a horrible reminder of the darkness that was out there. In The New Village all seemed peaceful and well. I hoped it would remain like this, and that I could concentrate on my studies and having fun with my friends.

My best subjects at school were English and maths. One of our maths teachers was a Karen woman called *theramu* Baby – teacher Baby. For our mid-term exams she promised a special reward if any student scored 100 per cent: a cup of coffee. I had only ever had coffee on very special occasions, or when I was sick. We made coffee with instant Nescafé and hot condensed milk. It was sweet and creamy and so delicious.

I was determined to win that cup of coffee on offer from *theramu* Baby. I prepared for those exams as carefully as I could, and sure enough I did score full marks. But somehow, *theramu* Baby forgot to buy me my promised cup-of-coffee reward. I was pretty annoyed, but nowhere near as upset as I had been at getting *thera* Jacob's zero.

But before I could raise the issue of my missing coffee with my maths teacher, the enemy attacked our village.

We started our Year Nine exams on 9 February 1997. We had arrived in the village the previous March, so we had been there almost a year. On 11 February we didn't have any exams, because it was Karen National Day. There would be speeches in the village square, and everyone would shout the popular rallying cries of the Karen resistance.

After the ceremony one of my school friends insisted on coming home with me as she wanted some help with her maths revision. I was annoyed, because the maths exam was the following day and I needed to study myself. On the hill behind our house I had made a clearing overlooking the lake. It was there that I would sit and study in peace. We spent an hour or so going over my friend's maths problems, when suddenly I heard a voice crying out from below.

'Little Daughter! Little Daughter! Come quick! Come quick!'

It was my mother. We rushed down the hill, only to find her frantically stuffing possessions into bags. She glanced around at me, a wild look in her eyes.

'We're under attack!' she cried. 'Quickly! Pack your bag! We have to run!'

Immediately she said that I heard a horrible screaming whine from the far side of the village, and a mortar shell crashed into the forest. My friend seemed frozen in panic.

'Quick! Run! Run!' my mother cried at her. 'Find your family! *Run!*'

Without another word my friend rushed off down the path along the lake. I glanced around myself in shock and confusion. How could the enemy be here? Now? In the midst of my Year Nine exams? What should I do? What should I pack?

'Don't just stand there!' my mother yelled. 'Where's your bag? The one we fled with before? Get packing! Get packing!'

My mother's harsh words shocked me into action. With the crash of the mortar shells growing louder and louder, I started throwing things into my black rucksack. There was the crackle of gunfire now, a noise that I had wished never to hear again. It was coming closer and closer, and I could hear voices from the far side of the lake crying out in terror.

I glanced up. A crowd of people was surging through the village. Men, women and children were running for their lives in the direction of the Thai border. Children were crying and wailing as they stumbled and fell. Parents screamed at them and dragged them to their feet, the little ones sobbing in bewilderment. How could this be happening? I wondered. How could it be happening again?

The noise of the fighting drew closer still. I heaved up my bag and slung it on to my shoulders. Oh my God, I told myself, if they catch me my life will be over. Say Say had told us what had happened to the women at Papun who were captured. The SLORC soldiers would rape us all. I was rooted to the spot with terror.

'Are you ready?' my mother yelled. '*Are you ready? Let's go!*'

She grabbed a cooking pot and stuffed some cold rice into each of our mouths to give us some energy. The she shoved me out of the door.

'Everyone – GO!' my mother yelled as if she was commanding a military unit. 'GO! No stopping until we reach the border!'

Slone, Bwa Bwa, Aunty Black, my mother and I ran from the house and into chaos. There were almost a thousand people in the village and they were all running to find their families or grab their possessions. People were running in every direction shouting and screaming. Animals were bellowing or squealing in panic. Children were screaming and crying, the crackle of gunfire rose above the uproar, and then there would come the crack-BOOM of the mortar bombs landing, as if every glass window in the world had shattered at once. Sometimes there was just one, sometimes three – one after the other. With everyone running the dry earth turned into a suffocating dust that I could barely see through. I was terrified.

Bwa Bwa and Slone were in front of me, Aunty Black behind me, and my mother last, pushing us ahead. Another mortar bomb landed, so close and so loud I fell to the ground. 'UP, MOVE!' ordered my mother and I climbed to my feet and ran on.

Every now and then I lost sight of Bwa Bwa, and I was scared I would never see her again. The dust got so bad it was almost like night. I couldn't breathe, I couldn't see, my legs were aching with running, my lungs burning, my whole body shaking with fear. I just knew I had to keep going or I'd be killed. If we slowed down my mother would yell 'MOVE!' and we'd run faster again.

Another mortar bomb landed, scaring me so much I fell to the ground again. It was so loud my ears popped and then I could not hear properly. "MOVE!" yelled my mother and again I was up and running. I wanted to cry but knew I couldn't. I had to keep running.

All around us were people running, but there were so many families with several small children. The parents could not carry them all. Tiny children were stumbling through the dust, screaming with fear, pushed on by their parents who had babies or younger children in their arms. I wanted to help but I couldn't. I was too weak to carry them, and my mother wouldn't have let me. She had her own children to protect and she was determined to save us.

My bag was so heavy I took it off my back and rested it on my head as I ran. My whole body ached. I desperately wanted to rest but knew I couldn't. I knew if the Burmese Army caught me I would be raped. I knew I would be tortured, I could imagine the soldiers beating me. I kept running. Boom, another mortar exploded and I was on the ground once more. I scrabbled around in the dust trying to find my bag, 'MOVE!' yelled my mother again and I ran on.

We were lucky our family was together. We passed men desperately shouting the names of their wives and children. Old people separated from their families, crying out for help. And still there was the dust, the explosions, the gunfire, animals and people screaming. I couldn't believe it was happening. Just one hour before, everything had been peaceful.

Finally we reached the edge of the jungle and the road that would lead us to safety in Thailand. It could only have taken thirty minutes to get there, but it had seemed like for ever. We stopped running and stumbled on to the dirt road. Everyone was jammed together into the small space. The air was still full of dust.

There were more explosions and gunfire in the village now. KNLA soldiers had rushed to the village to stop the Burmese Army and give us time to escape. But we knew the KNLA were outnumbered, and we were still scared the Burmese Army would come after us.

It started to get dark as we walked down the road. It was uneven and had ruts from cars and carts on it. I kept stumbling and falling, hurting my knees. One time I tripped and twisted my ankle, making every step painful. But every time my mother was there, urging us on, and on we went.

Hundreds of us walked in the darkness hoping to reach safety. No one spoke. We were too shocked, too exhausted, and too scared to make a sound in case it brought the Burmese Army to us. We could not use torches either for fear of alerting our attackers. The only noise was of people's feet on the road and the crying of children and babies. The crying never stopped. 'Keep walking, keep walking,' I thought to myself. The world seemed to shrink around me as I focused only on walking. My legs ached so much it was as if they were burning. 'Keep walking, keep walking.'

The night seemed to go on for ever. At last the first light appeared in the sky. And in that light on the road ahead we saw a soldier. Bwa Bwa and I froze in fear, but my mother told us to keep going. 'It's okay, they are Thai,' she said. The soldier waved us forward with a torch, and once again I was a refugee in Thailand.

There was a small camp just over the border where there were Karen refugees, and, frightened and exhausted, we entered it.

Bwa Bwa, Slone, Aunty Black and I collapsed to the ground, but straight away my mother started cooking rice for us. She had saved our lives, and as tired as she was her first priority was to take care of us.

As far as the eye could see there were the humped, shadowy forms of people slumped among the trees. Old people, children, breast-feeding mothers – all around us were the dirty, frightened inhabitants of The New Village. Some had crudely bandaged injuries. Piles of salvaged possessions lay everywhere. Each and every person had the same vacant stare in their eyes. Yesterday, these had been our neighbours and our friends. Today, we were the haunted and the dispossessed.

On the flight through the forest huge leeches had sucked our blood and mosquitoes had eaten us alive. Conditions here were little better, for whole families were squatting down on the jungle floor. But at least we had made it to Thailand, which might offer us a little sanctuary and security.

In spite of my exhaustion, I tried to ask around and find news of my friends. One of my fellow students, Star In The Sky, had volunteered to stay behind and fight. He had done so to help buy the women and children time to escape. It had cost him his life. One of those first mortar shells that had crashed into the village had torn Star In The Sky to pieces.

As for my other friends, I could see no sign of Nightingale, Moo Moo or Collective Love Flower. I searched everywhere among the shifting mass of traumatized humanity, but they were nowhere to be seen. I hoped and prayed that they had escaped. It didn't bear thinking about if any one of them had been captured.

In among the shapes humped beneath the trees I did notice the unmistakable forms of teachers Tom and Jacob. The white foreigners had been forced to flee the enemy, along with the rest of us. The difference was they had their passports and their ability to travel home to their countries of freedom. Once we had stepped across that border line we became non-people again.

Once again we were illegal immigrants in a foreign land.

Chapter Twenty

REFUGEES AGAIN

Tens of thousands of refugees were created by this new wave of attacks on the Karen. They converged upon a patch of land near a Thai-Karen village called Noh Poe. We were among them. In contrast to the first refugee camp that we had lived in, at least this one was granted official UN recognition.

Once again, my mother set about building us a temporary bamboo shelter. We registered with the United Nations and received our first rations of food and medical supplies. After that, it was the same regime as it had been at Mae Ra Moe camp: no lights after dark; no singing or loud noises; and no one allowed to go beyond the camp boundary. And that was it: we were back in refugee hell once more.

There were no grown men to help us this time – no Ter Pay Pay, or the two young Karen soldiers who'd been with us at Mae Ra Moe. It was only us now. We had to cut the bamboo and build the hut frame, make the split bamboo walls and floor, and thatch the roof with leaves. How many houses and shelters had we built now? Was this the seventh or eighth? No one was counting any more.

A couple of weeks after our arrival I woke with a start in the middle of the night to the staccato bark of gunfire. *Oh my God, not again. Not again.* My mother yelled for us to take cover under the floor of the shelter. We squeezed ourselves in there in a frantic rush of terror. For ages we sat and cowered in the cramped darkness, until one of the camp organizers came to speak with us. It turned out that it was just a drunken Thai soldier loosing off some gunshots.

We climbed out and found our beds once again. But I was so scared I just couldn't get back to sleep. I lay there thinking about what my life had become. Here we were – refugees once more. I did not want to be here. I really did not. Anything but this. I racked my brains, trying to think about how we could get out. But what could we do? There was nothing. This was our life now. Welcome to hell.

My mother was taking it the hardest. The terror and trauma of the flight from The New Village had really taken its toll. She was depressed and weak, and she was bottling everything up inside. During the day she worked feverishly, trying desperately to rebuild our lives. But during the night I would wake up to find her sleepless and racked with fever.

I kept asking her what was wrong and to go to the clinic in the refugee camp. Eventually, she agreed to. But the medics couldn't work out what was the matter with her. They told her to try to rest and relax, which was impossible in the refugee camp. And so my mother's condition steadily worsened.

Over the coming weeks I was reunited with Nightingale and Collective Love Flower. It was great to see them, despite the fact that we were now in a refugee camp. Mostly, we talked about absent friends. We missed Moo Moo hugely, but no one knew where she, and many others, might be. They had either been killed or captured in the attack on the village, or they had fled into the deep jungle, or they had been picked up by the Thai police and deported to Burma.

Life in this camp was harder than before, because this was when our hope truly died. We were exhausted and traumatized, but worse than that we had no hope for the future. We went through the rituals of living, but with none of the irrepressible joy of children. I was sixteen years old now, and the harshness of my last three years had put a very adult head on my young shoulders.

My eyes had been opened to the suffering of our people. In each place where we had tried to build a future we had ended up fleeing for our lives. People in the camp talked about what had happened to them. They came from many different villages, but everyone's story was like my own: the enemy attacking; the bombs and the bullets; running and hiding in the jungle; and trying to find a route to safety.

The suffering was so widespread. Where in the Karen areas was anyone safe now? Where was anyone free from attack? The killing and burning and raping and horror were on a shockingly massive scale.

Why did the United Nations and the international community allow this to happen? And where especially were the British? We had been their allies. We had fought and died beside them in the Second World War. Why had they abandoned us? I dreamed that they would come and rescue us. But they never did.

I had thought our own escape traumatic enough, but others had worse stories to tell. One evening our neighbour in the camp, Nant Than Htay, told us what had happened to her. At first she had been too traumatized even to speak about it.

When Nant Than Htay's village was attacked she had fled with her three young children. She had a five-year-old, a three-year-old and a little one-year-old baby, and somehow they had all made it into the safety of the deep forest. They hid there for days on end, surviving on what little food they had managed to carry with them.

One day they were resting in an open area as they tried to make their way towards Thailand and safety. All of a sudden the grassland all around them burst into a massive wall of flame. Nant Than Htay didn't know what had caused the burning, but they had to run for their very lives. She put her smallest child on her back and holding the other two tightly by the hand she started to run, away from the place where the blaze was at its fiercest.

Within minutes the fire seemed all around them. Vegetation turned into a roaring mass of flames, as thick, acrid smoke filled their nostrils and choked them. Nant Than Htay was totally disorientated, and terrified. All around her fallen leaves and grass roared and crackled; her terrified children screamed and cried out with fear. She was certain she was going to faint with suffocation and be consumed by the flames.

She didn't know how they had made it out of the inferno alive. Once they had done so, there was no respite. They forced themselves to continue with their epic trek to the refugee camp. Hearing her story put my own into perspective. It had been hard enough for me, yet I was practically an adult. How on earth had she managed alone, and with her three little children? It must have been a nightmare, yet she was one of the lucky ones, for they had all escaped with their lives.

In Noh Poe camp my mother was plagued by a fear of losing us. At all times she wanted us within her sight, and after six o'clock we had to stay inside the hut. The camp was at a high altitude, and it was the coldest we had ever been. During the day we didn't have enough clothes to keep warm. And at night the two blankets the UN people had issued to us weren't enough to keep out the cold. My mother's health worsened. Her skin dried and cracked. She developed a painful, racking cough and her night fevers worsened.

Life went on. I enrolled in Year Ten at Noh Poe camp school, the highest level of schooling available to refugees like us. The school was very similar to the one at Mae Ra Moe: it was run by Karen Refugee Committee volunteers, with basic educational supplies provided by NGOs. But there was a new threat here, one that menaced us everywhere. The Thai soldiers who were supposed to provide camp security were becoming sexually aggressive and harassing Karen girls. We were warned to be always vigilant.

One day I went to get some water from the camp borehole. There was one water point per camp section, and about 300 people per section. In the rainy season it wasn't so bad. People stored rainwater using bamboo guttering running into a big pot. But in the dry season the queue for water was interminable. It was the dry season now, and I joined the queue with a sense of resignation. I daydreamed as I shuffled forwards closer to the single tap.

But I became aware of a menacing presence off to one side. I glanced over, and there was a Thai soldier staring at me. He was just staring and staring, and not even trying to hide his interest in me. He was thin and wiry-looking, and not the slightest bit handsome. I noticed he didn't have his gun with him, which was a small relief. He was dressed in a mixture of uniform and civilian clothes, so I guessed it had to be his day off.

He seemed to be muttering away in Thai, almost as if he were talking to himself. I couldn't even hear, let alone understand, a word. More likely than not he was drunk. We'd been repeatedly warned about drunken Thai soldiers attacking Karen girls, and I was scared. I did my best to ignore him, but he just kept on staring and muttering.

Eventually I reached the front of the queue. I filled my plastic bucket as quickly as I could and turned away from the tap. I hoisted it on to my head and hurried off up the path to our hut. I marched ahead as fast as I could and tried to resist the temptation to glance behind. If I did it would only betray my fear. By the time I'd reached our hut I was sure I had lost him.

As I climbed the stairs I chanced a glance behind. I almost fainted. There he was, right on my very heels. I raced inside, spilling some of the water as I did so, but he followed me in. Luckily my mother was home. She ordered me into the bedroom. I ran inside, closed the door and crouched down with my back to it, my body shaking.

I could hear the soldier arguing with my mother in Thai. She just kept telling him that she didn't understand a word, and that he should leave the house immediately. He had no right coming in, she told him, bravely.

Just as his voice was becoming more and more insistent, I heard footsteps on the stairs, and then my mother was yelling at Bwa Bwa to get into the bedroom with me. The Thai soldier was now faced with my mother, two hiding teenage girls and my 15-year-old brother, Slone, who had returned with Bwa Bwa. He must have been hoping to catch me in the hut alone. After a few further menacing-sounding utterances he turned on his heel and was gone.

My mother was so angry. How did he come to be in the house, she demanded. I told her what had happened and how he had followed me home. The Thai soldiers had all the power, of course, and we refugees had none. If we reported him to the camp authorities, it was far more likely we would be the ones to be punished.

My mother became even more protective of us. Whilst she hadn't understood his words exactly, she had understood the soldier's intentions. I found myself starting to resent my father's absence. Why was he always away? I wondered. Where was he when we needed him to protect us?

One day a friend of my father's came to visit. He told us that our father was well, but busy with his resistance work. It was then that my resentment really flared up. The visitor would be seeing my father soon, and I asked him to take a letter. This is what I wrote.

Dear Pah,

Well, I think you must have completely forgotten us – especially your Little Daughter. Well, it's okay I suppose . . . But I don't want to be a refugee any more. Life in the refugee camp is so horrible. Do you know what it's like? What it feels like to be a refugee? The Thai soldiers are so horrible to us . . .

When I wrote that letter I was feeling depressed and angry. I was angry that the Thai soldiers could treat Karen girls so badly. We were trying our best to avoid them, but such harassment was commonplace. I didn't want to blame my father, but I did want to get it out of my system. My letter was like a cry for help. At least I wanted to let my father know the reality of our lives as he was never with us.

My father did write back, but he addressed the letter to my mother and she read it out to us. He wrote that he trusted in our mother to look after us and to care for us all. He wrote words of encouragement for her and for us. He wrote that there was suffering all around, and that it was the same for all the Karen. The only option was to be strong in the face of such adversity.

We tried as best we could to go on with our lives as normal. I had my Year Ten studies to occupy myself, but poor Bwa Bwa had nothing. Year Ten was the most important, for this was my final year before graduating from high school. Collective Love Flower had enrolled in the refugee camp school, and I often found myself helping her with her homework. In spite of everything, I was determined to do well in my exams. As I studied, a spark of hope was rekindled within me.

I didn't know what the future might hold. I couldn't see a way out of the refugee camp, except maybe one leading back into Karen territory. But where would be safe now? It seemed to me that we Karen were being hunted and killed and burned out of our homes all across our land. Even so, I nurtured that spark of hope. I told myself that if I believed in something strongly enough, then it had to be possible.

We had been in that refugee camp for ten months when my mother decided that Bwa Bwa and I had to leave. The harassment from the Thai soldiers had worsened. It seemed as if it was only a matter of time before a soldier cornered us somewhere where we had no one to defend us and no room to escape. Bwa Bwa and I were so scared.

A long-standing friend of the family had come to visit. He was trying to find a way to get his family out of the refugee camps and into Australia. This was what so many Karen families were hoping for. They had no chance of returning to Burma as long as the regime was in power and the international community did nothing to stop the attacks. Rather than returning to a life of insecurity and fear, the way to escape the camps was to resettle in a foreign country. If he managed it, then he might be able to take Bwa Bwa and me with him.

There was our chance to continue our studies – in Australia! He reckoned he could get a pass for us to leave Noh Poe camp. But my mother and Slone would have to remain behind. I was torn. On the one hand, I didn't want to leave them. On the other, I wanted to complete my Year Ten free of harassment and danger. It was my mother's concern for us that clinched it: she was convinced that we were in serious danger in the camp.

It was an emotional parting. I had just turned seventeen years old, and I had never lived apart from my mother for more than a few weeks. But now the family was being broken up, and we were leaving her and Slone behind. I said a tearful farewell to my friends, and we left the camp in the back of a pickup truck, knowing that we were leaving so much behind. I was barely weeks away from my end of year exams, and I hoped this was the right decision to have made.

The rules were that you had to apply for overseas resettlement in person, in Bangkok. But first we had to go to Mae Sot to get the official letter that we needed from the Thai authorities to travel to Bangkok. My father was staying for a while at a friend's house in Mae Sot and we went to stay with him there. He was full of stories of the horrors across the border, of civilians being killed, and of the SLORC's military machine continuing to steamroller onwards. The Karen resistance had taken a battering and the enemy had seized its second headquarters. Life in the villages sounded hellish, and perhaps we were lucky to have escaped as we had done.

One evening after dinner my father told us that he had just received a message that the Burmese Army had launched a new offensive. It was in Kler Lwee Htu district, in the far north of

Karen free state, an area that had seen little fighting. Karen villages had been shelled and burned. The survivors were hiding in the jungle and starving. When they were too ill to run any more, they were caught and used as forced labour. And when they were too exhausted to go on, they were killed.

Some days later my father gave a press conference, to explain to the media what was going on in Karen lands. As I watched him speak I could tell what a heavy toll it was taking on him. When he was young my father had had a dream – a dream of joining the resistance and winning freedom for all peoples of Burma. He was deeply troubled by what was happening now, and sometimes he was stressed and short-tempered. But he hadn't given up hope that the resistance would overcome.

I thought about that letter I had written in the refugee camp, complaining to my father that he had forgotten us. When I saw what he was dealing with on a daily basis – the annihilation of our villages and the despoliation of our homeland – I forgave him for leaving us behind. Not that there was anything to forgive. He had chosen not to do what others were doing. Rather than concentrating on saving his family, he was living a stressful, dangerous life in the midst of very tough times.

He felt the pain of the people so deeply that he tried to rise above all that. He sacrificed the needs of his family for the wider cause. What I had learned about the torment and horror in Kler Lwee Htu district had made me understand this. He had made a choice to stand beside those at the sharp end of the suffering. My father was a deeply humane man, and he couldn't turn away from all that.

He showed us what was happening to Karen who had fled the horror and ended up identity-less in Thailand. Young girls were on the streets of Mae Sot, working in the sex industry. And young men were labouring on building sites. In both cases these illegal non-persons were being treated little better than slaves. When not 'working', they were restricted to their rooms, for on the streets they could be arrested and deported. He pointed out the truckloads of young men and women getting shunted back across the border by the Thai authorities.

One night I was sitting outside in the garden and I noticed something odd in the trees. Instantly I felt a shudder of horror and a cold chill went up my spine. Something with a body of fiery red light and a burning tail was flitting from tree to tree. It was the size of a small kite, but the ghastly light made it seem far bigger. I had no doubt what it was – it was a ghost or a demon. I could sense its evil, and I was terrified.

I called out to Bwa Bwa in fear, and she came running. But by the time she reached me it had gone, flying off behind a coconut tree. Bwa Bwa could tell that I was scared. I explained to her what I had seen. Bwa Bwa didn't say whether she believed me or not, she just told me to come inside. Many Karen believe demons appear as a sign that something bad is about to happen. We tried to ignore it.

We just didn't need any more misfortune.

Chapter Twenty-one

MAE LA CAMP

It actually took our friend years to get his family resettled in Australia. Bwa Bwa and I had realized the difficulties he faced, and we chose to take our chances in a refugee camp called Mae La. Mae La camp had been in existence for more than twenty years, itself testimony to the duration of the Karen struggle. It was well established, with a greater level of support from the NGOs and the United Nations.

It had a boarding school called the Mae La Further Studies Programme. The headmaster was called Pu Taw – Grandfather Honest. He told us that the Burmese Army had attacked Mae La camp twice before, so we had to be careful. But at least in the boarding school we reckoned we would be safe from the Thai soldiers. And our greatest joy was being reunited with Moo Moo and Collective Love Flower, who were both already enrolled in the school.

Because this was a Further Studies school, and the Thais would allow no formal study in the refugee camps post-high school, the only subjects on offer were mushroom cultivation and vegetable farming. As we were refugees, with no land to call our own, the subjects were strikingly inappropriate. Where would we be establishing any mushroom or vegetable farms any time soon?

But the Further Studies school opened up other exciting opportunities for us. One day we had a visit from an American lady, who proceeded to give us a talk about something called the OSI Scholarship Programme. The OSI is the Open Society Institute, a charity set up by George Soros, the international investor, which gives grants to support human rights and democracy work. The American lady told us that scholarships were available to refugees like us who wanted to study for a degree. Anyone over a certain age could apply. We had to pass an entrance exam, to show we could satisfy university level requirements. And the OSI required us to write three essays, one on how we would use our education to help our country. Bwa Bwa, Moo Moo, Collective Love Flower and I all decided to apply!

It was April 1999 when we sat the OSI scholarship exam. Dozens of hopeful students did so in our camp alone, so it was anyone's guess how many eager applicants there were across all the camps. I was desperate to have done well, although I knew competition for places was fierce. But when it came to it only five people from our camp were accepted. They included Bwa Bwa and Moo Moo, but not me.

I had passed the exam, but there just weren't enough places for everyone. I knew it was right that Bwa Bwa and Moo Moo went ahead of me – they were a year or more older. In Bwa Bwa's case she had been sitting around for months on end with precious little to do. But even so, I was bitterly disappointed. For at least another year it looked as if I would be stuck in the camp.

I had put so much of myself into getting a scholarship, and when I heard that I had failed my spirits took a nose dive. I felt absolutely hopeless and I ended up in tears. Bwa Bwa tried to comfort me. She told me not to worry, for I was still young. I was sure to get one the following year.

Bwa Bwa left in September to begin her studies at a university in Bangkok. The day she drove out of the camp I was so happy for her, yet unhappy in myself. As I stood at the gates and watched her drive away, I wondered what the future held in store for me. I waved at my big sister until her hand was lost in the dust and the shadows, and then she was gone.

I went back to the school dormitory feeling so alone and so disappointed. I plonked myself down in a chair. As I did so, my eyes came to rest on the school motto, which was painted on one wall:

1. To learn
2. To live
3. To serve

Somehow, that motto gave me strength. To me it seemed to mean that we endured, in spite of all that was ranged against us. And if we endured, we could learn. And if we could learn, we could still hope to do good in the world, in spite of everything.

Yet I missed my sister so. At times I cried myself to sleep. I had always relied on having her around me. I wondered if she missed me, or if she had forgotten me as soon as she reached Bangkok. For the first time in my life I found myself without any of my family around me. I felt as if a great void had opened up in my life. My family had been scattered to the corners of the earth. My spirits were at a real low, and all I was living for was next year's OSI exams.

A few months back my mother had written me and Bwa Bwa a letter. I was missing her more than ever now, and I felt that I really needed her. I reread that letter. 'My lovely daughters,' it said. 'Look after yourselves, take care of your health. I am sorry you didn't get the chance to go to Australia, and hope your education in Mae La is going well.'

I felt a bit happier. It was good to know that that she and Slone were well. A few weeks after she had left, I received a letter from

Bwa Bwa. She wrote that everything was going well. She was so impressed by the university facilities – the lecturers, the computers, the literature. It was like being in another world. She told me about the space-age escalators and the electric lifts with glass doors. As I read her letter it only made me feel all the more left behind and abandoned. I missed Bwa Bwa so much.

I wrote a letter to my mother telling her that I was happy, and that I had made lots of new friends in the camp. I said that I would apply again for an OSI scholarship next year. I didn't want to worry her by telling her how I really felt. When we had left her she was depressed and ill. I didn't want to make things any worse.

But I did feel I could be honest with my father. I wrote to him about my failure to get accepted by the OSI, and that I was disappointed and feeling down. I told him I felt as if all my hopes had been dashed. He wrote back telling me not to be so hard on myself. He said I should see that first OSI exam as a dress rehearsal. Next time I would know what to expect and would be sure to do well.

It wasn't long after that that I became ill. At first I felt as if I had a cold, but it soon became a very high fever. I was shaking so much that by the time I was taken to one of Dr Cynthia's clinics I was unable to stand. I had never in my life felt so cold. I lay on the bed piled in blankets and shivering uncontrollably. I could hear the headboard knocking against the wall as my whole body shook. It was frightening.

The medics diagnosed me with cerebral malaria – the type than can and does kill. I was told by my doctor that I had only just reached the clinic in time. Any longer, and it would have inflamed my brain to such an extent that I would have died. I lay in bed for two weeks on a quinine drip, and I could keep little solid food down. It took me an age to recover my strength. And that was the second time that Dr Cynthia's clinics had saved my life.

The Thai government was very unhappy having hundreds of

thousands of Karen refugees in the country. They refused to formally recognize us as refugees, but in 1999 did allow those in Mae La camp to formally register with the United Nations. Only those people would be allowed to get rations. The Thais did this to discourage more refugees coming to the camp, but of course people kept coming because the Burmese Army was attacking them, not because of the camp rations.

As the attacks continued more and more people arrived, and more refugees made for the camps. Soon, there were thousands of 'ghost refugees' in Mae La – ones who might be physically present, but officially didn't exist. The Karen Refugee Committee estimated that there were some 20,000 refugees in the camp, but as many as one quarter were ghost refugees. Some 15,000 official refugees were secretly feeding the 5,000 'ghosts', which meant there was never enough food to go round.

There was an influx of students from Huay Kaloke refugee camp. One night the Burmese Army had attacked their camp and burned it down. Many had burned to death in their huts. The camp was devastated and everyone had to flee. As with most camps, the Thai soldiers had been paid by the United Nations to protect it. But all they had done was run away. There was little official welcome for those who made it to Mae La camp; they, too, had to join the ranks of the ghost refugees.

I was angry with the enemy, but this was what we expected from them – attacking and killing innocent people, even in the camps. I was angry with the Thais, for instead of providing security they had run away – but it wasn't the first time they had done so. But as for the United Nations, what excuses were there for their failings?

I knew the United Nations had money and resources. I knew it represented all nations on earth. I knew it was aware of how bad things were for us. So why didn't it stand up to the Thai government or the military junta in Burma? My father had often talked about the United Nations as the one organization that could really affect our lives. But it seemed useless to me. If even the United Nations wouldn't stand up for our rights, then who would?

In June 2000 my mother and Slone made it to Mae La camp. They had always intended to try to join us, and so they entered the ranks of the ghost refugees. Officially they didn't exist. Slone was allowed to enrol in school, but neither he nor my mother was entitled to any rations. In spite of all we had been through there was a strong community spirit in the camp, and no one was left out. One family would give them some rice; another, a little fish paste; a third, some of their cooking oil.

I hadn't seen my mother and little brother for approaching two years. He was growing into a handsome young man, but my mother had aged so much. I was shocked. Her arms and legs had swollen up, and if you pressed her skin it would stay in the shape it had been pushed into. Her ankles and wrists were the worst. Only her hair had retained its rich, lustrous shine. It struck me that she was looking like an old woman long before her time.

The camp clinic could only do so much. They told us she had liver and heart problems, and that the swelling was water retention. Within a matter of weeks she was seriously ill. Her arms and legs were heavy, her joints painful. She could hardly walk. I was so sad, for my mother had always been the strong one, even in difficult times. I looked at her and thought about what a wonderful mother she was.

Luckily, a little help was at hand. A 14-year-old orphan girl called Thu Ray Paw came to stay with my mother, plus a teenage boy called Saw Nu. Both were alone and in need of parents, and my mother was happy to take them in. She 'adopted' two other homeless boys, one of whom was Say Say's 10-year-old nephew, Poe Thay Doh – Baby Big Tree. He was the youngest and my mother adored him. He was treated like the baby of the family.

This was my mother's surrogate family, and she was the matriarch to whom the lost were drawn. They helped her in her day-to-day living, and she in turn gave them much-needed love and security. My father tried to visit my mother as often as he could, but it wasn't easy getting into and out of the camp. Whenever he did manage it he was relieved to find her surrounded by her adopted family.

Eventually, my mother realized the pills from the clinic were not doing her any good. So she asked Uncle Lay Pyoe, a traditional healer, to come and see her. Uncle Lay Pyoe used herbs from the forest and other traditional remedies to cure people. He gave my mother a bottle of the medicine that he'd prepared for her. She had to drink a capful every day.

It looked like home-made lemonade. One night I dipped my finger in, but it was bitter, and I was surprised that my mother could even drink it. It made her go to the toilet much more regularly, and at first she did seem to get better. She seemed happy with his treatment, far happier than she had been with the pills. For a little while she seemed somewhat recovered.

There was a tarmac road that went past the gate of Mae La camp. Converted pickup trucks would pass by carrying passengers to and fro. One day I saw one stop at the camp fence and there was a white girl sitting in the back. She didn't look a lot older than me, and on the spur of the moment I decided to speak to her.

'Hi! Would you like to come and visit us?'

'Why?' she asked me, in bemusement. 'What is it?'

'It's a refugee camp,' I told her, with a smile of welcome. 'And we are Karen refugees.'

For some reason she seemed to trust me. She got down from the truck, heaved her rucksack over the fence, and we found her a hole that she could squeeze through. I took her straight to the school dormitory where we could keep her hidden. There were other foreigners working in the camp, but none were allowed to stay there. They would come in the morning and return to their houses in the evening.

Once we were safely ensconced in the dormitory, she told me her story. Her name was Linda and she came from Holland.

230

She was a tourist and she was on her way from Mae Hong Song to Mae Sot. She was in her early twenties and travelling alone.

It had been a spur of the moment thing me calling out to her like that. We were all so eager to talk with foreigners about our situation so they could spread the word. I just wanted to let people know what was happening. I told Linda we were Karen refugees from Burma, and that our villages had been destroyed and so we were forced to live in the camp. She had had no idea that there were refugees in Thailand. She had just presumed Mae La camp was a poor and overcrowded village.

The rest of the students thought it was great having her visit. That evening I cooked dinner – rice and fish paste for a change! After she'd eaten we found her a bed in the girls' dormitory for the night. Linda stayed for two days. The only downside was that we couldn't let her walk around freely in the camp, for the Thai authorities might have caught her.

When it became time for her to leave we sneaked her out through the fence by removing a couple of the bamboo poles. Linda had given me her email address and phone numbers. But, of course, I had no way of communicating with her, so they were useless to me. But I kept them just in case. One day I might get out of the camp and contact Linda – my friend from the outside world.

In March 2000 I sat my second OSI exam. I had to write essays in English about myself and what I would like to do in the future and why I wanted to study for a degree. I wrote that I was a refugee from Burma, but that I would like to become a successful person so I could help my people in any way that I could. That's what I wanted to do when I had finished my studies.

Some sixty students from our school took the exam. The headmaster told us that hundreds more were doing so all along the border. Overall there were nine refugee camps, housing over 100,000 refugees. Yet the OSI could offer only a handful of scholarships. I didn't want to build my hopes up too much, for I knew that if I failed again it would destroy my self-confidence, and my hope would die with that failure.

Two months after sitting the exams our results were handed around the class. Each student received a sealed letter. I ripped mine open, barely daring to hope for a place. I couldn't believe it when I saw that I had passed, and been accepted on to an OSI scholarship. My results also meant that I had won a scholarship from Prospect Burma, a charity set up by friends and relatives of Aung San Suu Kyi. All my fears had come to nothing. I had a route out of the camp by studying for a degree.

Nightingale had also won a place, along with three other friends – Tha Say (Silver Heart), Saw Poe Htoo (Mr Baby Gold) and Saw Winworld (Mr Winworld). Five from our school had got through. The other fifty-five had failed. There were tears of joy for us lucky few, and tears of sadness for the others. I knew exactly how it felt to be rejected, for I had been there last year. It was so easy to lose hope and resign oneself to rot in the refugee camp.

That afternoon the headmaster, Grandfather Honest, took me to one side to have a private word. He was very proud of me, he said. Of the hundreds of students who had applied for an OSI scholarship, I had the highest mark of all.

It was 27 September 2000, and approaching my twentieth birthday, when I left Mae La camp. I was heading to Bangkok to join Bwa Bwa at the same university. I had to be smuggled out of the camp, because I was still a refugee with no formal ID. I only existed as a name on a UN list in the camp.

I said goodbye to my mother and Slone with mixed emotions. On the one hand, I was so excited at what lay ahead. On the other, I felt guilty to be leaving my mother. She looked so ill. She was trying to be happy for me, but she couldn't shake off her depression. As for Slone, he was overjoyed that I was getting this opportunity. His plan was to follow in the footsteps of his big sisters as his own escape route from the camp.

I had known that leaving my mother would be tough,

especially now when she needed me most. But she didn't complain. She wanted us all to find a way to escape, for she knew the desperation of being trapped in the camp. I hugged her and my little brother one last time, jumped into the vehicle, and then I was gone.

And I had no idea when I might be back again.

Chapter Twenty-two

BANGKOK DAZE

After my life in the Karen jungles and the refugee camps, Bangkok was like another planet. It was my first time in a big city. I looked around in wonder at the tall, beautiful buildings, all sheets of concrete and glass, and thought to myself, wow! Amazing. If only my country could find peace my people might leave the squalor of the refugee camps and live in places like this.

At first, I didn't really notice the noise and the smell and the car fumes, and how busy everyone was. I was blind to the Bangkok traffic jams and the dark underbelly of the city. All I could see was the development that was all around me: the smooth, mirrored glass, the shiny vehicles gliding through the streets on tarmac roads, and everywhere people buzzing about on motorbikes and scooters.

Life in this huge, chaotic city was going to be a challenge for a girl from the jungle. Luckily, I had Bwa Bwa there to help me. Bwa Bwa had rented a little flat in a block of apartments populated largely by students. It consisted of one small room, with a shower and toilet cubicle inside it, and the one bed to share. We had to cook in the room using an electric cooker – a portable ring that we plugged into the wall.

Our flat was situated in an area called Ratchda Piseit, about ten minutes' walk from college. This isn't a tourist area: it's more a business and banking district, with a mix of residential apartment blocks and offices. My sister had decorated the flat by hanging a photo on the wall of my father, herself and me taken on Karen Resistance Day. There wasn't much room for anything else.

The money we got from the OSI scholarships was barely enough to go around. It paid for our university fees, with 5000 Thai Baht – about £70 – left over each month to cover our living expenses. With that we had to buy our food, clothes and books and to pay the rent. We also wanted to send some money home to my mother and Slone, and by sharing a flat we might just be able to afford to do so.

This was the first time in my life that I'd lived in a concrete box, as opposed to a house made of bamboo and leaves. Even with the window open it was stale and airless. Yet here I had to stay if I wanted to study. Our tiny apartment had to be locked every time we went out, in case of burglary, whereas even in the refugee camps we'd not had any doors or windows to lock.

Luckily, Bwa Bwa and I had some of our friends nearby. Nightingale lived in a neighbouring apartment block, along with her sister, Paw Wah – White Flower. They had both won OSI scholarships, although White Flower had done so from a different refugee camp. And Moo Moo – my friend from The New Village – was living in that same building with her sister, Khu Khu. Khu Khu and I were to become the best of friends.

I wasn't able to choose my degree subject. The scholarship was available in one subject only – Business Administration. There were ten OSI scholarship students in my year, coming from some of the main ethnic groups in Burma – Karen, Mon, Karenni, Arakan and Burman. What united us was that we were all victims of the Burmese military regime and opponents of the Generals who had seized power illegally in our country.

Our college was called the St Theresa Institute of Technology. It was an international school affiliated to Bradford University in the United Kingdom. The majority of the students were either the children of affluent Thai families, or foreign students from China, Taiwan, Cambodia, Sri Lanka, India, the United States, Canada and the United Kingdom. In that first term I had little time to make friends, for I had to spend my every waking hour studying if I was to have any hope of catching up with their level of education.

My biggest challenge was learning how to use a computer. I had to study late into the evenings to acquire that skill. The friends I did make were invariably other OSI scholarship students, and we bonded over frustrating evenings spent in the computer studies hall trying to master the use of a PC!

Everything at the college was done with computers, so we were lost if we couldn't use one. The teachers would send their lecture notes by email. Our research was to be done via the internet. Our essays were supposed to be typed, printed out and handed to our tutors. I was on a very steep learning curve, with masses of catching up to do.

If I had been able to choose my degree I would have opted to do Southeast Asian Studies. Business Administration was my least favourite subject, for it was so alien to me. I didn't understand many of the most basic concepts. I had no idea about the practices of international business. As to the relative benefits of Kimberly Clark's logo versus that of Toyota, or Tesco – I was completely lost. What was a logo? What was a superstore? Who were Tesco, Toyota and the rest?

I felt frustrated by the huge amount of 'catch up' that I faced. The style of teaching was also very different from what I was used to. In Karen schools we had copied down lessons from the blackboard and learned by rote. Here we had an hour's lecture on a subject, and then we were supposed to spend time in the library or on the internet doing our own research. This was a real challenge, but I soon discovered that I liked developing my own thinking in this way.

We had one module called ASEAN Studies, and this was my favourite subject. ASEAN is the Association of Southeast Asian Nations, an alliance of nations similar to the European Union. The ASEAN block consists of Thailand, Laos, Cambodia, Vietnam, Singapore, Malaysia, the Philippines, Indonesia, Brunei and Burma. In theory we were free to choose to study the economy of any ASEAN country.

But no one chose Burma, for there was more or less nothing to study. There wasn't a single textbook in the library on the economy of Burma. For decades the dictatorship had run the country for its own benefit, under a chaotic and corrupt rule. I chose instead to study Thailand – and that's how I found out about the way in which you run a nation's economy so that anyone can benefit, as opposed to making a handful of military leaders obscenely rich.

At first I had been awestruck by the city of Bangkok, but once I had been there a few weeks I realized it wasn't so great. It was all tall buildings and neon lights. Cars, trucks and swarms of motorbikes clogged the streets, spewing out a choking cloud of pollution. Dirt; crowds of people; snarling traffic; locked doors – I began to realize that life in the village had its own benefits.

I had no idea how to use an escalator, a lift or even an electric kettle. There was no electricity or mod cons in the jungle or the refugee camps. Crossing a busy road was a real trial. And it took me an age to learn to recognize window and door glass. If it was see-through, then it had to be air, or so my brain told me. On several occasions I walked right into a glass door. It was very embarrassing.

Whilst this had a funny side to it, it was also worrying. I was living in Bangkok without any legal papers, and the more I stood out as a misfit the more chance that I might attract the attention of the Thai authorities. At first I couldn't speak any Thai, so I couldn't communicate on the streets. I was an illegal alien. If I was stopped by the police I was in big trouble. Whenever I saw a policeman I felt scared.

The bottom line was that I had no legal papers or ID card to show to the police. So I had to hide, even as I went about my daily studies. Whenever I saw the police I would try to melt into the background. I tried to spend as much time as I could on the college campus or at home studying – for then I knew I was safe. Bwa Bwa and I had gone from living in a camp with ghost refugees to being ghost citizens ourselves.

Most Burmese in Bangkok had no papers, so we were living a life similar to an awful lot of others. The Thai police stopped people all the time. They would demand their papers, and if they had none they were invariably deported to Burma. Those with money could bribe the Thai police into letting them stay. There were millions of illegal immigrants in Thailand, and every day they lived in fear.

The Thai police would set up roadblocks or they would be on foot roaming the streets. They would stop anyone who looked out of place. Not being able to speak Thai or wearing scruffy 'rural' clothes was a dead giveaway. I tried to make myself look 'Thai'. I wore trousers, not the traditional Karen longyi that I was used to. I cut my hair in a short, Thai-style bob. On the streets I spoke the few words of Thai that I had mastered, or not at all. I did everything I could to keep under the radar.

At college I quickly realized how different I and the other OSI students were from the rest of our class. We were all human beings, and yet we had lived a life of hell, while the rest of the students had comfortable lives. I kept myself to myself at college, for if I talked too much people might realize I was an illegal, and that might cause me problems. But I knew that the other students were from wealthy backgrounds.

They would turn up at college driving their own cars. They talked about going to expensive restaurants and the cinema and playing golf. They wore trendy designer clothes. Their parents were business people, doctors or diplomats. They had enjoyed freedom and privilege all their lives, whilst we had been in the jungle running from bullets. I wondered why. Why were people so different, just as an accident of their birth?

I had been born a Karen, and I had faced a life of fear, persecution and oppression. By accident of their birth those students had never faced one fraction of the hardship that we Karen had experienced. I had never been around people from such backgrounds before. They complained about the fact that they'd ripped their designer jeans; or their parents wouldn't buy them the newest mobile phone; or that their car had got bumped on the street. And I thought to myself: 'This is nothing. What are you complaining about?'

I had been driven out of my homeland and shunted from refugee camp to refugee camp, places where I had nothing, absolutely nothing – not even a future. And here I was among people who seemed to have everything, yet they complained about trivial things. In fact, they seemed unable to appreciate the life of privilege with which they had been blessed. Sometimes they'd skip class or turn up late or they'd miss study deadlines and not even seem to care.

I was amazed that people could treat education with such a lack of respect. We OSI scholars had fought so hard to be here. This education, this degree course – *this was my dream*. But to them, it was just another chapter in their lives. There were so many thousands in the refugee camps who would give anything to have a carefree life of opportunity like theirs.

In among the designer clothes, the rounds of golf and the partying, there was never any mention of my country or its suffering. It wasn't far away. It was just across the border. It was in the newspapers and on the TV news. These students had access to the internet and the global media, and there was no excuse for them not to know. But it was never once a topic of conversation at college.

At times I did feel inferior, as if I was not their equal. The only way I had to combat such feelings was to try to succeed in the exams. I had to prove that in spite of being a Karen 'jungle girl' and a refugee, I could be the equal of anyone no matter who they might be.

One of our course modules was economics, and as part of this we had to study the 1997 crash in Thailand. Several factors had contributed to the meltdown in the Thai economy, and one of those cited was currency speculation. The 'guilty parties' were named, and imagine our surprise when one of them turned out to be George Soros. No one – not the professors, nor the rest of the students – knew that we were OSI scholars, and we weren't about to own up to it either!

Whenever we felt as if our lives of study, study, study were getting on top of us, Bwa Bwa, Nightingale, Moo Moo and I might treat ourselves. If we could afford it, we would go to the cinema. The first film I saw in Bangkok was *Black Hawk Down*. It had been my idea to go and see it. I knew it was about a country called Somalia, and about the United Nations sending in a peacekeeping force. I had thought to myself: 'If they could have peacekeepers in Africa, why can't we have them in Burma? Why can't the United Nations do the same for us?'

But the film was only about war. All we learned from it was that war was hell, and we knew that anyway. Worst of all were the emotions that the movie stirred within me. It was so graphic and so realistic that it brought back dark memories – memories from Manerplaw, from Per He Lu village, from the refugee camps, and of fleeing from bullets and bombs. At one stage I almost walked out, but I told myself that I had paid for it, so I would see it through to the end.

During that first year of college I missed my parents and brothers very much. My one link to home was my father's phone. He split his time between Burma and Thailand now, and if he was on the Thai side of the border we could often raise him on his mobile phone, which was the most contact I'd had with him for ages. We were further away physically than ever, but united by this phone link.

The news from 'home' was mixed. Slone was doing well, coming top of his class in Mae La camp. And Say Say had given up the life of a soldier to help my father with his work. But my mother wasn't well. My father wanted to get her into Dr Cynthia's clinic in Mae Sot, but he needed a car to carry her there as she was too ill to make it any other way. He needed money to hire a car and to buy petrol, and to pay off the refugee camp guards to let her leave. I told him that Bwa Bwa and I could save some money and help, but he said that he would manage.

I desperately wanted to go and visit my mother, but I didn't want to take the risk of travelling all that way and getting caught. My fears had been fuelled by a Thai neighbour of ours called Pi Dao. She and I had become good friends, and it was through her that I learned about the fate of many of the Burmese illegal immigrants in Bangkok. Pi told me that every Thai person knew of a Burmese who was living in the city as a virtual slave.

Pi herself knew of a Burmese refugee who had worked for years for a Thai family as a domestic. She was never allowed out of the house and never paid. Eventually, that girl had killed herself. Pi said it was terrible what was going on. Most Thais knew about it, but didn't care. There was a dark side to the city; people lived and slaved away and suffered and died there, unnoticed.

An underground support organization had been formed to help the illegals, called the Overseas Karen Refugee and Social Organization (OKRSO). They had an office in someone's house, but they worked in constant fear of the Thai police. It was actually against Thai law to run an organization that helped illegal immigrants, or so the Thai police argued. So the office had to carry on in secret.

The first time I went to hear about their work I was really impressed. They helped illegals to find proper work; they tried to get them released from police custody; they even paid the necessary bribes to free them. For the Thai police this was a source of extra income, and so they would arrest the same person over and over again. They would hold that person until someone – either family or OKRSO – came to pay the money to release them.

Burmese girls were vulnerable to being abused by the Thai

police. Men could be savagely beaten, sometimes half to death. This was the normal way to treat 'illegals'. They regarded them as less than human somehow. I learned all of this via OKRSO, and also from friends and my own experience. I ended up hating the Thai police.

Thai people could be good or bad, just like anyone else. A few of them were openly racist, but most were just getting on with their lives. None was ever racist to me, but that's because they thought I was Thai. My friends called me by my nickname, Poezo, which means 'baby Zoya'. So I had a name, and an appearance, which could just as well have been Thai. That was my greatest protection.

During that first year I studied as I had never done before. In the end of year exams I scored 60 per cent, which put me about average in the class. My biggest failing had been IT. But bearing in mind that I'd only learned to use a computer that year, it was a miracle that I hadn't failed.

The girl from the jungle and the refugee camps was holding her own.

Chapter Twenty-three

CITY GIRLS

During my second year Bwa Bwa, Khu Khu and I decided we had to do more to help our people along the Thai–Burma border. Together with other Karen students we set up the Karen University Students Group (KUSG). Our aim was to use the skills that we had learned to help those trapped in the limbo of the refugee camps. At our first KUSG meeting we had some twenty students present. We charged a membership fee of 500 Thai Baht, the money from which would fund a prize for the top student in the refugee camps.

We decided to make a 'medal', which would display the KUSG logo of a book, a candle and a Karen drum. One of our members, Saw Eh Tha Shee – Mr Clear Love Heart – drew up the design in gold, silver and bronze. We got some Thai metalworkers to make it up for us. Our aim was to give a medal to each of the top three pupils graduating from the refugee camp high schools, plus a Karen–English dictionary.

We couldn't give the prizes in person, but we could send them to the schools for the head teacher to officiate. The first year we ran the KUSG prize-giving scheme we had such positive feedback. It had really motivated the students. They wanted to follow in our footsteps, which meant that the OSI scholarships would be in even greater demand. It was good to give something back, even just a little.

That September – 2002 – Bwa Bwa left Bangkok. Her wildest dreams had been fulfilled, and she was going to finish her final year of study in the United Kingdom, at Bradford University. I was sad to see her leave, but happy that she was following her dream.

With Bwa Bwa gone a Karen girl called Tha Say – Miss Silver – moved in to share the flat with me. Tha Say was another OSI scholar, and she likewise had won her scholarship from the refugee camp. She was a couple of years older than me, and her life had been full of tragedy and horror. One evening she told me her story.

She was born and brought up in a village in Du Pla Ya district, far to the south of Manerplaw. Her family were impoverished rice farmers. There was no school in the village, and the Burmese soldiers were forever coming and demanding money from people. Those who couldn't pay had to face the horror of forced labour, carrying weapons and food for the army. Those who weakened or faltered were beaten and killed.

When she was thirteen a Karen lady had adopted Tha Say. As with my elder brother, Say Say, her parents had given her up in an effort to secure her a better future. Tha Say's adopted mother had treated her as a much-loved child. She had put Tha Say into a school in a village near the border, where she could get educated along with the rest of the village children.

But the village had been attacked, and they had fled through the jungle to the refugee camps. Like me, Tha Say had been driven out of her homeland.

Shortly after Tha Say moved in with me I began my internship, which was part of my course. I would be spending three months working with Telecomasia Corporation. Telecomasia was based in a gigantic glass tower block not far from the college. I could hardly believe that I would be working in such a place. Hordes of people passed in and out, and each was dressed in a smart business suit.

This was the uniform of those who worked there, and in keeping with my general strategy – *do not stand out* – I set about making myself look like them. Tha Say and Nightingale offered to take me shopping. I needed to buy myself a smart jacket and skirt, a blouse and *high heels*. All the women at Telecomasia wore high heels, so I would have to do likewise.

I tried on several pairs, but they hurt my feet and I couldn't for the life of me imagine how anyone could walk in them – especially the stilettos! I had broad, flexible feet more used to jumping in rivers, sliding down mudslides or gripping on to bamboo. Eventually I found a pair of platform shoes that gave me the extra height but didn't threaten to kill me.

Luckily, Tha Say knew how to do make-up. She taught me how to apply foundation cream, rouge, lipstick and eyeliner so that it didn't look overdone. She was also great at helping me choose my outfits, and telling me which colours went with which. She seemed to have an eye for such things.

The first day of my work placement I checked myself in the mirror before leaving the flat. I barely recognized the person I had become. I looked so smart dressed in all my finery, but it felt somehow unnatural. At the same time I felt a shiver of excitement. I looked so professional, like someone I had never imagined myself becoming. It was a long journey for the girl from the jungle to where I was now. It was as if I had grown a new skin.

But as soon as I was out the door I realized how difficult it was to walk in those silly shoes. Then I had to fight my way on to a crowded Bangkok bus, and for the forty-minute journey to Telecomasia I was crammed in like a sardine, breathing in petrol fumes. Most Thai bus drivers seemed to have a death wish, and this one was no different. I arrived at the office bang on 8.30 a.m. – the time to start work – feeling frazzled.

One of my managers was a Thai woman whose nickname was Pi Mao. She received me in her office on the twenty-eighth floor of the Telecomsasia building. She was perusing my CV, and seemed pleased that I spoke good English, for that would help with their international clientele. She was friendly and helpful as she showed me to my desk and explained what was expected of me.

I had a desk on the twenty-second floor right in the middle of the building. The office block had a steel and glass exterior, and was fully air-conditioned. I couldn't see much from my desk, but I could go to the windows whenever I needed a break. As far as the eye could see the view was of the city. There wasn't a mountain or a river or a patch of forest in sight. I could hardly believe that so many people could live in such a vast area of concrete and glass and tarmac.

Pi Mao was patient with me and very supportive as I went about learning the ropes of the telecoms business. At first I stayed in the office, and was taught how to market telecommunications services and to enter customer details on to spreadsheets. Then I was sent out to the shopping malls selling six-month contracts for landlines. Mobile phones were hugely popular in Thailand, and selling landline services was a real challenge.

People were friendly at the company, but it wasn't exactly fun. Everyone worked too hard to have much fun – that was the corporate work ethic. The highlight of the working week was when Pi Mao took me out to lunch. We would go to a Thai restaurant just around the corner. Usually, I would have fried rice with egg and she would eat noodles. She would drink iced coffee, and I would have iced tea. This was a real treat, for I had never been taken out to eat in a proper restaurant.

Over lunch, Pi Mao would outline for me the challenges and opportunities facing Telecomasia. At present they had a virtual monopoly on landline sales. But in 2006 the telecoms market in Thailand was going to open up to global companies. Orange was already investing heavily in Thailand, and there was going to be more and more competition. Telecomasia needed people with language skills, especially English. After my placement there might well be a job for me.

I learned a lot from working at Telecomasia. Whilst the direct sales side was boring, I did like learning about different marketing strategies. And I enjoyed meeting people who worked in the industry and hearing them discuss their international strategies. At the end of my internship the head of the department called me into his office. I had done very well, he told me, and everyone at the company was very pleased with my work.

'You should feel very proud of yourself, Zoya,' he said. 'And if you would like to come back and work for us, we would be happy to have you. Let us know.'

I couldn't believe it: he was offering me a job! I thought, wow, what an opportunity! I could work here and learn the ins and outs of the telecoms industry, with a view to taking my knowledge into Burma when freedom came to our country. We would need a telecoms industry. There was no better place in which to learn. And I would have all the necessary experience to start a Burmese telecoms company.

I allowed myself to imagine what it would be like to have a normal life. I would have a proper job, security and a bright future. I would have money, and I would live in peace. I could build my life, support my family, and perhaps even have my own children in time. I could invest in my own future. And when Burma was free, as surely one day it would be, I would be ideally placed to help build the new country. Every way I looked at it, it really wasn't such a bad idea.

It was on the cusp of the year – 2003 was all but upon us – when my father phoned with some worrying news. My mother's condition had worsened and she had been admitted into Dr Cynthia's clinic. The whole of her body was horribly swollen. The medics had diagnosed her with liver failure, compounded by a heart condition. My father sounded really worried, which was unusual for him. He normally took every adversity that life threw at him firmly in his stride.

A week later my father phoned again. My mother had been admitted to a Thai hospital, and he was visiting her every day and praying that she might recover. I was torn. I so wanted to go and see my mother, but at the same time I knew the risks of making that journey back to the border. If I did and I was pulled off the bus and arrested, I knew only too well what the consequences might be.

Two weeks later I had another call from my father. I was dreading more bad news, but he sounded lighter. My mother had responded well to treatment and the swelling had gone down. The Thai doctors had let her out of hospital. She was staying for a short while with my father, in Mae Sot, to recuperate. Over the coming months this was to become the pattern of my mother's life. Once she was out of hospital the swelling would slowly build up again, and eventually she would go back in.

I was in my final year and my biggest challenge was studying for my final exams, whilst coping with the worry over my mother. It was eating away at me. My biggest fear was that she would die before I could get back to the border to see her. When I wasn't occupied by study that fear played on my mind.

I saw two options ahead of me once I had finished my degree. The first involved me going back to the border, to work with the Karen community in and around the refugee camps. This meant becoming a stateless person based in the camps, but at least it would mean that I would be around my ailing mother.

The second option was to take the job with Telecomasia. That would mean a life of luxury and freedom, of good food, money and fine clothes. I would have status, and no Thai policeman would ever think of arresting a smart 'Thai' telecoms employee. I could turn my back on poverty, death, suffering and the indignity of life as a refugee. I could turn away from the struggle, the never-ending path of resistance, and I could enjoy life. I could earn good money and send it to my parents, and get them out of the camps.

In March 2003 I sat my final exams. I had worked very hard and desperately hoped I had done well. The day the results were issued I rushed over to check on the college notice board. I was excited and worried all at the same time. When I found my mark on the list I practically jumped up and hugged the board: I had got a 2.1! Tha Say had also got a 2.1 and she was likewise overjoyed. Nightingale had scored a 2.2 and she was pretty pleased.

I phoned my father with the news. He told me that he was so proud of his Little Daughter. There was no formal degree ceremony. Instead, the dean of the college handed us each our degree certificate. It displayed the name and logo of Bradford University, plus the words 'Bachelor of Arts in Business Administration'.

And now I had to choose. My OSI grant was finished, and living in Bangkok was expensive. I would have to take the job with Telecomasia if I wanted to keep my little flat. But first, there was one thing I had to do. I had to travel back to the border to see my mother. I couldn't wait any longer. Now I had my degree I had to go.

I travelled back to the border region by bus. I was dressed in my smartest clothes, and had donned my armour of make-up and platform shoes. Then the bus was stopped at the first checkpoint and a Thai policeman came on.

'Get out! Get out! Karen and Burmese – out!' he ordered, fiercely.

I stayed where I was, but I was practically shaking with fear. I knew what awaited those people forced to get off the bus. Many would be making their first journey 'home' in many years, with whatever money they had saved from the pittance they earned in Bangkok. And now the Thai police were about to fleece them. Most would pay the bribe and be allowed back on. The unlucky few wouldn't have enough money, and they would be sent back to Burma.

We finally reached Mae Sot after running the gauntlet of several further checkpoints. At each I had bluffed my way through in the same manner as before. My father had rented a house in Mae Sot for him and my ailing mother, which doubled as his office. It was here that he briefed the media on what was happening across the border and met politicians and others of influence.

In spite of what my father had told me, I was shocked at my mother's appearance. She was so very, very, very thin. The swelling had gone away, all apart from her tummy, which was extended like a hard drum. Her face was wrinkled, and for the first time in my life she had cut her hair. When I realized that she didn't even have the energy to care for her beautiful hair, then I really knew how sick she had become.

She could walk in the garden, but only slowly and with help, and she couldn't cook any more. She was having her food prepared for her, and she would eat it in her room. She could still read, so she was able to lose herself in her books. And that was about her one joy in life now. She had no vegetable patch, no chickens and no pigs and ducks. My mother was so unhappy.

When things got very bad she had to go on to oxygen in order to keep breathing. She needed to be somewhere where she could have access to such treatment, and that wasn't the refugee camp. My father knew that she had to stay close to the hospital, as did she. It was the hospital that was keeping her alive.

After a few weeks of having me home and caring for her, my mother's spirits seemed to improve a little. She told me how proud she was of my degree mark, and now and then I even managed to make her laugh. We would go into the garden in the afternoon, and I would tell her stories about my life in Bangkok: how I used to walk into glass doors; how I got stuck on the escalators; and how I got crammed into those buses with the mad Thai drivers.

My mother smiled. She said Bangkok sounded like a mad house. After talking for a while I'd get up and make some lemonade. I'd squeeze fresh lemons into a jug, add a little sugar and a pinch of salt, and top it up with water. It was my mother's favourite treat. I'd take the jug out to her in the garden, and maybe a glass to my father in his office. Before bed I'd massage my mother's shoulders and stroke her back. But I had to be gentle with her, for she was as thin and delicate as a little bird. I'd light a candle in her room, tuck in the mosquito net and leave her to sleep.

In the morning I'd prepare a pot of water over the fire. I'd take her to the bathroom, and bathe her with warm water and a sponge. After that my mother would insist on me plucking out her grey hairs. We'd do it in the privacy of her room, and it would take an age. Often she would drop off to sleep.

As I plucked out the grey hairs I thought about when I had done this as a child. Back then, she had very few grey hairs amidst her thick black mane of hair. It was so hard to find any. When I did pull out a grey one I'd show it to her, and then pluck out a black one a few minutes later, and show her the same grey one again. Eventually, I'd tell her that all the grey ones were gone!

I'd been home about a month when it became time for the Karen University Students Group prize-giving in the refugee camps. In the past we had only been able to send the medals and the dictionaries to the camps. This time we wanted to do it in person. In fact, we wanted to do more than just the prize-giving. A number of the KUSG wanted to go across the border, to lead a fact-finding mission into the areas where the refugees were coming from.

Over the past few weeks I had learned from my father just how bad things were across the border in Burma. I was shocked. I had first fled my country when I was fourteen years old, and then again when I was sixteen. I was twenty-two years old now. Yet nothing seemed to have changed. Those three years in Bangkok had put a distance between me and the reality of what was happening across the border. But now that I was back it was all before me again.

I hadn't been in Burma for many years. Perhaps I should have been scared at the prospect of going back, but for some reason I wasn't. My father reassured me that the people we were visiting knew how to look after themselves and to avoid the State Peace and Development Council (SPDC) soldiers.

In a way I was surprised that my father supported me in my aim to go back into Burma. I had told him we were going to Papun district, and he knew how far inside that was. He knew we'd be dodging enemy soldiers the whole time and passing through great swathes of their territory. But he backed me in my desire to go, and in spite of the risks.

Some of my fellow students' parents banned them from going. They said it was too dangerous. As for my father, he dug out his mosquito net and his hammock – things that he used on his regular journeys inside – to lend to me. The hammock was particularly precious, he explained. He had carried it with him for a decade on his travels. He gave me his advice on which clothes to wear and which medicines to take.

And then he gave me his blessing for the journey ahead.

Chapter Twenty-four

———————

LAND OF EVIL

In the jargon of the aid industry the people we were going to visit were called Internally Displaced Persons (IDPs). They were people driven from their homes, with no permanent place to resettle. If they had crossed an international border they'd be called refugees, but as long as they were trapped inside Burma they were IDPs. And, mostly, they were ignored by the world. Our aim was to learn about the situation they faced on the ground, to see what they most needed, and how we might be able to help them.

There were thirteen students in the group going over the border, including my friends Khu Khu and Nightingale. And there was a Karen man called Hsa Pwe Moo – Full Star Life. He was originally from Papun district – the area we were going into – so he would know the lie of the land. He had also come from an OSI scholarship but at a different university, one where he had been able to study ecology. Our expedition fell under his informal leadership, for he knew the area well.

We sneaked across the border in a long-tail boat and began our journey on the Salween River. At last, we were heading back into my homeland. We would remain on the Salween for some four hours, and we knew that this would take us through several enemy checkpoints. These consisted of a hut flying a Burmese flag, each manned by a unit of soldiers. Full Star Life told the Karen boat driver not to stop for anything – and especially not those checkpoints. If they tried to flag us down, he was to outrun them.

We had a sixty-mile boat journey ahead of us, followed by two days walking in the jungle. In all it would be a hundred-mile round trip during which we could be in danger from the enemy. We could have chosen to head for an area where the Karen resistance fighters were still firmly in control, but that wouldn't have taken us to the places of most need. The aim of the mission was to get into those areas that the media and human rights workers were seldom able to visit.

The boat driver agreed to run the checkpoints, in spite of the risk of being chased or shot at or worse. He did so because he believed in the mission, and because we paid him well above the odds to do so. On the advice of Full Star Life we had all dressed like local villagers. The hope was that we would blend in with the rest of the traffic on this busy river. Our cameras and recording equipment were well hidden out of sight in the bottom of the boat.

We had been on the river for half an hour or so when we were waved in to a Thai checkpoint. The boat driver went to sign his name in the register. Other boats had pulled in to do the same. One was a huge craft that was being used to transport a herd of water buffalo, with a hut built on it for the boat driver to shelter in. I wanted to take a closer look at that big boat.

I hopped over a number of others, which were tied loosely together. Khu Khu came with me, as she was likewise curious. After inspecting the boatload of water buffalo, we returned the way we had come. I jumped from the last boat into our own, and Khu Khu went to follow me, but my leap was already forcing the two boats apart. Khu Khu landed with a splash behind me. Only her arms had made contact with our boat, and she was hanging on for dear life.

The sight of her head peering above the side of the boat and her thrashing legs was just too funny. Everyone cracked up laughing. But an instant later we heard Khu Khu's terrified cries: she couldn't swim! The boys raced to her rescue and hauled her out of the water. She lay in the bottom of the boat gasping for breath and dripping water. Khu Khu was in a huge grump with us all.

'I'm soaked and terrified,' she declared accusingly, 'and all you can do is laugh! I was that close to getting swept away, or forced beneath the boat, and all you could do was laugh!'

I was the worst of all, Khu Khu declared, for I had caused the problem in the first place by forcing the boats apart. She was most in a huff with me.

She glared at me accusingly. 'You! You caused this problem – but yours was the loudest laugh of all!'

I didn't know what to say. It's a fact of life that Karen people find other people's discomfort funny. If I had fallen in everyone would have laughed at me. The moment we realize that it is serious, however, all the fun goes out of the situation. Then everyone turns their mind to helping. We wrapped Khu Khu in the towels that we had with us, and tried to convince her that we really did care.

We set off again, and a half-hour later we approached our first Burmese Army checkpoint. We lowered our heads and stared at the bottom of the boat, no one saying a word, as our boat driver stuck to the far bank on dead slow. He hoped that the soldiers wouldn't even hear us. The tension was unbearable, but little by little we inched along the riverside, and then we were past the checkpoint.

The boat driver gunned the engine, and as we picked up speed the tension and fear evaporated. If we had made it through that checkpoint, there was no reason why we shouldn't do the same with those that lay ahead. We approached the second one to find the enemy soldiers stripped to their shorts and taking a bath in the river. It was such a stroke of luck. They were preoccupied with their washing, and none of them thought to stop us.

By the time we reached the third, the river had swollen to some 500 yards across. We sneaked past on the far side, where it was all but impossible for the enemy to intercept us. The soldiers stared over, but even if they did open fire it was an awfully long way to try to hit a long-tail boat bobbing about on the water. And they had no vessel that we could see in which they could chase after us.

A half-hour after that we reached a fourth checkpoint. We sighed with relief when we realized that this one was flying the Karen flag. Full Star Life announced that this marked our entry into safe Karen territory. We pulled in to the checkpoint, but there was worrying news. The Karen soldiers had just received a warning by radio that the enemy were massing to attack the next village. We were free to continue our journey, but we might run into fighting up ahead.

There was no question in any of our minds of not continuing. This is what we had come for – to witness for ourselves the plight of the villagers deep inside our land. A few minutes later a hilltop village came into view. We could see Karen soldiers leading women and children down to the river. A long-tail boat had pulled up at the riverbank, ready to ferry them to safety on the far side of the Salween. We altered course and came to a halt at the riverside.

We arrived at a scene of panic and chaos. Women had babies clutched in their arms and bundles of possessions balanced on their heads. Mothers turned to their children and cried for them to run faster and to keep up. Little children were crying and stumbling as they tried to reach the river. Karen soldiers were passing children into the waiting boat and helping the mothers aboard with their heavy loads.

It broke my heart to see this. It was exactly the same as had happened to me all those years ago. I had felt scared earlier, but now fear turned into anger. I felt helpless. What could we do for these terrified families? I didn't yet know how, but I felt determined to stop this happening.

Part of me wanted to do as my mother had done, and pick up a gun and fight. But at the same time I knew the power of bearing witness, and communicating that to the outside world. I knew in myself I could achieve more that way than ever I could by becoming a resistance fighter. But the desire to fight and to kill those who were doing this to my people was overwhelming.

I realized that I recognized one of the Karen soldiers from somewhere. His name was Saw Lah Doh – Mr Big Moon. I grabbed him by the arm, and I could tell that he knew me right away. As hurriedly as I could I explained why we had come.

'Great!' he enthused. 'It's great what you're doing. Thank you for coming to witness this. You must go and tell the world what is happening to our people, right here and right now.'

I watched Saw Lah Doh as he put his radio to his ear to listen to an incoming message. He looked stressed and exhausted beyond words. The three years since I had last seen him seemed to have aged him a dozen or more. I heard him issue various instructions. He was ordering his men to round up the villagers and bring them to the riverside, whilst other units protected the beachhead from the advancing enemy. He was using his soldiers to buy the villagers time to escape, which had been the main task of the KNLA for many years now.

He turned away from his radio, and his eyes met mine. 'You must go. There's no time to lose. The enemy are very close. It's time to leave.'

We said our farewells. 'You're doing great things,' I told him. 'You are my hero, Saw Lah Doh. I'll keep you in my thoughts.'

And then we were hurrying down to the riverside and our boat. The boat driver gunned the engine, set the prow upstream and we thundered onwards into Burma.

As we powered ahead I was lost in my thoughts. It was six or more years since I had last been in Karen lands, but what, if anything, had changed? Here I was again and the killing and the horror and the darkness continued. I couldn't believe that my people still weren't being allowed to live in peace.

We pressed on through the gathering darkness. Eventually we arrived at another Karen village, where people made us welcome as best they could. I was so exhausted from the day's events that I quickly fell asleep.

We were awake at five o'clock the following morning. We had to cook food and prepare for the long day's journey ahead. It was too early for me to eat, and I decided to carry my rice breakfast with me.

We began the next stage of our journey by scaling a high mountain, and I quickly realized that I'd forgotten how to walk in the jungle. After three years of life as a city girl I was unfit and unsteady on my legs. I had to wrap a towel around my neck to soak up the sweat, which was pouring off me. In my pack I only had some rice, water and extra clothes, but it felt like a dead weight on my back. Luckily, one of the male students offered to carry it for me, and I accepted.

By mid-morning I was so hungry that I had to stop and eat my rice breakfast. We had two Karen resistance fighters with us who were acting as our guides. We all knew that they weren't there as a protection force. Two soldiers would not be able to defend us. All they would be able to do was try to show us where to run if we came under attack.

At first we chatted and admired the beautiful forest. Full Star Life pulled out a little book that he carried with him, so he could identify the plants and birds. But as we drew closer to a Burmese Army post, the resistance fighters told us to keep quiet. We were on silent routine now, and we had to walk in single file with at least a yard or so between us, so as not to present an easy target to the enemy. We were warned not to stray from the path, in case there were landmines.

We crept past that army post soundlessly. Every now and then the resistance fighters signalled for us to stop and crouch down in the undergrowth. We would remain like that for a minute or more as they listened out for danger, and then we would get the signal to move quietly forwards. We pressed ahead fearfully, casting furtive glances into the shadows beside the path.

Once we were over the mountain summit we entered a secret and incredibly beautiful land. It was a lost world of tall forests and plunging mountains. Few people lived here now, for most had been hounded out by the enemy. We were going to visit some of the stubborn few who remained. At the foot of the mountain we stopped to refill our water bottles from a sparkling stream. One of the male students climbed a tree and threw down the fruit, which had a sour-sweet flavour and was hugely refreshing.

That night we stayed in a tiny village deep in the jungle. Again, we were made welcome. They had so little but they shared everything with us. We had brought a little food with us but they insisted on feeding us themselves. It was to be the same everywhere we went.

The next morning I asked the lady of the house I was staying in if I could use the loo. She told me to use 'the toilet by the side of the hill', which was a euphemism for using the bush.

Nightingale came with me, and as we walked out of the village we realized there was a herd of pigs coming after us. They were squealing excitedly as if they knew what was coming. We left the houses behind and headed for a patch of thick bush. Nightingale gathered a couple of stout sticks, and as we crouched down and went about our business we had to fight off the pigs from all directions.

On the count of three Nightingale said we should finish and run, which is exactly what we did. By the time we made it back into the village we were laughing fit to burst. One of the other students asked us where the toilet was, and we told them that all they had to do was follow the pigs. But beneath the humour we were starting to realize the poverty and hardship that were the daily life of our people.

On the evening of the third day we reached our destination, Village Three. The following morning there was a celebration in the village, and we were all invited. But the celebratory feast turned out to be pork! After my experience with the 'toilet beside the hill' I had to force myself to eat it. Perhaps I really had become a city girl!

The villagers told us their story. Some months back their village had been attacked for the fourth time. The Burmese Army had rampaged through it, burning down many of the huts. The villagers had fled into the jungle, where they had remained until the danger was past. Each time there was an attack they rebuilt their homes, but no one knew how long it would be before the enemy returned and attacked again.

It was the same story for most Karen villages around here. Recently, the neighbouring settlement had been burned down, and the villagers there had to rebuild their homes and their lives. Village Three was special, in that it did have a school. Each time it was attacked they rebuilt the school anew. But how could you possibly rebuild your school *four times*, I wondered. And how could you find the strength to do so never knowing when it was next going to be burned to the ground?

All the school consisted of was a bamboo frame and a leaf roof. There was an old, battered blackboard and a couple of dog-eared textbooks. Children came from miles around to attend lessons. The teachers had little more than a stubborn determination to teach, and the students an insatiable hunger to learn.

We organized a workshop at the school, in which we sang and play-acted and did our best to lift the children's spirits. Then we asked them to share with us some of their stories. The happy atmosphere that had resulted from our 'show' didn't last long. Just about every child had survived an attack on his or her village, some several times over.

There were dozens of orphans, and even more who had lost one or more family members. It was impossible for them to hide their trauma. Listening to their tiny, faint voices telling their stories of horror, one after another after another, really broke my heart.

The headmaster told us that he never expected to complete a whole school year, for the enemy always found the school and destroyed it. Often, the soldiers planted landmines. If anyone ventured back into the village – to try to retrieve a blackboard maybe, or some textbooks that had survived the burning – they risked getting their legs blown off by a mine.

He chose a handful of students to talk to us privately. One was a 10-year-old boy who came from a poor farming family. His family's supply of rice was exhausted, and they were reduced to eating the green shoots of the rice plants growing in the fields. Sometimes he went without food altogether, and the pain of the hunger gnawing at his stomach was unbearable. His family were charged a nominal school fee of 5 Thai Baht, or less than 10p, a year. But this coming year his parents would struggle to pay even that.

As I listened to his story, I felt myself close to tears. He spoke in a soft, quiet voice, and without a hint of self-pity. And what was most amazing was that there wasn't a trace of hatred or anger in his words. Instead, he spoke matter-of-factly, almost as if there was nothing exceptional about his story. Life had always been thus for him and his family. Wasn't this what happened to every child?

And the tragedy was that here in Papun district his was every child's life. His story was normal. *Normal.*

Here, every child lived a life like his, or worse.

Chapter Twenty-five

THE AWAKENING

A few days later we set off on a triangular walk that would take us back to our starting point on the Salween. We prepared to leave in the bitter cold of dawn. The villagers had few clothes or blankets, and only the heat of the fire to keep them warm. They couldn't afford candles or oil lamps, and so they lived in darkness until the sun lit their world.

On the march through the forested mountains from one village to the next we came across a family in the middle of nowhere. They had fled from a village further inside Burma, which had been attacked and burned down by the enemy. They had been on the move for weeks now, spending each night in a different makeshift shelter.

The poor, frightened mother gestured to her two little girls – indistinct bundles wrapped in rags. One was on her lap, the other lying on a bed made of leaves. She explained how one had the high fever typical of malaria, and the other had chronic diarrhoea, which was most likely cholera. They had no medicine and no means of getting any treatment, other than reaching a refugee camp in Thailand.

At the pace they were able to move, carrying their meagre possessions and their dying children, that was weeks away. In the interim, they were terrified of being caught by the enemy. It was unspoken, but I read the pleading in the mother's eyes: would they make it before one or both of her little girls died?

I gave them all the medicines I had. My friends and I pooled our money so we could give them something more. It was only 100 Thai Baht – £1.50 – but for them it was a fortune. And we gave them what clothing we could spare.

They were so poor and destitute that even the clothes they stood up in were in shreds. The man of the family had tried to maintain his dignity whilst his wife told us her heartbreaking story, all the while holding up a pair of threadbare shorts with one hand. We left them building a temporary shelter next to a little stream. I glanced back once and saw the mother squatting by the water. In the shadows of the forest she produced a withered breast and tried to get her youngest to feed – the little girl who was dying of cholera.

I felt something change within me then. I felt tears pouring down my face. I knew that this was a turning point. I couldn't go back to the good life and work for Telecomasia, not when my people were suffering and dying like this – like animals hunted in the jungle, bereft of all dignity and comfort. It was this family's bitter tragedy that turned my mind away from a soft, moneyed and easy future and brought me back to my people, to the struggle, to the resistance.

There was no holding back in the face of such suffering. And there was no end to the need. The next village was full of families in similar circumstances to the one we had just left. I visited one hut and the need just screamed out at me. They had nothing. *Nothing.* No pots and pans; no blankets; precious little to eat; no medicines (of course); and no school for their children. Their little children were sickly and ill-fed. Their eyes had a listless, hollow look. How could they live? I wondered. How could they survive this?

Their plight so touched my heart that I just wanted to give everything away. I wanted to give something to each of them, just to ease their pain a little. But there were hundreds of families like this – maybe 300 in this village alone. Each had the same chilling story of running from the Burmese Army, of hiding in the jungle, of darkness and terror. The farmers told us about the hunger. The Burmese Army had destroyed all their food stores.

To the family whose hut I visited I gave away my father's hammock. It was one of the last possessions I had remaining, and I figured I could do without it. It was all so hopeless here. In the refugee camps at least we had the basic requirements to sustain life: food rations, clean water, shelter, a little medical care. Here there was nothing. They died from hunger, from simple, curable diseases, or from the bullets and bayonets of the soldiers who hunted them.

Occasionally, a team of backpack medics might come through this area. But the last one had been a year ago and they didn't expect another one any time soon. The villagers had thought at first that we were a backpack relief team. They were so disappointed when they discovered that we weren't and that we'd only come to *record information*. Of course, they didn't tell us as much but we knew it for sure, for we could read it in the hopelessness in their eyes.

There was one lady I shall never forget. She was a young mother with three small children. She was trying to build a life for her family in the midst of such hopelessness and despair. She was still beautiful, but because she had to work so hard she was ageing fast, her skin cracking in the sun. I tried to imagine for one moment being her, having her life, bringing up her family. But I couldn't visualize what it would be like. I couldn't even begin to comprehend living a life like that.

'My husband spends most of his time on the farm,' she told me. 'In the rainy season we feel a little more secure. But come the dry season, we live in fear every minute of the day.'

I took her hand and held it tightly in my own. She lived a life in daily fear of the Burmese soldiers coming. What could I say?

'We really need your help,' she continued. 'Please do something about the suffering here. Go and tell the world.'

I cannot forget that woman and what she told us. She was speaking from the heart, and her words are for ever burned into my own heart.

Once again I thought of the United Nations and how they had failed us. Where were they? I knew they were operating in Burma. But not here. Here the need was so desperate. Surely they should be delivering aid to those who needed it. The regime told the United Nations they could not come here, and they just accepted that. But the denial of aid to these people was part of the ethnic cleansing policy, and as effective at killing them as a bullet.

We set off for the final leg of our journey – the return to the Salween River. On the way we came across yet more families fleeing in destitution and fear, trying to make a break for Thailand. Each was like a blow to my heart. And with each I felt my anger and the spirit of resistance rising within me.

Before reaching the Salween we had to scale a high mountain. It would be three hours up and two down, and by now we knew that the Burmese Army were after us. We started the climb in the dark. A handful of Karen resistance fighters scouted the way ahead, searching for the enemy. We reached the summit without incident, but I was dripping with sweat, my legs shaking with exhaustion.

We began our descent, keen to reach the comparative safety of the Salween. But the scouts reported that they had spotted Burmese troops to the rear, and so they urged us to hurry. Without warning we blundered into a towering wall of flame. It completely blocked our path. A Karen farmer had set alight a patch of dry, cleared forest to prepare an area to plant rice.

With the enemy at our backs we had no choice but to push on through the burning, smoking heat, dodging the flames. We probed ahead, Full Star Life and some of the others beating a path through the withering heat. Halfway across the flaming hillside we realized there was no choice but to make a dash for the far side. If we delayed, we knew we would collapse from the suffocating fumes. I dashed ahead with the rest, arms flailing at the walls of smoke and sparks.

We reached the far side and collapsed on to the ground. From there we stumbled and staggered the final few miles to the foot of the mountain. I had never felt so relieved to see the wide expanse of the Salween River stretching away before us. From here the village at which we had commenced our journey was only a short stroll away. It had lasted less than a fortnight, but to me it had felt like a lifetime. It had been a descent into a living hell, for which none of us had been prepared.

I knew that the horrific memories of that journey would live with me for ever, and I made a solemn vow to myself: I would return to this place, to this land of suffering, and when I did return it would be with the ability truly to help. I didn't know how yet. I didn't know when. But I knew that I had to do this. My eyes had been opened. This journey had been my awakening.

The boat ride back to Thailand was a repeat of the journey in. We sneaked past the first few checkpoints without incident, but then we approached another and spotted soldiers waving us down. We expected the boat driver to gun his engine and force a way through on the far side. But instead he slowed his engine, and turned the prow of the long-tail in towards the shore where the soldiers stood waiting.

I heard Full Star Life let out a strangled hiss of alarm, but by then it was too late – we were too close to the shore, and within easy range of their guns. I was terrified. What on earth was going on? Full Star Life issued some hurried instructions. If anything happened, we were to jump into the river and swim for our lives. Whatever else, we mustn't let ourselves be captured.

There was a soft crunch as the boat hit the riverbank. Not a word was spoken as we waited in trepidation for whatever was coming. The nearest soldier spoke to the boat driver. They needed a lift down river. They came on board and sat on the prow of the craft, facing backwards – *towards us* – and with their assault rifles clutched between their knees. The boat driver backed the craft out into the river, and we set off downstream.

The two soldiers sat there, their eyes expressionless and their bush hats buffeted by the boat's slipstream. Surely it was only a matter of time before they started to question us. Whilst we out-numbered them, they were armed and we were not. Fear gnawed at me, as I tried to avoid looking in their direction or showing any interest. Maybe if we ignored them they would just go away?

All of a sudden Full Star Life turned to face me and burst out laughing. What on earth was he doing? I wondered. Why was he drawing attention to us like this? Laughing in the face of the Burmese soldiers! Surely he of all people should know better.

'Why're you looking so worried?' he asked, as he tried to con-tain his laughter. 'Check out their sleeve badges. They're ABSDF. *ABSDF*. That's all!'

The ABSDF is the All Burma Students Democratic Front – a group of students who took up arms after the 8/8/88 uprisings. They were Burmese soldiers all right, but they were *on our side* – they were part of the resistance. In our unreasoning fear we'd missed all of the obvious signs, like the ABSDF flashes – a yellow fighting peacock and white star over a red background – on their sleeves. They shared the same struggle as us, to liberate our suf-fering land.

The two ABSDF soldiers sat there chatting away in Burmese, completely oblivious to how our fear had transformed itself into relief and joy. As they were sitting right on the prow of the boat, our words would be drowned out by the buffeting wind and the roar of the engine. I'm sure they didn't have the slightest clue as to how terrified we had been of them!

We reached the Thai border without further incident. It was then that we heard that the SPDC's soldiers had followed in our wake, and that people were running and hiding in the jungle behind us. The soldiers had come hunting us, because they didn't want anyone to do as we had done – to witness the horrors that they were perpetrating in my homeland. And so I left my country as I had always done, being hunted by the enemy.

When I got home I told my parents and Say Say everything that I had seen and experienced across the border. They were hardly surprised. That was the daily reality of life beyond the border, they said, as it had been for many years. Why would it ever have changed?

But when I told my father about giving away his hammock he was really annoyed. He'd had that hammock for ten years, and never lost it or given it away. I tried telling him how I had been compelled to give everything away in the face of so much suffering.

And then I had to confess that I'd also given away his blanket and all the medicines that he'd loaned me!

Chapter Twenty-six

CHILDREN OF DARKNESS

After my return from that journey I faced a major life decision. I had been offered a place at Bradford University, studying for a Master of Arts in marketing. I would have to find my own funds, but there was a place open for me. At the same time my mother's health was deteriorating fast, and I knew that I couldn't leave her. I moved in with her and my father, in the house in Mae Sot, and resigned myself to pursuing my studies at some future date, if at all.

My parents had two adopted boys living with them. There was nothing so unusual about that: they had spent their lives taking in the children of suffering. But these two were very different: they were ex-child soldiers. Each had been seized when he was just eleven years old. One had been on his way to the cinema when he was taken from the street and bundled into a military vehicle. And that had marked the end of his childhood.

In the Burmese Army they were given barely any training before being sent to the front line. They were made to carry weapons that were as tall as they were. Anyone who refused to fight was threatened with being shot, and when they weren't fighting they were used as forced labour. They were given amphetamines and other drugs to raise their aggression levels, and they were ordered to rape and kill ethnic women – Karen, Shan and others – wherever they found them.

One of the boys had seen soldiers doing this. He had heard the Karen women crying desperately: 'Please help me! Please help me!' The Burmese Army has the greatest number of child soldiers of any military in the world. There were many child soldiers in the boys' unit. Some had tried to run away, but they blundered into the minefields that surrounded the camp, or they were shot by the sentries.

One day the two boys had decided to try to escape. They had sneaked out of camp and found their way across the jungle to a Karen military base. Eventually, the Karen soldiers had managed to get them to my father.

My father had taken them in and given them a home in his. He treated them like his own grandchildren, and they in turn called him 'grandfather'. They were around fifteen years old by now, and my father knew there were dangers in taking such ex-child soldiers into his home. He knew there was a plot by the enemy to assassinate him, although he never talked about it to us. And friends had warned him that the Burmese intelligence services might try to use the boys against him.

But he also knew what danger they would be in if they were forced to return to Burma. As most children would, they would try to find their families, and they were sure to get picked up by the police or the intelligence services. They would be tortured into revealing their story – how they had escaped, who had helped them – and likely press-ganged back into the army. He felt that they had suffered more than enough, and so he welcomed them into his home.

Normally, we would all eat breakfast together as one big family. But one morning the two boys were nowhere to be seen. My father was worried, and together we set out to search the town, but we could find them nowhere. My father was convinced that they had left to try to find a way back into Burma and to their families. My father had called them his 'grandchildren', but the pull of their real families had been too much to resist.

Two weeks later my father had a telephone call. It was one of the two boys.

He said: 'Grandfather, I've come back. I'm sorry I ran away. Will you let me come to stay with you again?'

'Of course,' my father replied without hesitation. 'You know you're welcome.'

Yet my father was worried. He suspected that the Burmese intelligence had picked the boy up and sent him back into Thailand to cause trouble. Why else would he have returned? He would either still be on the road searching for his family, or if he had been caught he would have been held as a 'deserter'. When the boy arrived at home my father welcomed him in as if nothing had happened. He didn't ask a single question, or make any accusations. He just welcomed him as a grandfather would his grandson.

Three days later the boy sat down in front of my father and confessed all that had happened. Just as my father had suspected, he and the other boy had crossed over the border to try to find their families. But in no time they had been picked up by the Burmese intelligence. They had been taken into separate interrogation rooms, but each could hear the other cry out as the beatings began.

The interrogators had pulled out two photo albums. First they had shown the boy lots and lots of pictures of my father: in his car around Mae Sot, speaking at official functions. Then they had shown him the second album full of photos of . . . *me*. They showed close-ups of me in my father's car, plus me on the streets of Mae Sot.

The interrogators asked the boy if he knew me. He told them he did not. So they beat him around the head. Did he know who

271

I was? they asked. He confessed that he had seen me at my father's house. They asked him again who I was. He refused to answer, and so they pulled out a set of crocodile clips connected to the electricity and attached them to his bare arm.

They asked him again – *did he know who I was?* If he refused to answer they would shock him. He refused to speak, and so they turned on the power. The boy confessed to my father that the electric shock was such a horrible, unbearable agony that he couldn't remain silent any more. Tearfully, he recounted how he had told them that I was my father's daughter, and that I was staying in his house.

They explained that they wanted us both 'dealt with'. They offered the boy an ultimatum: he could either return to Thailand to assassinate my father, or go to prison for deserting the army. He wasn't just to deal with my father; he was to kill me, too. If he refused to do the killing, they would not only imprison him, they would also ensure that his family was made to suffer.

When faced with the threat to his family, the boy made his decision: he would return to Thailand to kill us. They offered him a bayonet or a pistol with which to do the killing. He refused to take the pistol. It was too obvious, and if he was stopped by the Thai police he would be in serious trouble. The knife he might just get away with. And so the Burmese intelligence officers drove him back across the border into Mae Sot.

Before dispatching him, they had instructed him to kill my father over breakfast, when the two of them normally ate together. He was to do so by driving the bayonet up under my father's ribcage and into his heart. Then he was to kill me. If he couldn't kill me, he was to rape me. And if he couldn't manage to kill my father he was to rape me and leave me alive. I was my father's 'heart', they told him. If I was raped then my father's heart would break, which would be almost as good as killing him.

They had dropped the boy in the centre of Mae Sot. They had shown him where they would be hiding and observing his collection by my father. And then they had got the boy to make the phone call. But he had been unable to carry his terrible mission through. He loved my father dearly for helping him and giving him a home.

My father knew that there was only one way to treat the boy now, and that was with compassion. As he had failed in his mission the Burmese intelligence would want their revenge on either him or his family, or both. In his time my father had actually helped dozens of ex-child soldiers. Nothing that this boy had told my father had come as a shock to him, apart from the revelations about the plot to kill his daughter – *me*.

By now my father was the Secretary-General of the Karen National Union – which meant he was highly placed in the resistance. And, of course, his position made him an obvious target. But his family? It had never crossed my mind that the junta would have us in their sights. Yet what the boy had told us made perfect sense. If they managed to kill one of us – Bwa Bwa, Slone, Say Say or me – then it would cause my father untold pain. And in doing so they hoped to break him.

Over the coming months my mother's health worsened. In the spring of 2004 she was again admitted into Mae Sot hospital, where the doctors told us she had both liver and heart problems. They made it clear that she had to remain in hospital. She lay there for a month with a tank of oxygen by her side. She developed bedsores on her back, and once again her body became horribly swollen. And every waking hour she was in so much pain.

Each night I slept in her hospital room, on a roll-up mattress that I carried with me. I'd spend half the night massaging her back, to try to relieve the pain of the bedsores. As I did she'd tell me stories of her time as a Karen soldier in the jungle. She told me how she had felt guilty at not being able to spend time with and look after her parents in their old age. I told her not to worry. Even though she had been unable to do so, she should be proud that she had achieved so much in her life. And I reassured her that I and my sister and brothers would look after her.

Sometimes, Say Say or friends would visit, and even stay the night at the hospital. My father came every day, but couldn't stay overnight because of the threats to his life. The nurses kept telling my mother to eat and to take her medicine, but she could hardly keep anything down. She tried to do as they said, and I could see that she didn't want to die. She was putting so much effort into trying to live. But seeing her like this – racked by pain and suffering – made me feel so torn up inside.

Eventually a nurse put a tube into her nose to feed her food and medicine directly. My mother hated it, and she kept pulling it out. I tried to explain to her how important it was, but sometimes my mother was unconscious and she pulled it out without realizing. The doctors put drips into her arms, and then her legs as well.

Finally, one of them asked to have a private word. 'I don't know quite how to tell you this, but your mother is very ill now. There is no more treatment that we can give her. If there are family members who need to see her . . . you should call them home.'

The doctor told me that my mother was alive only because of the drips and the oxygen mask – her body had already 'died'. On hearing this I felt as if my heart were breaking. I went outside the hospital and I cried.

I called Slone, who was away studying in Bangkok on an OSI scholarship, and I called Bwa Bwa in England. They both said they would drop everything and come. I told my mother that Bwa Bwa and Slone were coming to see her soon and to hold on.

I could tell that she was happy at the news, but she was too weak to speak. I asked the doctor if he would keep her alive long enough for her children to see her. He agreed to give her two more weeks. But after that there was nothing more they could do; the life support machines would have to be switched off. Then he gave me a document to sign, giving him clearance to turn them off so my mother could die.

I talked to everyone, and we decided it was the right decision to let her go. Even so, my father and Bwa Bwa couldn't bring themselves to sign the consent form. My father was in tears, for losing my mother was such a blow. Neither he nor Bwa Bwa had it in them to sign her life away. Eventually, it was Say Say and I who signed the form to let our mother die.

Now my mother – who had fought and survived so many battles – had only days left to live. I told her to be strong and to hold on for my sister and little brother, but I knew that she was leaving us. Her mind was still working, but only just. She was unconscious a lot of the time, but I knew she was holding on so my sister and little brother could get to see her.

Four days before they turned off the life support machines Slone made it back to see her. My mother smiled her love at him, but she was too weak to speak. And two days later, Bwa Bwa made it to my mother's bedside.

She called out to my mother, gently – 'Mummy, Mummy – it's me.'

My mother opened her eyes and saw my sister. She knew that she had come.

'I've come back to be with you,' Bwa Bwa whispered. 'So don't worry. Don't worry.'

My mother just smiled and nodded.

They turned off the life support machines on the 31 July 2004. My brothers held her hands as she faded before our very eyes. Just before she breathed her last breath she called out a name: 'Say Say!' It was Say Say, her adopted child who had stayed with her all through the time when she was really ill, when the rest of us had run off to chase our dreams.

We held the funeral in a Buddhist monastery on the Thai–Burma border. Buddhist monks prayed in the morning and Christian priests in the afternoon. The way animists mark a loved one's passage into the spirit world is by calling out a message: 'You do not belong to the human world any more, so you must now find your own way.' And this is what was done for my mother.

What amazed me about her funeral was the massive crowd of mourners that gathered to pay their last respects. Thousands turned up. Mostly they were the Karen refugees, orphans, illegal immigrants and the dispossessed – those that my mother and father had spent their lives trying to help. They had come to mourn her passing.

Even though she had been suffering, I never wanted to lose my mother. Now she was dead I felt guilty that I hadn't spent enough time with her. I hadn't had the chance to return all the love that she had given me. The last few years of her life had been ones of suffering, poverty, indignity and illness. Even in her old age her life had remained so tough. I felt as if I never had the chance to try to make her well and her life an easy and happy one.

Two weeks after my mother's death we celebrated Karen Martyrs Day. It takes place on 12 August each year and is a day for remembering all those who have died during the decades of resistance. As a family we went to the Moei River with my mother's ashes. We scattered them under a spreading tree and into the river itself.

Animists believe that a person's spirit endures in the world after their death. We knew that my mother's spirit would be happy residing in such a beautiful place – by the banks of the Moei, the river she loved so much.

The same month that we scattered my mother's ashes Slone won a scholarship with the World University Service of Canada. He would leave for Canada at the same time that Bwa Bwa returned to the United Kingdom. As for me, I had accepted an offer to study for an MA at the University of East Anglia in the United Kingdom.

However, with Bwa Bwa and Slone already leaving the country, I faced a quandary. I knew that my father needed me to stay longer, to help him cope with his loss. But if I didn't get to the University of East Anglia by September – the start date of my course – I would miss my chance.

So I made up my mind to take up that offer and head for the United Kingdom.

Chapter Twenty-seven

LONDON WITH BWA BWA

Two weeks later I found myself in Bwa Bwa's tiny London apartment. My journey from Bangkok to London had been far from easy. I had travelled to the United Kingdom on false papers, the only way for a stateless 'non-person' like me to do so. But it is part of my story the details of which have to remain untold, for many reasons – not least to protect those who helped me.

Bwa Bwa was working in a pharmacy to help pay her way through college. That first day she went off to work. I really fancied a shower after my journey, but for the life of me I couldn't get the complicated tap-contraption to turn on or remain at the right temperature. And then I wanted a cup of tea, and the kettle proved beyond me. In Thailand we had boiled water over an electric ring.

When Bwa Bwa got home she had a good laugh at me – the girl fresh from the jungle! The following day I told myself I would do better. I was determined to work the washing machine. I put in my dirty clothes, twisted some dials and pushed some buttons and hoped for the best. There was a satisfying hum, followed by the hiss of incoming water, and the drum started to turn. It seemed to be working.

An hour later it stopped making its noises and I opened the door. But when I reached in the first item came out baby-sized. I had shrunk and ruined most of my wardrobe. This time when Bwa Bwa came home from work she really did have a good laugh at me. As she inspected each of my tiny items of clothing you'd have thought she had never seen anything so funny before.

When she'd recovered from her merriment she explained that I had pressed the button for the very high temperature setting. She made up for laughing at me by giving me some of her own clothes to wear. Otherwise, I would have had nothing. Bwa Bwa put me on a train for Norwich. She had arranged for a Burmese friend to meet me the other end and see me safely to my university accommodation.

I had chosen to do an MA in Politics and Development, a subject that was truly close to my heart. I wanted to understand what was happening in my country and take my skills home to help my people – like those I had met on my recent journey into Papun district. And I wanted to learn to communicate to the world the horror, as that young mother I had met on that trip had asked me to.

I had a room in the university halls of residence. It was small, but clean and neat, and it looked out over a beautiful green lawn running down to a lake. I had a little bed, a sink and a desk, which I positioned to maximize the wonderful view. There was also a shared bathroom and a shared kitchen.

Things were completely different here, as opposed to how they had been at college in Bangkok. I could talk openly about the story of my life: fleeing my village; the refugee camps; the ongoing crisis and the life of those affected by it. I had even brought with me newspaper articles and reports about the crisis in Burma, and I was determined to talk to as many of the students as I could about it.

From the very start of the course I loved my chosen subject. One module was called 'Government, Democracy and Development'. Naturally, I chose to study my own country, Burma. I learned the basic tenets of good governance: transparency; accountability; the rule of law; the will of the people (one person one vote); providing the means of survival (clean drinking water, healthcare, education); respect for human rights and religious freedom; and freedom of expression.

It sounds strange, but it was not until I escaped from Burma and came to the United Kingdom that I actually had the chance to learn about the truth of what was happening in my own country. In Burma all news is controlled by the regime. Education is limited, there is no freedom of speech; even poets and comedians get jailed if they say something negative about the government. In ethnic areas such as I came from we are also cut off from news, not by a government, but by poverty and geography.

Learning about the history of my country, the full scale of the human rights abuses and the role of the international community was a revelation to me.

I learned about how they used torture in Burma's jails. The iron rod rubbed up and down on shins until the skin and flesh were worn off and the rod scraped on bone. I learned how rape was used as a deliberate policy by the regime, even against girls as young as five.

I learned about Aung San Suu Kyi, leader of the democracy movement, who had spent so many years under house arrest. I learned of the cruelty of the regime in not allowing her English husband to visit her for one last time before he died of cancer.

The human rights abuses I had witnessed myself were just a fraction of what was going on countrywide.

On my course we had broken into groups of four to study different aspects of Burma more closely. In my group was a Canadian man called Hugh, a German called Mike and a girl from Cyprus called Rana, who was as beautiful as Collective Love Flower.

We looked at the role of the international community in my country. What we learned left me shocked and angry. There had been a lot of talk about sanctions against Burma, but, in fact, British, European and other companies had been doing business with the Generals for years. As the Burmese Army attacked my village, a British trade delegation dined in Rangoon with the regime that ordered the slaughter of my people. And while Britain was now a strong critic of the regime, many other countries were still doing business with the Generals.

We could see how the increase in trade and investment had enabled the Generals to buy more weapons and double the size of the army. But Burma had no external enemies. Those soldiers were for attacking people like me.

I was disgusted with the European Union and United Nations for failing to act. How could there not even be a UN arms embargo against my country? I wished all the people in Burma had the chance to discover the truth, as I had. It was crazy that I had to be thousands of miles from my country before having the freedom and opportunity to learn of it.

Again, two scholarships were paying for my studies. One was from Prospect Burma, the other from the Burma Educational Scholarship Trust. But they weren't enough to cover all of my fees and my living expenses.

Bwa Bwa suggested I should try to find work waitressing in a Thai restaurant. So I went around the nearby city of Norwich asking at all the Thai restaurants if they had any work. Several of the restaurant managers took my phone number, and said they would call if they had any need of me. The very next day I had a phone call.

I went for an interview at a restaurant called Sugar Hut. The manager asked if I had worked as a waitress before. I told him I had not, but that I was willing to learn. I told him I would make a good waitress, because I liked talking to people. He said he'd give me a try. First, I had to be taught how to open a bottle of wine, for I had never done so before. I had to learn how to pour it properly, so that the diner could taste it and declare it good to drink.

That first evening I tried to open a bottle of wine, but I managed to knock it over and break a wine glass. I was so embarrassed. But the customers were really nice to me, and the restaurant owner told me there was no need to apologize so much, for everyone makes mistakes. I had to try to memorize the wine list, but I couldn't even pronounce most of the names. But I liked talking and joking with the customers, and they were so forgiving of my mistakes, and so generous with their tips!

I experienced a wholly different learning style at the university. It was all about challenging ourselves, about debate and questioning others. This didn't come naturally to me. It was so much more mature and critical and incisive. It was the opposite to how I had been taught in Karen schools. Luckily, my friends on my course were supportive and they helped me pull through.

For Mike, Hugh and Rana it was a unique experience to be studying a country together with a victim of that nation's oppression. Prior to this they had known next to nothing about Burma. None of them even knew who the Karen were, let alone about the suffering of my people. I had to explain it all to them starting from scratch. I took them through the process of learning about the destruction and enslavement of my country, and I could see how it shocked them.

It was ten months into my MA course when Bwa Bwa called me and invited me to go to a demonstration in London. On 19 June 2005 people would gather to celebrate the birthday of Aung San Suu Kyi, the leader of the National League for Democracy. A Burmese man called Dr Win Naing, one of the pro-democracy leaders in exile in London, had asked Bwa Bwa to attend the demonstration to mark her birthday. And he had asked Bwa Bwa to bring me along.

I was really excited at the idea of going. I had no idea what a demonstration was exactly. I'd never been on one, and all I could imagine was that it had to be something similar to the 1988 uprising that had taken place on the streets of Rangoon. I imagined students and monks marching the streets of London calling for an end to the dictatorship. I knew we were gathering outside the Burmese Embassy in London, but what were we going to do there? And how would the British police react? In Burma, they would shoot and beat such protesters.

On the morning of 19 June I headed for London. My sister had given me very specific instructions for the journey. At Norwich station I would board a train for London, and I was not to get off again until it reached London Liverpool Street station. A couple of minutes before my train was due, a train pulled into the station. I got on board and settled down for the journey. Not long after that I had a call on my mobile phone. It was Bwa Bwa.

'Hi. I'm on the train,' I announced happily.

'But you can't be! Your train doesn't arrive for another few minutes!'

'Don't worry, I'm on the train. I'm on the one that departed from the London platform.'

'There's no such thing as a "London platform". All kinds of trains go from the same platform. You'd better check you're on the right one, Zoya. Just ask someone where it is going.'

I turned to an elderly man sitting next to me. 'Excuse me, d'you know where this train is going?'

'I do. Its final destination is Peterborough. Why? Where are you trying to get to, young lady?'

'Oh dear. London. I thought it was the London train.'

I told Bwa Bwa the bad news. 'It's going to somewhere called Peterborough. What should I do?'

'Find the train guard and ask him how you can get to London.'

The man sitting next to me pointed me in the direction of the guard. As I hurried off to find him I wondered how I could have messed up. I had no idea that trains went from one platform to many different places. I found the guard in his smart uniform, and he was very helpful. He told me to get off at the next station and wait for the very next train. Check the displays to make sure it was for London, and if it was then I should jump aboard.

A couple of hours later I was in London. I made my way to a

place called 'Whitehall', by asking directions from people along the way. There I found a crowd some several hundred strong, with banners displaying Aung San Suu Kyi's photo. Bwa Bwa had been unable to get away from work, so Dr Win Naing explained what was happening. We were on the pavement just across from the Prime Minister Tony Blair's house – No. 10 Downing Street.

'Wow,' I thought to myself, 'we are making a show of force right outside the British Prime Minister's house!'

It struck me as being a funny little place for Prime Minister Tony Blair to live. I had seen images of the White House on TV, and that was a suitably grand and impressive residence for the US President. But here the Prime Minister seemed to live in a house like any other, in a row of similar houses. I took out my mobile and dialled my father's number, to see if I could reach him in Thailand.

'Pah! Pah!' I cried, just as soon as he answered. 'You're never going to believe this, but I'm at a demo for Aung San Suu Kyi's birthday, and we're trying to tell Tony Blair all about the problems in Burma! We're right outside his house!'

'My Little Daughter!' my father exclaimed, with laughter in his words. He was so happy. 'That's my Little Daughter.'

We started the march from there to Charles Street, the location of the 'Embassy of Myanmar' as the junta call it. In 1989 the military dictatorship renamed Burma Myanmar. However, the name isn't recognized by most countries of the world, including the USA and the European Union, who continue to use the name 'Burma'. None of the pro-democracy resistance groups have recognized the name change either.

As we walked, a couple of policemen placed themselves at the front and rear of the column of marchers. At first I watched what they were doing a little nervously, but their main concern seemed to be to stop the traffic at various points so we could march safely onwards. They certainly did nothing to stop us. It was amazing. No one was arrested. No one was carted away.

This is what a free country ruled by democracy must be like,

I told myself. As we marched through the streets more and more people joined us. There were Burmans, Karen and people from other ethnic groups, but also a lot of white people. I was really touched. I hadn't realized that white Europeans cared so much for our country. I was so pleased to see them demonstrating alongside us.

I was wearing a traditional Karen dress, which was hand-woven in a refugee camp. It was sky blue in colour, with red and white tassels hanging off it, and it dropped from my shoulders to my ankles. I'd decided to wear it because that's what I would have worn to an event back home. But now that I was here I realized I was the only Karen person dressed in traditional clothes, and it did rather make me stand out.

As we marched, a young white guy approached me. He was dressed in smart casual clothes and he had cameras slung around his neck. He had to be a journalist.

He smiled at me. 'Hi. I'm a freelance photographer. And who might you be?'

'My name is Zoya and I am a Karen refugee from Burma.'

'Great. Mind if I take your picture? And ask you a few questions?'

I told him it was fine. I didn't mind. He asked why I had fled my home in Burma, and what had brought me to the United Kingdom. I told him a little of my story, and as I did so he started snapping some photos. It felt a little odd at first, especially as people in the crowd were staring at me. I could tell what they were thinking: who is she? But I tried to act naturally and keep walking straight ahead.

By now we had reached the embassy. I looked up and recognized the Burmese flag flying from the roof. It is a simple slab of red with a square of blue in one corner, within which are fourteen white stars (representing the seven divisions and seven states of Burma). The last time I had seen that flag it was flying from a Burmese Army checkpoint on the Salween River. We had sneaked past in our long-tail boat, fearing that the soldiers would discover us and open fire.

I felt a tap on my shoulder. It was Dr Win Naing. 'Zoya, would you like to be the MC?' he asked me.

'The MC?'

'Master of Ceremonies,' he explained.

I had no idea what an MC did, but I said I'd be honoured to. 'Can you just explain to me what an MC does?' I added.

'Well, it's just introducing the speakers, that sort of thing. Plus saying a few words about Daw Aung San Suu Kyi's birthday. Okay?'

'Fine,' I said, although at that point I knew little about the details of her life.

He handed me a funnel-shaped device. It was very heavy.

'It's a megaphone,' he explained. 'Press that button and speak into this end and everyone will be able to hear you – even the people inside the embassy!'

I was feeling quite excited. I had never done anything like this before, and his request had come completely out of the blue. He knew my father, of course, so maybe he just presumed that I, too, would be good at public gatherings. I put the megaphone's thin end to my mouth and pulled the trigger.

'Ladies and gentlemen,' I began – that was always how my father had begun such things. 'Ladies and gentlemen, today is the sixtieth birthday of Daw Aung San Suu Kyi. We are here because we care about her and what she stands for. We are here because she is not free and is under house arrest. We are here because she cannot be here herself. And I know you are all here because you care about Burma, democracy and human rights. Now, our first speaker is U Uttara, a Buddhist monk and a leader of the monks in the United Kingdom.'

U Uttara stepped forward to speak. I handed him the megaphone. He looked superb in his rich saffron robes and with his shaven head bathed in the summer light.

'Today is a very important day,' he began, in his soft, gentle voice. 'It is important because we are here to remember—'

As he spoke I gazed around me. We were surrounded by a

crush of photographers, video journalists and people scribbling into reporter's notebooks. I thought to myself then: 'Wow! This is great! This is democracy and free speech and a free press in action – all of the things that we do not have in Burma.'

As U Uttara finished speaking I took back the megaphone. 'What do we want?' I shouted. 'De-mo-cracy! De-mo-cracy!'

'Democracy! Democracy! Democracy!' the crowd thundered back at me.

'When do we want it?' I shouted.

'Now! Now!' the crowd cheered.

As the chanting thundered around the streets I saw the curtains twitch on the upper floor of the embassy building. All of a sudden people were in the window with cameras snapping photographs and videoing the crowd. But still the crowd continued chanting, and no one seemed the remotest bit scared. So I thought to myself: 'Well, let's shout and chant as loud as we can, because we certainly can't do anything like this in Burma, or Thailand for that matter!'

For some reason I didn't find it at all nerve-racking to MC the rest of the event. In fact, I found myself enjoying it. Afterwards, I was surrounded by a crowd of journalists, all of them asking the same questions: how long have you been here; what happened to you in Burma; why did you come to the United Kingdom; what is your birthday message for Aung San Suu Kyi; and what is your message for the Burmese junta?

As I answered their questions the words and gestures just seemed to come naturally to me, and it struck me then that perhaps they were a gift from my father. It reminded me of the first time I had ever heard my father speak, at the rally in The New Village. That was the first time that I really understood what his role was in the resistance and what a gifted man he was. And now I was here, following his example.

At the end of the interviews a smart-looking white man in a business suit approached me. He had chosen a quiet moment in which to speak with me. I instinctively liked him, for he had smiling eyes and a friendly face. He introduced himself. He was Mark Farmaner, from an organization called the Burma Campaign UK, based in London.

'You did a great job today,' he said. 'We don't know a lot about the current situation with the Karen. Would you come into the office to brief us?'

'I'm studying for an MA at the University of East Anglia,' I replied. 'So I'm really busy, and it's hard to get to London. But I'll try.'

That evening I settled back into my seat on the train – the right one this time – and thought about the day's events. It was one of the most empowering and exciting things that I had ever done. I called my sister and told her every detail I could remember. Then I phoned my father and told him what I'd been up to.

'Oh my Little Daughter!' he exclaimed. I could hear the pride in his voice. 'Now that's my Little Daughter – following in the footsteps of your old dad.'

I didn't know then how true his words were. This was to be a life-changing day for me, setting me on a new path that would fulfil my ambitions to help my people, but also put me in a new kind of danger.

For the first time in my life I had been able to stand up to those who had ravaged my country, murdered my people and driven me out of my homeland. All my life I had been a victim, but today I had felt what it was like to fight back.

And it was the most amazing feeling in the world.

Chapter Twenty-eight

IN THE FOOTSTEPS OF MY FATHER

A week later I was in my little room at college working on an essay when there was a call on my mobile. It was Mark, the man from the Burma Campaign UK whom I had met at the end of the demo. At first I couldn't remember who he was, but I was too polite to say so. There were so many people that I'd lost track of who they all were.

He told me that a British human rights researcher called Guy Horton had produced a new report, *Dying Alive*, detailing the genocide committed against the Karen people. The BBC's *Newsnight* was preparing a story based on that report.

'They'd like someone from the Karen to do an interview,' he explained. 'Someone who can speak with personal experience about what is going on. Is that something you'd be willing to do?'

'Yes,' I said, without even thinking about it. 'Of course. What do I need to do?'

I didn't know who or what *Newsnight* was, but of course I

recognized the name of the BBC – an institution from my child-hood and my mother's evenings spent listening to the World Service on her tiny, long-wave radio. I knew that this was a chance to speak out, and I wasn't about to turn that down. Mark told me to expect a call from the BBC, and shortly there was one.

'Hi, it's Tim Hewell here from the BBC,' the voice told me. 'I got your number from Mark.'

'Yes, I know,' I told him. 'What would you like me to do?'

'Well, first I'd like to ask you a few questions over the phone. Can you tell me a bit about your story.'

I gave the man an outline of it.

'Right, well, if you're happy to do the interview, we need you on tonight, okay?'

'Okay. But how do I get there.'

A few hours later I arrived by taxi at the BBC's offices in White City. I met Tim, and he took me outside to film the interview in the grounds. I was a little nervous as it was so formal, but all they wanted was for me to tell my story. At the time I had no idea that this was such an influential programme, one watched by millions. All I knew was that the BBC were doing a report on the genocide of the Karen, and this was my chance to speak out. After it was over I hoped I'd done okay.

A couple of days later I received another call from Mark. He had watched the programme being broadcast. I had missed it, as I had no TV in my college room.

'Congratulations, Zoya!' he told me. 'Well done. You were bril-liant. We'd like you to work with the Burma Campaign UK. Would you be interested in meeting to discuss it?'

I had to finish my MA first, but I agreed to meet Mark for lunch so we could talk about it some more.

I also faced another momentous life decision now. My scholar-ship money was all but exhausted. Sometime soon it would be time for me to return home. But the question was: where exactly was home? Where did home exist for me? It wasn't Burma, that was for sure. Was it Thailand? The refugee camps? Bangkok?

It was now July 2005. I had six months left on my visa, and then I would have to make a decision. At the beginning of the month I received some news from Thailand. In Mae La refugee camp they were holding a second UN registration programme. Officially, my refugee status relied upon my registration in that camp. If I remained in the United Kingdom, I would be struck off the camp's list of refugees.

I couldn't go back. Even if I could somehow scrape together the money for the flight, I only had a single entry visa for the United Kingdom. If I flew to Thailand to register, I wouldn't be allowed back into the United Kingdom. And I still had to complete my MA. It seemed that I had no choice but to allow my United Nations refugee registration to lapse. But if it did I would then be even more of a stateless person bereft of identity.

All this was on my mind when I went to meet Mark in London. We went to a pub and he passed me a big menu. As usual I ordered sausage and mash. My English friends thought that this was my favourite food. Whenever I ate out I would have it, and they would joke: 'Zoya – you really love your bangers and mash.' Actually, I didn't like it that much. It was more that I didn't know what any of the other foods were, and I still hadn't learned how to use a knife and fork properly. Sausages were easy to cut, and mash didn't need cutting at all.

I picked at my mash as Mark explained about going to work at Burma Campaign UK. But my heart was with my people. I didn't know how, but I wanted to go back to the border to help them. I explained this to Mark, and without hesitation he told me I could do more to help them in London than I ever could on the border.

'This white man is crazy,' I thought. 'What's he talking about? How can I help them when I'm thousands of miles away?' I agreed to think about it.

Soon after meeting Mark there was more worrying news from the border. I received a phone call from my father. The KNU had intercepted a Burmese Army radio message. It was a 'hit list', and my name was on it. Perhaps by speaking out as I had done on the

BBC, I had attracted the notice of the Burmese security services – *again*. First they had sent the ex-child soldier to kill my father and me. And now this.

I discussed it with Bwa Bwa, and she told me that there was no way I could risk going back to live in Thailand. I should make a claim for refugee status here in the United Kingdom. That was what she had done, and she had already been issued with official papers recognizing her as a genuine refugee in Britain. That meant in turn that she was safe to stay in the United Kingdom for as long as was necessary.

With my UN refugee status in Thailand about to expire, and the Burmese regime determined, it seemed, to kill me, I guessed I had little choice. On 7 July I tried to go to the Refugee Legal Centre, in London, to lodge my claim, but the entire city was paralysed by the terrorist plot to blow up the underground. I tried again on 21 July but there was a terrorist scare and the underground was closed. So I tried again on 5 August, and this time I managed to speak to a Refugee Legal Centre lawyer. She sent me directly to the Home Office, in Croydon, to submit the paperwork for my claim. When I got there I was amazed at the size of the queue. There were people of all nationalities and religions, and all of them were claiming a right to remain in Britain on the grounds of the fear of persecution.

I understood the concept of giving asylum and protection to refugees, but I was surprised by the numbers – so many of whom seemed to be so obviously the victims of suffering. It said a great deal about the tolerance of the British nation and people that they extended their kindness to so many from all corners of the world.

But as I went to lodge my claim I was a bag of nerves. I feared the Home Office people might arrest or detain me, due to my false papers. If they did so, all they had to do was deport me to Burma and then I would be finished. I was known to the regime; I had openly criticized them; *I was on their hit list*. I had little doubt that they would show no mercy.

I took my numbered ticket and waited for it to be called. I was there from lunchtime until six in the evening, and still no one had seen me. Finally, I was called to one of the booths. I was asked a few questions relating to my Refugee Legal Centre forms, and then I was told to come back on Monday. It was Friday evening, and things were closing down for the weekend.

I spent the entire weekend worrying about what would happen when I went back again on Monday. I returned to the Home Office at seven o'clock in the morning. I was fingerprinted and photographed and given an asylum seeker ID card, but by the end of that day I still hadn't seen anyone. I was asked to come back again the following day.

It was so frustrating. I was staying with Bwa Bwa on the outskirts of London, and the journey to Croydon took hours. The train fare was costing me a fortune. But I returned the following day as asked. I was there before the office was even open, and already the queue had to be several hundred strong, just as it had been on each of the previous occasions that I had been there.

At lunchtime I was called into an interview room. I sat on one side of the table facing my interviewer. He asked me how I had got my passport. I explained it was a false one. I also pointed out that all of this was detailed on my form, as completed by my lawyer at the Refugee Legal Centre.

The man warned me that it was a very serious offence, procuring a false passport.

'Don't you know what trouble you're in?' he said. 'You can be imprisoned for twenty years for doing what you've done. Don't you know that?'

'No, I didn't know that,' was all I could think of to say.

He scribbled down a few notes on the interview form, and then he got up as if to leave. I asked him for a copy of what he had written. It was what my Refugee Legal Centre lawyer had advised me to do.

He shook his head. 'You don't need a copy.'

He left the room. I was on my own once more. I had expected sympathy, but he had been so rude. I imagined him returning with two policemen, like the nice ones that had been on the demo with us, but this time they would be looking fierce and coming to arrest me.

I thought all my dreams were over, that I was going to spend twenty years in jail. After all I had been through I couldn't believe it. I tried to hold back the tears. I had hardly ever felt so low. Somehow, this seemed almost as horrible as when I had first been forced to flee my village. Had everything that I had struggled for been for nothing?

All of a sudden the door swung open and a new man walked in. He had with him a worried-looking lady whom I guessed had to be Burmese. Without anything of an introduction he started to fire questions at me. He spoke in English, and before I could answer the Burmese-looking woman translated into Burmese. This was completely crazy. I didn't speak Burmese. I could understand his English, but only half of what she said.

'Look, I've already said I don't need interpretation,' I objected. 'I don't speak Burmese. I'm Karen. *Karen*. We have our own Karen language.'

The woman repeated the question in Burmese. 'Look,' I said to her, 'I've already told you – I do not speak Burmese.'

I turned back to the guy. 'I don't need an interpreter. I don't speak Burmese, she doesn't speak Karen. So, let's do this in English.'

He snorted derisively. 'So, you're from Burma but you don't speak Burmese. How d'you explain that one?'

'As I have already explained, and written clearly on my form, I am from a separate ethnic group,' I said. 'I am a Karen. We Karen have our own traditions, culture and language. Our Karen language is not the same as the Burmese language. That is why we are unable to understand each other. In fact, there are several dozen separate ethnic groups in Burma, many of whom also speak—'

The questioning continued – in English – for an hour or more.

'Right, that's it,' he finally announced. 'I think I might have to detain you.'

A look of real concern flashed across the interpreter's face. As for me I was terrified. I knew what that word 'detain' meant. It was the first stage on the road to being deported.

'But why?' I blurted out. 'Why would you detain me? What have I done wrong?'

'You entered the country illegally,' he fired back at me. 'You came here on a false passport, didn't you?'

'And that means I have to be detained?' I queried.

I was terrified now. What had I been thinking of, coming here, if this was how they were going to treat me?

'All right, look, maybe there's another way,' he announced. 'Perhaps we don't have detain you, after all. But if we don't you'll have to report to your local police station, every week, to sign. And that's the best I can do for you.'

I left that room feeling emotionally exhausted. But at least I hadn't been 'detained', I told myself, as I headed for the exit. Once I was back at Bwa Bwa's place I told her all that had happened. I told her how horrible it had been. Bwa Bwa gave me a hug and told me not to worry. She had won her claim for refugee status, and so would I. My case was stronger than hers, she said, for by speaking out I had made myself a public enemy of the Burmese junta.

Now I had claimed asylum I was banned from working in the United Kingdom, but I still wanted to work with Burma Campaign UK, and joined as a volunteer.

It was an exciting time to join the campaign. The demonstration I had been to at the Burmese Embassy had been part of a global effort to raise awareness about Burma. It was so successful that the United States raised Burma at the United Nations Security Council, which had never discussed it before.

But Russia and China had blocked the talks, saying Burma was not a threat to international peace and security, and so the Security Council could not intervene.

This prompted Archbishop Desmond Tutu and former Czech President Vaclav Havel to commission a legal study by a US law firm, DLA Piper. The report was published in September 2005, and found that Burma did, in fact, meet the criteria for the Security Council to intervene, as Burma had many of the problems that the council had taken action on in other countries, including the overthrow of a democratically elected government, HIV/AIDS, conflict resulting from its attacks on ethnic minorities, severe human rights violations, refugee outflows and drug trafficking.

The report recommended that the Security Council pass a resolution requiring the restoration of democracy to Burma and an end to the attacks on ethnic civilians. If it were passed the regime would be forced to stop attacking the Karen, or face serious consequences.

Two days after the report was issued, the United States announced that they would support a resolution. I felt so happy – the most powerful country in the world would take action on my country.

But the UK was sitting on the fence, and our job at Burma Campaign UK was to get it to support the resolution as well. I learned how to campaign, lobbying MPs, putting pressure on the government through the media, giving public talks. It was challenging, there was so much to learn.

One evening Mark and I travelled back from Oxford together, where we had been speaking at the University. During the journey he told me how he had been moved to tears by my words, and what an impact I was having when I spoke to audiences. I knew I had to grab every opportunity to let the world know what was happening in my country, and was really encouraged by his words. I felt at last that I had found a way to make a difference.

After almost three months of campaigning the British government said it would support Burma being taken to the United Nations Security Council. Now I could see that campaigning could change things. In December 2005 we finally got nine countries on the Security Council to support Burma being discussed, and so for the very first time in history, the most powerful body in the world discussed my country. The discussions were only informal, but it was a significant step forward. We kept up the pressure, and in September 2006 they held their first formal discussion, another step forward. In January 2007 the United States and the United Kingdom put forward a resolution on Burma, calling on the regime to enter into negotiations, but China and Russia vetoed it. Even more shocking was that South Africa voted with them. How could they do that after they had depended so much on international support for their own struggle against apartheid?

But all the time I never forgot my journey back into Burma and the people I had met there. In early 2006 the Burmese junta stepped up its attacks against the Karen still more. Tens of thousands of people were being driven from their homes. Horrific reports of abuse were filtering out of Karen areas: women and even children were being raped; villagers were being horribly mutilated, with ears, arms and breasts cut off. There were even beheadings.

The British government seemed content to ignore what was going on, and so did the United Nations. As the regime brutalized my people, the new United Nations Envoy to Burma, Ibrahim Gambari, visited the country. But instead of demanding an end to the killings, which the United Nations later described as breaking the Geneva Convention, he smiled and posed for pictures with the Generals, and even talked about how they had opened a new page in their relations with the world community. I was so angry. It seemed he believed their lies.

No aid was getting to those people who had been forced to flee their homes, and I became more and more upset. We had to do something. One Friday night I got home and read emails from friends on the border about villagers being tortured and killed. I called Mark to see what Burma Campaign UK could do. But I hadn't realized how late it was. I had woken him up. He was exhausted from working so hard, and was going to go on holiday the next morning and had to get up at 4 a.m. At first he was grumpy at being woken up, but then he agreed that Burma Campaign UK must act. On the plane he drafted a campaign plan, and as soon as he got to his hotel called me. He gave me a jobs list. It meant asking lots of people to take action, even Yvette Mahon, the Director of Burma Campaign UK. How could I ask her to do things for me? Mark had put me in charge of my first campaign. I was so nervous, and I knew that if I wasn't successful more of my people would die.

Our priority was to get aid to those homeless people in the jungle. The only way to get it to many of them was cross-border, as the regime blocked aid from inside the country. But the Department for International Development (DFID), the UK aid department, was refusing to fund such aid. They only wanted to work from inside the country. But aid could not get to people from inside. I could not understand why they would not just help people who were so desperate. I felt even more angry when we found out that another government department was funding a survey of wild bats in the same area. No aid for people, but they were counting wild bats!

Newsnight were just as shocked. They interviewed the minister from the DFID, and after that he ordered a policy review. But the months dragged on and still the review wasn't published, and in the meantime my people were dying.

In October 2006 things were ratcheted up a level. Benedict Rogers – a human rights campaigner working with campaign group Christian Solidarity Worldwide – contacted me. He told me that William Hague, the Shadow Foreign Secretary, had wanted to invite Aung San Suu Kyi to speak at that year's conference of the Conservative Party – one of the main political parties in the United Kingdom. But they couldn't even get the invitation to her because she was being kept under house arrest in Rangoon. Her phone line was cut, her post intercepted and no visitors were allowed. And so they asked me to speak instead.

I had actually met Benedict Rogers once before, on the

Thai–Burma border. In 2003 he had come to see my father, in the company of the cross-party peer and human rights campaigner Baroness Cox and John Bercow, an MP. Benedict and I had stayed in touch since then, and recently he'd seen me giving interviews. He explained that they wanted me to speak for six minutes at the conference, which would be a high-profile event. I figured if I prepared well I would be fine, and so I agreed.

I chose to wear a plain white Karen dress for the conference, in order to make a simple statement as to my identity. The day before I was scheduled to speak I travelled down to Bournemouth by train. I went to collect my conference pass, but it wasn't ready. The police said it would take them some time to get clearance to allow me to enter the conference secure zone, especially as I was an asylum seeker. In fact, it wouldn't be possible until the following morning.

As my hotel room was inside the conference centre I now had nowhere to stay. I was tired and stressed and nervous about my big day tomorrow, and all of a sudden I just started crying. The conference organizers apologized profusely, but they had to follow procedures. Luckily, Benedict Rogers was there. He spoke to a conference organizer and he finally managed to find me a hotel room.

Unfortunately, by the time I reached the hotel their kitchen was shut, so I went hungry. It was the worst possible way to prepare for the biggest public event of my life so far!

The next morning my pass was ready. I was whisked into the conference hall itself, and suddenly I realized the true scope of what I had taken on. The hall was simply vast, with thousands of people seated there. I was amazed, but undaunted.

I was rushed to the Green Room, where I was given some make-up and a mic was clipped to my Karen dress. I was instructed to sit in the front row on one of the chairs reserved for speakers, and to prepare myself to appear immediately before William Hague. The other guest speaker that morning was John McCain, the soon to be US presidential candidate, but I had little time for worry before I was on.

I was ushered on to the stage. I turned to face the audience. A sea of faces stretched before me, and the hall was silent as they waited for me to begin.

'Good afternoon, ladies and gentlemen,' I began. I gestured behind me, at the green wall of the Green Room. 'With this green background I feel like I am back home in the jungle of Burma again—'

There was a ripple of laughter.

'It is an honour to be speaking to you today . . . When I was just fourteen years old the soldiers came to my village. Mortar bombs exploded and they opened fire. There was no warning. We fled for our lives, but many people were killed. My family ran, carrying what we could on our backs, leaving our home and everything behind. I still remember the smell of the black smoke as our village was destroyed—'

'My country is ruled by one of the most brutal dictatorships in the world. It is eleven years since the attack on my village, but nothing has changed. Earlier this year the regime launched yet another offensive against the Karen civilians . . . Shooting children, mutilating and beheading people, forcing 20,000 from their homes. And still the British government has done nothing to stop companies investing in Burma. How many more generations will have to suffer whilst the world looks the other way?'

As my question died away, a round of applause erupted, filling the momentary silence.

'In many countries trade and investment can have a positive impact, bringing jobs and prosperity, and opening up countries to new ideas. In Burma the reverse happened. The regime used trade and investment to double the size of the army, and reduce spending on healthcare and education. That is why Burmese people are asking for targeted economic sanctions, to cut the lifeline keeping this regime afloat.'

There was more applause; it seemed as if I was doing all right.

'What is more important than the basic right of all of us to live in peace, without fear? How can governments stand by whilst in

Burma innocent children are shot, whilst girls as young as five years old are raped by soldiers, whilst over a thousand political prisoners face torture every day? Whilst Aung San Suu Kyi remains under house arrest, her life in danger?'

I continued speaking, and at the end I made a simple point, one that came from my heart.

'There are millions of people like me around the world who have been forced from their homes by brutal regimes . . . We just want to go home. But I can't without your help. Please help us to go home. Thank you.'

As I stopped speaking the audience started to rise to their feet, and all of a sudden 3,500 delegates were giving me – the Karen girl from the jungle – a standing ovation. I had done it. I had spoken for five minutes freely from the heart. At the end I hadn't even needed my speech notes. I was relieved it was over and thrilled with the result. I hadn't expected such a positive response. It was a plea that had come from the bottom of my heart.

William Hague mounted the platform. 'Ladies and gentlemen, what a wonderful speech by a brave young lady from Burma—'

After the session I was asked to do lots of interviews. The next day *The Times* praised my speech, and my appeal to go home was quote of the day in the *Mirror*. In the taxi on the way back to the train station the driver recognized me. He showed me the local newspaper which had printed my whole speech. I felt like I was getting the message across that action needed to be taken to help the people of Burma.

However, with a higher profile came greater danger. More than ever now, I was putting myself in the firing line.

Chapter Twenty-nine

IN THE FIRING LINE

I still had to go and sign at the police station every week, but there seemed to be no further progress in my claim for refugee status. The Home Office wrote to my solicitor, saying they needed proof of my status as a refugee in Thailand. But by now I would have been crossed off the UN list in Mae La camp. It just added to my worries. I still feared that they were going to try to deport me to Burma. Sometimes, alone at night, I would cry silent tears.

By February 2007 I was staying at a friend's house in London. I was returning one evening with Satoko, a Japanese girl I knew from university. Bwa Bwa was going to be there for dinner, and I was looking forward to seeing her. Satoko and I walked up the dark, rainy street and approached the door. I stood back to let Satoko in. As I did so I saw two shadowy shapes detach themselves from a phone box on the street, and suddenly they were upon me.

I felt a stab of intense pain as one dragged me by the hair, pulling me back towards the street. I started screaming as loudly as I could. I had my handbag on my shoulder, but neither made any attempt to grab it. Instead, they tried to drag me out towards the road. As my screams cut through the night, I saw Satoko turn to help me. I screamed even louder for help, and suddenly my attackers had let go of me and were running away.

I was shaking and in shock. My friends helped me inside the house. My hair had come out in great, painful clumps. Once I had recovered a little, I tried to work out who it was who had attacked me. But I had no idea. They had been wearing hooded jackets, and their faces had been in shadow. I had been able to make out nothing of their features. All I was certain of was that I hadn't been robbed. My mobile phone and my handbag were untouched.

The next day I went to the police station and filed an incident report. Funnily enough, that day was 14 February, Valentine's Day. Around lunchtime a courier arrived at the office with a lovely bunch of flowers. All the girls who worked there were laughing and joking – 'Who're they for?' 'They're gorgeous!' 'Are they for me?' My head was hurting too much for me to really care. God, it hurts, I kept telling myself, as I ran my hand over the swollen scabby wound.

But it turned out the flowers were for me! It was a bunch of roses, sent anonymously. It was good to know that there was someone out there who cared about me, I thought. But I was feeling sorry for myself, and all I really cared about was the pain in my head. I tried to get my mind to focus on the flowers, instead of the pain.

'Gorgeous red roses!' one of the girls teased me. 'Wow! Who's the anonymous admirer, Zoya?'

'If I had to choose between being pulled by the hair by those men or getting flowers,' I remarked, 'well, I'd prefer the flowers!'

That raised a laugh, but I was still teased remorselessly, especially when the post brought me two anonymous cards as well!

My claim for refugee status was almost two years old when I was finally given permission by the Home Office to work. I could start working full time with the Burma Campaign UK, who would pay me a living wage. I was appointed their Campaigns Officer, with special responsibility for parliamentary work.

That August I moved into a two-bedroomed flat in North London. I shared it with a married couple, both of whom were Karen. The lady was a medical doctor, called Pasaw Htee – Mist Water. Her husband, Saw Htoo Tha – Mr Golden Fruit – had already won his refugee status in the United Kingdom, and he was working full time. They were 100 per cent supportive of my work, and they knew the risks I was taking. They knew my safety was threatened, and we instigated certain measures to make things more secure at the flat.

The Home Office had given no reason why they had to verify my refugee status in Thailand, but that was the reason they were using to justify my claim taking so long. I had given them my father's phone number, so they could speak to him and verify my story. But I knew from speaking with my father that no one had ever called.

As my claim ground onwards my solicitor applied for judicial review – a process by which the courts can compel the Home Office to make a decision. It was the threat of judicial review that finally forced their hand. At last, in August 2007 I was granted full refugee status in the United Kingdom. I was overjoyed. I felt as if an enormous weight had been taken off my shoulders. At least now I knew that I couldn't be deported to face the vengeance of those who rule my country.

My friends at Burma Campaign UK decided to throw a little party. Mark went out and bought a carrot cake, with white icing and little carrot-shaped biscuits on top. We had it with champagne in plastic cups to celebrate. Or it might just have been sparkling wine – I'd not be able to tell the difference anyway! Mark asked everyone to raise a glass for the toast.

'Congratulations, Zoya, on winning your refugee status! It's been a long two years!'

'To Zoya!' everyone echoed. 'Congratulations!'

'I'm so happy to finally be a legal person existing in the real world!' I told them. 'This day really means so much to me.'

Since the age of fourteen I had been a ghost citizen. I had been a refugee of sorts, but one with no formal status. Even my UN refugee registration hadn't meant much. I had no ID card, no passport, and was pretty much bereft of any identity. This was the first time that I had existed, legally for real, and by now I was twenty-six years old. My time as a 'non-person' had been twelve long years.

Winning my refugee status made me feel safe for the first time in more than a decade. Now I could be 'human', like everyone around me. I could open a bank account, work, rent a home, and soon I could travel abroad – things most people just took for granted.

That weekend my sister came to visit, and she, Mist Water, Mr Golden Fruit and I had a celebratory meal. I cooked chicken curry, spiced with chilli, pepper, salt, garlic, coriander and turmeric. I could afford to buy these things now and to treat my friends and my big sister. And, of course, we had a big bowl of fish paste!

We celebrated the fact that, for all of us, life seemed to be coming good. I had my status, a country to call my home, a flat and nice flatmates, a job, an income and a bank account. Soon I would be issued with my refugee travel documents. Bwa Bwa was likewise a refugee in the United Kingdom. Slone Phan had gone to Canada to study, as part of a UN resettlement programme, and for now at least that was his home. The three of us were safer and more secure than we had ever been during the last ten years.

As for Say Say and my father, things for them were pretty much as they had always been. They had no formal ID, no homeland, and no way to travel out of Thailand. Say Say was married, and he now had a little son and daughter. His Karen wife had taken up the offer of resettlement under the UN programme and moved with the children to Norway. But Say Say had remained on the Thai–Burma border, working with my father.

The campaign on cross-border aid that I had been given responsibility for was making real progress. We had persuaded the British government's International Development Committee to hold an inquiry into the situation. They issued a report supporting what we had been campaigning for – that aid should go to the Internally Displaced Persons and be delivered cross-border. Once again the DFID reviewed their policy. Finally, they agreed to double Britain's aid to Burma, and to fund cross-border aid!

I was overjoyed. The increase in aid might save the lives of thousands of desperate people. But tragedy was to strike my country again. In August 2007 the Burmese regime raised the price of fuel by up to 500 per cent. For people already living in abject poverty it was too much. They took to the streets demanding change. Despite arrests and intimidation the protests grew, until hundreds of thousands were marching on the streets. Saffron-robed Buddhist monks led those protests, for they said they could no longer ignore the suffering of the people.

The press had dubbed the uprisings the 'Saffron Revolution'. It was headline news, and the Burma Campaign UK was inundated with media enquiries. For days on end I would get up at 4 a.m., go and do my first TV interview, and then go from studio to studio all day long. We were demanding action from the international community, not just sympathy. As the protests grew we allowed ourselves to hope that perhaps this was it, the regime would fall. But, finally, the junta reacted as it always had done, by opening fire and killing and maiming on the streets.

As they launched their brutal crackdown my heart wept. Yet at the same time I had to find the strength to continue speaking out. As the killings and arrests continued on the streets of Rangoon, media interest in Burma reached a massive peak. I was rushing from one interview to the next as Buddhist monasteries were being raided and thousands of monks arrested. It was vital that the world act.

The Conservative Party were holding their 2007 conference as the crackdown began, and they invited me back to speak. This time I held up the iron manacles with which dissenters are chained in their cells in Rangoon to demonstrate the brutality of such a regime. On the Friday of that week the regime cut phone lines and internet links, effectively isolating Burma from the outside world. That made it very hard to get any news out of the country.

I was in the office and Mark asked if I would take a phone call. 'Who from?' I asked.

'Prime Minister Gordon Brown,' he replied.

My eyes went wide. I couldn't believe it. 'For me!?'

Mark nodded. 'Yep. He's spoken with China, the French President and the US President about the crisis. Now he wants to talk to someone from Burma. He wants to talk to you.'

I was honoured and amazed. I asked him to try to get the United Nations Security Council to take action and for the European Union to introduce targeted economic sanctions that would stop money going to the Generals. European investment was helping to pay for the bullets we saw being used against the monks on the streets of Rangoon.

On Sunday morning the Prime Minister issued a statement on Burma. He said he would be pushing for the United Nations Security Council to discuss the crisis and for the European Union to impose new sanctions. It was exactly what I had asked him to do. I felt so encouraged that finally the world might take a strong stand against the Generals.

The following weekend Gordon Brown invited a delegation, including some Buddhist monks living in exile and myself, to meet him to discuss the crisis. It was so funny to be sitting in No. 10 Downing Street, when only two years previously I had stood on the pavement outside shouting slogans and phoning my father! He promised to do all that he could, and I could see his concern was genuine.

After that meeting I went on to address 10,000 people in Trafalgar Square on the Global Day for Burma rally, and then spoke that night at a concert that the musician, Damien Rice, was giving in Wembley Arena. It was one of the most amazing days of my life. By the time I got home I was exhausted. But my mind was buzzing with everything that had happened and it took me ages to get to sleep.

My journey from the jungle to the world stage had been a long and harrying one. But breaking the silence finally seemed to be taking effect. After the years of being a powerless victim, this was truly the best feeling in the world.

In November 2007 I was issued with a British refugee travel document. At first glance it looks like a normal passport, but it has 'Travel Document' emblazoned across the front. In January 2008 I prepared to make a journey back to Thailand and the border. The Burma Campaign UK was assembling a delegation of politicians and the media. I had been given the job of organizing it, and I was really looking forward to going back. I wanted to see again the situation for myself, and, of course, I wanted to see Say Say and my father.

The plan was to visit Mae La – my old refugee camp – and Dr Cynthia's clinic. And those of us that could intended to sneak across the border into Burma to spend time with those most in need – the IDPs. The delegation included a Spanish MP, called Carmen Garcia, together with a Spanish TV crew and NGOs, an Estonian MP, called Silver Meikar, and an Estonian journalist. Plus we had radio journalists from the BBC, and, of course, Mark would be going with us.

I spoke by telephone to my father about the trip. He told me the security situation was worsening. His name was at the top of the regime's hit list, and I would be in danger as well. I discussed this with Mark, and he decided we needed to be more security aware. He arranged for a former Royal Marine, called John Rowe, to visit the office. John taught us about surveillance and counter-surveillance; how to detect a tail and how to lose a tail; and how to do simple first aid, plus very basic self-defence.

This last bit was hilarious, and John had me cracked up laughing. He instructed me on what to do if I was grabbed from behind. But Mark had already shown me one trick – that I should stamp my heel into my assailant's foot. John wasn't expecting me to do this. He cried out in pain. This big marine wasn't expecting a small Karen girl to be so strong!

But there was a serious side to all of this. Once more I was heading back into the darkness. Only now I was doing so as an outspoken opponent of the people oppressing and enslaving my country.

They would have every reason to want to stop us.

Chapter Thirty

THE ROAD HOME

A few weeks after my self-defence instructions from John our delegation arrived in the Thai town of Mae Sot. I left the guests in the hotel, and Say Say picked me up and took me to my father's house. I was shocked by Say Say's appearance. It was barely three years since I had last seen him, but he had aged so much. The constant stress of his work had left him thin, haggard and exhausted-looking.

My father was waiting for me at the doorway of the house. He broke into a smile as soon as he saw me, and I tried to return the warmth and the welcome that was in his eyes. But in truth I was shocked at how old and tired he looked. His hair had turned grey, and for the first time I saw him as an old man.

He hugged me tight. 'Oh, wonderful! My Little Daughter has just arrived!'

I hugged him back as hard as I could. Disregarding the fact that my father seemed like an old man now, I still went and sat on his lap. I was a 27-year-old woman, but I didn't ever intend to stop doing so.

Yet it was clear that all the pressure he was under was taking its toll. He was at constant risk of assassination, he felt the pain and suffering of our people so deeply, and he had so many responsibilities as General Secretary of the KNU – representing the Karen to the world and doing media interviews every day. He was one of our most respected leaders, and everyone wanted his advice and support.

That night he invited the entire delegation to his house for a traditional Karen dinner. Later, once the delegation had left, he proceeded to tell the story of how he had come to name me 'Zoya'. I felt like I had heard it a hundred times before, but as he spoke, I could see how proud he was of me. That night I went away and researched the original 'Zoya' – the Russian partisan – on the internet. It was the first time that I had ever thought to do so.

As I read her story I was amazed at her youth and her bravery. She was only seventeen years old when she had joined the resistance. By the time she was eighteen the die was cast: her feats of daring would pass into legend. As I mulled over the original Zoya's story, I knew why it was that my father had named me after her. He wanted me to emulate her struggle.

In the morning we set off to visit two IDP camps. They were both situated on the very banks of the Salween River and only just inside Burma, but we still had to pass by Burmese Army checkpoints to reach them. The camps were full of hundreds of new arrivals, and they told us their stories of the ongoing suffering and horror.

In the first camp we met a couple with a newborn baby girl. The father had helped the mother give birth in the jungle, with no doctors or medicines to hand. It was a miracle that they had all made it through alive. The mother asked me if I would name the baby. I said I would love to but that we should offer the honour to the foreign guests. It was the Spanish MP who gave the girl a name, and she chose the word for freedom in Catalan, which is 'libertad'.

We met another young mother with children. She told us how her husband had been shot dead in the attack on their village. She had fled for her life with the children, escaping into the jungle. She was a widow now, with no one to care for her and her offspring. We had brought canned fish and biscuits with us to give out to the children. It was impossible to imagine how such simple, basic foodstuffs could be received with such joy by the half-starved kids in the camp.

We were told that more people were on their way to the camp, with Karen soldiers acting as their guides to ensure they reached it safely.

But even in the camp they were far from safe. A Burmese Army post was situated in the jungle not far away. An attack could happen at any time, and there had been several in the past year. Before leaving we went to visit the school. There were two teachers and 100 students crammed into a tiny bamboo hut with a bamboo floor and no walls.

I could tell that the foreign visitors were horrified. I didn't need to remind them how this compared to the schools of their childhoods. It was too obvious to require any mention. Each of those children had his or her tragic story to tell, but sadly we had precious little time to record them.

The following day we set out for Mae La refugee camp. It was my first time back there since 2004. It felt so strange entering the camp gate again, only this time knowing that I wasn't trapped. I was no longer a stateless non-person, a powerless refugee surviving on charity. There were scores of new arrivals, but most were 'ghost refugees'. The dreadful system that my mother, Slone and so many others had suffered under just seemed to go on and on.

We weren't allowed into Mae La camp officially. The Thai authorities rarely let politicians or journalists into the refugee camps. But we found a way to get in, and were able to meet the newly arrived refugees. Yet again these people had had their villages shot to pieces and burned down and then spent months hiding in the jungle before they reached the camp. And when they got here they had to join the growing ranks of the ghost refugees.

One man told us his story. He was a teacher back in his home village. One day the Burmese soldiers came and took him away. They tortured him and tried to make him confess to being a resistance fighter. First, he was beaten with bamboo poles, then he was tied to a tree and left there for days on end. Every day he would get beaten as he drifted slowly towards death. He showed me the scars from where he had been whipped. He told me he could never forgive those who had done this to him.

It was the village headman who had saved him. He had travelled to the army camp to argue for his life. He explained that the man was an honest, innocent teacher. Finally, the Burmese soldiers had let the teacher go. He was that close to death that he had to be carried back to his village by his friends. Once he had recovered enough to move, the teacher had fled with his family into the jungle and found his way to Mae La camp.

A lady from the Karen Women's Organization gave us a meaningful insight into the stark hopelessness of the camps. Some people had been there for twenty years or more. But most of those with any skills – the doctors, nurses and teachers – had left on UN resettlement programmes. Those that remained were the uneducated farmers and rural villagers, who in any case made up the majority of the refugees coming out of Burma.

As long as the Burmese junta remained in power the horror and the killing would continue, she said, driving more people into the camps. It was a vicious circle, which needed breaking. And the only way to break it was to get rid of the ruling regime and bring freedom and democracy to Burma.

At Dr Cynthia's clinic we met a mother with a young boy who was very ill. They were ordinary villagers from deep inside Burma, but the lack of any proper healthcare there meant the mother had had to walk through the jungle for weeks to get to the clinic. The boy had fallen into a high fever and was close to death by the time they arrived. He had been unconscious for days. She had heard that Dr Cynthia's clinic gave free treatment to refugees and IDPs, and so she had trekked through the jungle to find it, carrying her unconscious son in her arms. Whether she had got here in time to save him she didn't know, but she hoped and prayed that she had.

Her story reminded me of my almost-dying. The difference was that my mother had only had to make a short dash through the jungle before reaching a clinic. This woman was actually from the Shan ethnic group, and her journey from the Shan hills to Dr Cynthia's clinic had been a truly epic one. And all the time she would have been torn up with the worry that the son she was carrying in her arms was going to die before she managed to find help.

At the end of the week I did an interview with the media that were with us.

'I first fled Burma when I was fourteen. It is now thirteen years later and nothing has changed. Nothing. We have seen in the IDP camps that people are still running from bullets and bombs, just as I did years ago. We have seen in the refugee camps that people suffer there, just as I and my family did when we were refugees. Nothing has changed. We need to stop investing in this murderous regime; we need to stop buying their oil and gas and timber and gems; and we need to stop selling them arms with which they go about killing their own people.' The delegation departed, and I stayed on for a few days to be with my father, and catch up with old friends.

Just before we had arrived in Mae Sot the British International Development Secretary had visited there and gone to Mae La refugee camp and Dr Cynthia's clinic. For someone so senior to come all this way to this forgotten place was a sign of just how successful our campaign had been. I realized I needed to be in more regular contact with people on the border, and that Burma Campaign UK should work more closely with them.

The British government was now one of the fiercest critics of the regime. Within the European Union Britain was one of the strongest voices for increasing sanctions, and at the United Nations Security Council had co-sponsored the draft resolution on Burma. It was also one of the most generous aid donors. And I knew from meeting Prime Minister Gordon Brown that he personally cared deeply about what was going on, and wanted to help.

I told my father that I had started working on this book. And I told him that with the proceeds I wanted to set up a charity in memory of my mother, to fulfil our dream of providing proper education for the Karen. My father was so pleased. He said he'd like to write the foreword, if I would allow him to! I laughed at him teasing me.

'But let this book speak about the Karen struggle,' he urged me, 'and Burma's fight to be free.'

One morning we set off to attend a meeting – the Karen National Unity Seminar. With Karen inside Burma, in exile on the borders, and now many being resettled overseas, it is important that we all share information and organize how to work together. We had to take extra security precautions. A few days earlier we had learned of a plot to kill my father and me as we travelled to the meeting, and at the Unity Seminar another assassin with orders to shoot us was discovered. Luckily the plots had been found out, but they brought home to me that my father was in real danger.

On 31 January we went to attend a ceremony to mark Karen Resistance Day. But the people organizing the event discovered a bomb beneath the chair where my father was going to sit, hidden in a transistor radio. My father gave a speech and a press conference in which he described the continuing military offensive against the Karen people. Later, he received a phone call. An unknown voice told my father that he was going to come and kill him.

After that, my father told me to be very careful. He told me that the enemy knew I was here with him and that they also wanted to kill me. He made me promise that I would look after myself and be careful. He said I'd be much safer when I returned to the United Kingdom.

'They are closing in on me, Little Daughter,' he warned me. 'And if they cannot get to me, they will try to get to you.'

The Pakistani presidential candidate, Benazir Bhutto, had just recently been assassinated, and I was really worried for my father's safety.

'Look, Pah, you have to recognize that Benazir Bhutto got killed because she didn't take proper precautions,' I told him. 'I'm worried the same might happen to you.'

'I know! I know!' my father replied. 'The regime is trying very hard to kill me, so maybe I won't survive for long.'

'Pah – don't talk like that!' I said. '*Please.*'

'Little Daughter, even if they kill me they won't kill what I stand for, will they?'

'But I still don't like you talking like that. I want you always to be around, Pah, and to live into a grand old age!'

My father seemed to ignore my last comment. 'I am so proud that you are taking such an active role in the struggle now, my Little Daughter! When I meet people they speak about you so much. They tell me: "Ah, your Little Daughter, she is just like you."'

My father went on to tell me that he was tired. He had been fighting for a long, long time. He was feeling old and he wanted to retire after a few more years. Then he would write a book about his life and tend to his flower gardens. I told him that I would like him to be at my graduation ceremony for my MA in the coming July. He promised he would try to be there.

Although he didn't say as much, I knew that he would never give up as long as our people were suffering. He hadn't told me, and hadn't asked for it, but many others had said that he was likely to be nominated as KNU President in elections due towards the end of the year. My father was expected to be easily elected.

I returned to London in early February. Bwa Bwa and I had been invited to the premiere of the movie, *Rambo IV*. In the film

Rambo – played by Sylvester Stallone – travels into Karen areas to rescue some missionaries kidnapped by the Burmese soldiers. A lot of blood and mayhem follows, but finally Rambo wins the day, with the help of the Karen resistance.

Most people don't believe it when I tell them, but the film *Rambo IV* accurately portrays the horrors going on in my homeland. I had told my father that I had been invited to the premiere. He was pleased, and I promised to call him after to tell him about it.

When Bwa Bwa and I turned up on the red carpet outside the cinema, we were mobbed by the crowd.

'Who do you play?' someone yelled.

'Give us an autograph, will you!'

'Get us in to meet Rambo!'

People thrust autograph books at us. Cameras flashed in our faces. It was all very weird. But I signed away, and made sure we took the opportunity to tell them about the plight of the Karen people in Burma.

'We're not in the movie exactly,' I said. 'But we are Karen, and the film's all about our people. For decades—'

When I came out of the premiere I gave my father a call, but he had crossed into Burma on his work and I couldn't reach him.

I never did get the chance to tell him about the movie.

Chapter Thirty-one

THE FINAL CUT

Two days after the movie premiere I had an early-morning phone call. It was Bwa Bwa. A reporter had just called her from the BBC World Service. She was asked if she had heard news of my father being shot. As I listened to Bwa Bwa's words, I heard a text message come in on my mobile. It was another journalist, asking me if I had heard the very same thing.

I got off the phone refusing to believe what I had heard. *My father shot? Surely it couldn't be true?* I just had to hope and pray that the journalists had got it wrong and that my father was all right. I tried calling his mobile, but it was turned off. In mounting panic I tried Say Say, but his phone was also unavailable. In desperation I called a friend of the family called Pee La Sein.

Pee La Sein confirmed to me that the news was true. My father had been shot and he had died of his wounds.

I let out a cry that brought everyone in the house running. I broke down and sobbed out the news to them. I called poor Bwa

Bwa and heard her break down over the phone. Then I called Slone, in Canada, and woke him in the middle of the night. He knew immediately that something was wrong. I cried and cried and cried as I choked out the news to Slone that our father had been killed.

Our father, Padoh Mahn Sha, had been assassinated by those who for so long had been plotting and striving to kill him. He had been sitting peacefully on the veranda of his house in Mae Sot, when three agents of the Burmese regime drove up in a pickup truck. Two came up the stairs and shot him. Those are the simple facts of his dying.

But in the greater scheme of things, my father was killed because the Burmese regime feared him. For ever a man of principle and a man of the people, my father had enjoyed enormous support – not just from the Karen, but from the Burmese democracy movement as a whole and from freedom-loving people around the world.

As news spread of the killing more and more Karen turned up at my home. They were all devastated, and I realized some were looking to me for comfort. I thought of my father's iron determination and willed myself to stop crying. I needed to be strong now. They killed my father because they wanted to kill what he stood for. I was determined not to let that happen.

But underneath my heart was broken. My father was my best friend, my inspiration and my guiding light. Whenever I felt afraid it was his example that kept me strong. But now he was gone.

The next day Bwa Bwa and I returned to Thailand. The night before the funeral we went to see his body. I clasped my hands in front of my face and bowed down three times, which is the traditional way to pay respect. My father was in a bed surrounded by flowers – the flowers that he had always loved so much when he was alive. He looked so pale, but he seemed to be at peace. It was as if he had found it at last.

318

We stayed with him all night, for we knew that it was not safe for us to stay for the funeral. There were reports that many more assassins had been dispatched to kill Karen leaders and other democracy activists. My sister and I were so torn, we wanted to stay for the funeral and knew that our people wanted to see us, but the risks were so great and we were determined to stay alive and carry on his work. As dawn rose we had to creep away. It was the hardest decision we had ever had to make.

We had delayed the funeral as long as we possibly could, but Slone hadn't been able to get back to the border in time. Poor Say Say was alone when he prepared a final lunch for our father. He set a place for my father and asked him to come and eat with him one last time.

Friends describe it as the saddest funeral they had ever been to. Thousands turned up to pay their respects. It was a traditional animist funeral, but Christian and Buddhist services were also held. The KNLA gave a gunfire salute over my father's body. At the end it was burned on a funeral pyre, and a memorial was built to him there. His ashes were scattered in the Moei River and under trees and at the bottom of a mountain.

Shortly after that Slone arrived and we went to visit my father's memorial. Slone hadn't seen our father in years. As he was the youngest my father had always worried about him.

Later, we went to clear our father's papers. In among them I found the letter that I had written when I was sixteen, from Noh Poe refugee camp. I read it over again.

Dear Pah,
    Well, I think you must have completely forgotten us – especially your Little Daughter. Well, it's okay I suppose . . . But I don't want to be a refugee any more. Life in the refugee camp is so horrible. Do you know what it's like? What it feels like to be a refugee? The Thai soldiers are so horrible to us . . .

Some months later I was flicking through his diary and found a poem dedicated to all women in Burma.

To Beloved Daughter
Yin San [Padoh Mahn Sha's pen name]

O my beloved daughter,
In the long journey of life,
In broad daylight, under the sun,
As it's hard to know where north and south are,
There're also those who're standing still.

Though in the middle of the night,
A time hard to see the way,
As north and south are definitely known,
There're those who're journeying towards the
    destination.

In the stormy wind,
And the waves blasting,
Crying and wailing,
In abandonment,
There're also those who've sunk into depravity.

In the violent storm,
And the stormy sea,
There're also those who are journeying,
Against the current and vicious wind.

O my beloved daughter,
Keep sincerity and conscience;
Alertness and ethics,
Diligence and learning,
Faith and uprightness,
Courage and sacrifice,

As a base and journey on,
With fearlessness,
For the noble cause.

Published in the Thanu Htoo Journal of 31 January 1999,
on the fiftieth anniversary of Karen resistance

My father never had a peaceful life. It was one of sacrifice and struggle. My mother's also. When they died they left us no material possessions. But for me they left us something more valuable than a house or inheritance. They gave us compassion, principles and strength.

And whilst they may have killed my father, they could never kill my father's dream. That the Karen, and all the people of Burma, will be free.

Statement Written by Zoya Phan and Her Sister and Brothers for Their Father's Funeral

We have lost a great father and a great leader.

We were lucky to have a father who was caring and full of love. He gave us guidance and support, and taught us tolerance and to stand against injustice. He could not give us wealth or luxury, but ensured that we had an education and the opportunity to fulfil our potential.

He was always humble, yet a strong and brave leader. He dedicated his life to the struggle, and always put the welfare of his people and his country before himself. His example of determination to win our freedom won him the love and respect not just of the Karen people, but also of the Burmese democracy movement and of freedom-loving people around the world.

He will be remembered by many not only as an inspirational leader, but also on a personal level for the many acts of kindness he performed for those who needed help. We are proud to be his children as all Karen people, and all people who long for freedom in Burma, are proud of him.

Our father lived for the principles of freedom and democracy. He believed in the unity of the Karen people against a common enemy, and in the unity of all the people of Burma, knowing that only together can we bring freedom to our land.

What the junta is trying to do by killing our father is to try to kill what he stood for. We must not let them succeed. For the international community, the assassination of our father shows once again that the regime is lying when it says it has a road map for democracy. Our father dedicated his life to the struggle for a democratic Burma. That is why they killed him.

We know that many of you are feeling sad and downhearted. That is not what our father would want. He would want you to be strong and unified. If you loved our father, the best way to show it is to fight to fulfil his dream of freedom. Don't let what he stood for die with him.

Our father's death does not leave us weaker. It shows that we are strong. They killed our father because they are afraid of him and what he stood for. Our father did not live to see freedom for our people, but his dream lives on. The Karen, and all the people of Burma, will be free.

Epilogue

As I write this epilogue I am thinking of my home, the mountains and rivers, the people, and the food! But I can't think of it without thinking of the horrors going on there. It is 27 October 2008, my birthday, and I have just had a call from the Thai–Burma border. The Burmese Army is building up its military forces in Karen free state again, and there are fears of another big new military offensive now the rainy season is over. The Generals will say it is anti-insurgent action, but as before they will avoid the KNLA bases, and instead attack defenceless villagers.

When I had that first lunch with Mark back in 2005 and he said I could do more to help my people in London than on the border I had thought he was crazy. But when I returned to the United Kingdom after my father's funeral I received news that showed being in London did give me new opportunities. The campaign we launched back in 2006 was finally having an impact on the ground. The British government agreed to increase its funding for the refugees in the camps on the border of Thailand, and also gave its first grant to Dr Cynthia's clinic. When you are in the refugee camp, and even when you escape to a country like the United Kingdom, you feel helpless and useless, not knowing how to change things or to help. It meant a lot to me that I could help the people who lived in the camps as I once had and aid the clinic that had saved my life so many times.

At the Burma Campaign UK we are gearing up for a big new

campaign to raise awareness about the situation in eastern Burma, and I hope that we can finally get the international community to pay attention to what is going on, and even take some action. I am the International Coordinator at the Burma Campaign UK now. My task is to help link up campaigners around the world, building the international campaign to help my country. Former anti-apartheid activists, who campaigned for the freedom of the people in South Africa and to free Nelson Mandela, tell me the situation in Burma is much worse than it was in South Africa. But there isn't the same scale of international campaign for Burma as there was for South Africa.

I have visited many countries to tell governments, MPs and the public what is going on. I have met politicians, present and former presidents and prime ministers, even Prince Charles. Sometimes I have to pinch myself to make sure that it is all real. That the girl from the jungle really is meeting these people and having these opportunities to speak out. I feel such a responsibility to make the most of the opportunities I have been given. I know that lives depend on it. Sometimes I find it depressing that there is still so little awareness among governments, and that so few are willing to take action. But as my father said, freedom won't be given to us, we will have to work for it.

Many of my Karen friends who feature in this book are now scattered all over the world. The United Nations runs a resettlement programme to find new homes in new countries for those in the refugee camps. Tens of thousands of people, mostly Karen, have been resettled, some in Australia, the United States and even in the frozen landscapes of northern Finland. One ethnic Karenni woman in her forties whom I met on a lobbying trip to Finland told me she felt like she hadn't been born until she arrived there. She had lived her entire life in fear, she told me. But she said what everyone else says if you talk to them long enough. I want to go home. It is very good that the UN resettlement programme is giving people a chance to escape from the misery of the refugee camps and start a new life in safety, but I can't help thinking that the SPDC must be delighted with the United Nations for doing this. It drives us out of the country, and the United Nations, instead of taking action to stop the attacks, ignores why there are refugees, and instead whisks them thousands of miles away. It's exactly what the SPDC wants. And no matter how many people the UN resettles, more come to the camps to fill their place, because the attacks haven't stopped, and the United Nations isn't trying to stop them.

Zipporah Sein, my old teacher, has been elected to replace my father as General Secretary of the Karen National Union. She is a strong and experienced leader, and I am pleased it is her who has taken over from my father. She is also the first female leader of the KNU in its history. With Aung San Suu Kyi, and many other strong women leaders in our struggle, ours is a movement increasingly led by women!

Our struggle isn't just against dictatorship and oppression. It is also one for a better Burma, a better place for us to live, and I hope one day Burma will be a shining beacon of freedom and peace. My country is one of the most ethnically diverse in the world. We want to live in a Federal Burma. Regardless of our ethnicity we are one people, and we are engaged in one struggle for our country to be free. My dream is of a Burma where never again will a mother put her children to bed crying because they have not had enough to eat. I dream of a Burma where no more children die from preventable diseases because the government has spent money on guns instead of medicine. I dream of a Burma where no farmer lives in fear of being shot because of his ethnicity or used as slave labour. I dream of a Burma with no political prisoners, where we can choose our leaders. I dream of a Burma where we celebrate our cultures, different but equal. If every one of us takes action, no matter how small or big we are, then together we will be an unstoppable force and we will win our freedom. United, our will and determination are stronger than guns and bullets.

I hope that this book has been interesting for you to read. Maybe you will feel sorry for me after what I have been through in my life. Don't. I am one of the lucky ones. I am lucky I am still alive. I am lucky I haven't been raped. I am lucky that I am not still in a refugee camp that is like a prison camp, with no work, no freedom, and the same food for breakfast, lunch and dinner for year after year after year. And I am lucky to be able to work to help my people. I don't want you to feel sorry for me, I want you to feel angry, and I want you to do something about it.

The British actress and comedienne Maureen Lipman once introduced me at an event as a woman who would wrap my hands around your heart. But I told the audience, I don't want your heart, I want you to take action. I say the same to you now. So few people know what is going on in my country, but you do now. Will you do something about it, or just pick up another book? On the following pages are details of organizations working to help my people. I ask you to support them. We need your help.

I want to go home. Please help me.

About Burma

Burma is in Southeast Asia, with Thailand and Laos to the east, Bangladesh to the west and India and China to the north. The population is estimated at around 50 million. There are eight main ethnic groups, and more than 100 subgroups, making it one of the most ethnically diverse countries in the world.

It is a country rich in natural resources, but also one of the poorest in the world, as the dictatorship spends up to half its annual budget on the military.

Burma gained independence from Britain after the Second World War, but even under democratic rule the central government oppressed and discriminated against ethnic groups.

In 1962 General Ne Win took power in a military coup, and the country has been ruled by dictatorships ever since. A student-led pro-democracy uprising in 1988 was brutally suppressed by the regime, and a new dictatorship – the State Law and Order Restoration Council – took over. A combination of internal and international pressure led the regime to hold elections in 1990, which it expected to win. But instead the National League for Democracy, led by Aung San Suu Kyi, won 82 per cent of the seats in Parliament. The regime refused to accept the results, and instead arrested and tortured MPs and democracy activists. As of December 2008 there were more than 2,100 political prisoners in Burma, many of whom are tortured, kept in solitary confinement and denied medical treatment.

Aung San Suu Kyi is now in her third period of detention, and is the world's only Nobel Peace laureate in detention. She is denied visitors, her phone line is cut, and she is not allowed to send or receive post. She has grandchildren she has never been allowed to see.

Burma is a record-breaker for all the wrong reasons. It has the highest number of child soldiers, the longest-running civil war, one of the highest levels of infant mortality in the region and the lowest levels of spending on health and education. The regime has been accused by the United Nations of a crime against humanity for its use of slave labour, the highest in the world. It is engaged in ethnic cleansing in eastern Burma, is one of the few governments in the world that still uses landmines, and denies international aid to its own population. Burma also regularly comes top in tables on corruption and media censorship.

Burma Timeline

1947   Karen National Union (KNU) formed. Lobbies unsuccessfully for independent Karen state.

1948   Burma gains independence.

1949   KNU begins armed struggle after attacks on Karen civilians.

1962   General Ne Win seizes power in a military coup.

1975   National Democratic Front formed by ethnic groups opposed to the dictatorship.

1976   KNU drops demands for independent state, joins other ethnic organizations in calling for federalism in Burma.

1988   Democracy uprising across Burma. Ne Win regime toppled but thousands massacred in the student-led uprising. A new and even more brutal regime takes power, calling itself the State Law and Order Restoration Council (SLORC).

1989   SLORC renames Burma Myanmar. Democracy movement and many governments refuse to accept the name change, saying it has no right to decide what the country is called.

1990   Elections held. The National League for Democracy, led by Aung San Suu Kyi, wins 82 per cent of the seats in Parliament, but the regime refuses to hand over power.

1995   Burmese Army overruns KNU headquarters at Manerplaw.

1997   SLORC renames itself State Peace and Development Council (SPDC).

2004   SPDC and KNU make 'gentlemen's agreement' to end hostilities. KNU sticks to it but SPDC does not.

2005   SPDC gives just a few hours' notice that it is moving from Rangoon (Yangon) to a new capital, Nay Pyi Taw.

2007   January – China and Russia veto a resolution on Burma at the United Nations Security Council.

August/September – A democracy uprising led by Buddhist monks is brutally suppressed by the SPDC.

2008   February – Padoh Mahn Sha, General Secretary of the Karen National Union, is assassinated by agents of the SPDC.

May – Cyclone Nargis strikes Burma. SPDC fails to warn population that the cyclone is coming, and then blocks international aid.

May – Rigged referendum held on a new constitution for Burma that will enshrine military rule. SPDC claims 92 per cent support.

The Phan Foundation

The Phan Foundation was founded by Zoya Phan, her sister Bwa Bwa and her brothers Say Say and Slone. It is dedicated to the memory of their parents, Padoh Mahn Sha and Nant Kyin Shwe.

The Foundation aims to fight poverty and provide education for Karen people from Burma. It helps people in Burma and refugees forced to flee their homes. It also aims to protect and promote the culture of the Karen, one that is being systematically destroyed as part of the Burmese regime's policy of ethnic cleansing. In meeting its objectives, the Foundation has a particular focus on young people, encouraging and supporting a new generation of grassroots activists who will work to help their people.

Zoya's experiences described in this book are not unique. Each year tens of thousands more people are driven from their homes. Poverty is as bad as in the worst conflict-hit African countries, but the Burmese regime will not allow the United Nations or aid agencies to deliver aid to millions of people in desperate poverty. Parents are forced to watch their children die from measles, malaria or dysentery, when cheap medicines would save their lives. Children grow up without access to education. But there are ways to get aid in through underground networks. A small amount of money can make a big difference.

Please support the Phan Foundation. You can donate online at www.phanfoundation.org.

Other Organizations Working for Burma

Zoya is International Coordinator of the Burma Campaign UK, which campaigns for human rights, democracy and development in Burma. Find out more at: www.burmacampaign.org.uk

In the United States you can visit www.uscampaignforburma.org

You can find out if there is a Burma Campaign in your country at: www.burmacampaign.org.uk/links.html

The Mae Tao Clinic (Dr Cynthia Maung's clinic) on the Thai–Burma border saved Zoya's life several times. www.maetaoclinic.org

The Thailand Burma Border Consortium provides assistance to refugees who have been forced to flee to Thailand. www.tbbc.org

The Karen Women's Organization provides assistance to refugees and internally displaced people, and promotes democracy and human rights. www.karenwomen.org

The Karen National Union is the organization that Zoya's parents dedicated their lives to. It leads the Karen struggle for human rights and democracy. www.karennationalunion.net

Notes on the Authors

Zoya Phan is a 28-year-old ethnic Karen refugee from Burma. As a teenager she was forced to flee her country after her village was attacked by the Burmese Army. She now lives in London and works for the human rights organization Burma Campaign UK.

Damien Lewis has spent twenty years reporting from war and conflict zones around the world, including numerous visits to Karen areas and other war-affected parts of Burma.